The Adult Dyslexic
Interventions and Outcomes

The Adult Dyslexic

Interventions and Outcomes

DAVID MCLOUGHLIN, PhD, CPsychol, AFBPS

Visiting Professor, Department of Psychology, University of Buckingham
and Adult Dyslexia and Skills Development Centre, London

CAROL LEATHER, BA(Hons), PGCE, Dip SpLD, AMBDA

PATRICIA STRINGER, Cert Ed, Dip SpLD, AMBDA

Adult Dyslexia and Skills Development Centre, London

Consultant in Dyslexia
Professor Margaret Snowling
University of York

W
WHURR PUBLISHERS
LONDON AND PHILADELPHIA

© 2002 Whurr Publishers Ltd
First published 2002
by Whurr Publishers Ltd
19b Compton Terrace
London N1 2UN, England and
325 Chestnut Street, Philadelphia PA 19106, USA

British Library Cataloguing in Publication Data

A catalogue record for this book
is available from the British Library.

ISBN 1 86156 045 1

Printed and bound in the UK by Athenaeum Press Ltd,
Gateshead, Tyne & Wear.

Contents

Appendix 1

Appendix 2

Appendix 3

Preface

In 1993 we established the Adult Dyslexia and Skills Development Centre in response to a perceived need to provide a specialist service for dyslexic adults. We believed that they needed to be treated as a distinct group and that a particular approach is required to assessment, counselling, teaching and training. Since opening the Centre thousands of people have come through our doors. There has been an increased interest in dyslexia during the adult years. Practice has improved but there are still those who 'get it wrong', including ourselves. This book is an opportunity to pass on to others what we think we have learned. We have addressed conceptual issues and relied on evidence from systematic studies but, in the main, we have relied on our experience of working with dyslexic people on a daily basis.

Scientific research continues to focus on certain aspects of dyslexia but fails to provide a complete picture. We are constantly impressed by our clients' experiences: the anguish they have endured, the fortitude they have shown, their persistence and determination.

We have taken a lifespan approach as dyslexia is much more than an educational matter. Dyslexic people will seek advice from medical practitioners, counsellors, human resource specialists, teachers, tutors, their employers and volunteers. We hope that we have dealt with the important issues in such a way as to be of help to all these groups, and therefore to dyslexic people themselves. As we have aimed at a wide audience, a number of the chapters have been written with 'selective readers' in mind. There is, therefore, a certain amount of repetition as the same solutions apply in different settings.

Prologue

Professionals who wish to develop an understanding of learning and performance difficulties and their manifestation in personal, social and work settings must develop an understanding of their impact on the lives of real people. In doing so, it will become evident that even apparently mild problems can have considerable impact on employment, education, relationships and daily living (Getzel and Gugerty 1996).

While preparing this book we wrote to our clients, both former and current, asking them if they could comment either orally or in writing on their experience of being dyslexic. Some of their responses are recorded throughout the text. The ensuing is from a former client and is reproduced in its entirety as it encapsulates the journey too many dyslexic people have to undertake before gaining contentment in their lives.

The earliest memory I have of the impact of being dyslexic was when I was about seven. My teacher asked the class to write a story about an imaginary land. I remember writing this really long and imaginary story, no holds barred. I put all that I could into it. I handed it in and eagerly awaited its return. The teacher's reaction to something that I was so proud of was not what I had expected. She was really annoyed, she said I had put no effect into it and it was a terrible piece of work. She was blind to the substance, for she could only see the structure. I would take nearly twenty years before I would be so bold as to write so freely.

The next major impact dyslexia had on my life was when I was fourteen, I had to be assessed for my reading and writing. This was to see if I should be aloud to remain in the main stream and work towards my exams. The assessment was some what of a narrow-minded affair, I had to read and then spell, lists of words. An approach that is hardly the best way to determine any ones ability, let alone a dyslexic. In the real world of a classroom, I had long since employed methods and techniques, to enhance my ability, so evident in my successes in my other subjects. But based on this elaborate test I was informed that I had the reading age of a seven-year-old and I was not going to be put forward.

The head of English conclusions were clear. I was stupid, dim, a waste of time. The Education system fails a lot of people it a production line unable or unwilling to accommodate anyone who can't keep up. But it was its willingness to disregard me so readily and it failure to see beyond my bad English, without taking account of my success in other subject, was how it failed for me. This failure had such a negative impact on me. My school, may not have heard of dyslexia or worse chose not to, But that gave them no excuse and me no defence.

My biology teacher who could see my potential did succeed in changing the schools minds. She may not of have a better understanding of the problem then anyone else at my school, but she could easily see that I was not stupid nor a waste of time. With her and my mothers support, I left school with enough qualifications to secure an apprenticeship but school and education have proven to be a dreadful and very painful experience. One that would so soon start all over again.

After leaving school my approach to the problem, was to hid it, to avoid any situation where it would be exposed. I became very good at this. Some of my own family were unaware of the full extent of the problem. What else could I do? This approach worked well at first. I did not have to experience the humiliations that I had suffered at school but it came at a cost. I found myself in my mid-twenties, with limited expectations, a poor, dead end job, with no mental stimulation. This approach of hiding in the shadows, never daring to venture out, may have been safe but very limiting.

My teacher was right. I'm not stupid. So by the time I was twenty-five, I was very frustrated and unhappy, something had to change. Around this time I had started to hear about dyslexia and started to use the word about myself. I once told someone that I was dyslexic, who reply was 'why don't you do something about it?' This was a revaluation, it had never dawned on me that I could. It had been such a isolating experience till then. I did not tell anyone, so no one knew and those who had in the past, had acted so negatively. So who was there to help, who was there to understand. The ideal of change scared me but I started to think that maybe something could be done.

The turning point came when I met my future wife. She wanted to go travelling around the world. This would mean I would have to leave my safe little job. It was to be a work holiday so I would have to find work, not long-term but still in another country. On my return home I would also have to find a new job. To put it simply, all the demons were let loose. But just like when I had learnt to drive, something I had put off and put off, then bought a car, so I had to learn. I left my job and went travelling. This was the point of no return. I knew that things would then have to then change. Fear is a very powerful thing but nothing compared to love.

When I come back home, I got a new job in a scientific research group, talk about the deep end. I went to the Centre and met someone who could help and understand. This was a big turning point. With her I learnt many things, like how I can best learn. But the biggest thing was that I as person came out of the shadows to feel the warm glow of the sun without fear and limitation.

It has just occurred to me that until this moment I have never thought about what if? What if I was not dyslexic. This may sound surprising, but I am dyslexic. Just like I am a man. I have always concerned myself with no what I can't do, but with what I can do. I cannot change being dyslexic but I can change the effect it has. I think this realistic approach to dyslexia and life is one of the positive side to it. Another is the feeling that comes with success and achievement, such as to be able to participate in one of man kinds greatest achievement, the written word. The ability to pass knowledge and experiences from one generation to another. This, many may take for granted, as I would take walking. A simple and at times dull activity. But what joy and wonder one would feel, if achieved, when previously perceived as impossible. Every time I read a book and learn and remember the knowledge that is within, I achieve something that I once perceived as impossible.

So where am I now? I am 36 and have long since come out of the dyslexic closet. I also wrote what you are now reading, which is far in a way the best description of where I am and what I can achieve.

Acknowledgements

Our thanks go to Penny Carter, Betty Corcoran and Sissy Dewhirst for their contributions to preparing the manuscript, and to Colin Whurr for his infinite patience.

Dedication

This book is dedicated to dyslexic people of all ages from whom we have learned so much, to our families and to the memory of loved ones lost to us during the course of its preparation – Bill and Pauline Hooper, Margot Nott and Graham Stringer

Chapter 1
Dyslexia in the adult years

This chapter describes the characteristics of dyslexia in the adult years, and the scientific and theoretical explanations for some of these. A pragmatic model of dyslexia based on interactions within the working memory system is proposed as a way of empowering dyslexic people. The issue of degrees of dyslexia is also addressed.

Introduction

Dyslexic people seeking the advice, guidance and support of professionals usually want the answers to the fundamental questions, 'Why do I find certain tasks difficult?' and 'What can I do about it?'. Alternatively, those referring people for evaluation and advice are asking, 'Why is this person not learning or performing in the way we expect?' and 'What can be done about it?'. The subject of this book is the interventions that address these questions and enable dyslexic people to fulfil their potential.

The past decade has seen a greater interest in dyslexic adults but this does not mean they have been recognized as a distinct population, with needs that are quite different from their younger counterparts. Provision has often been an 'add-on', the same practices as employed with children being applied to adults, who are not and should not be regarded as 'children with a learning disability grown up' (Patton and Polloway 1992). There is a need for a fundamental shift in thinking on behalf of professionals, researchers and all the organizations concerned with providing for dyslexic people. The emphasis should be on empowerment or enablement rather than a model of disability that perceives the 'dyslexic as a victim'.

Although there has been more research into the problems facing and the needs of adults, studies have concentrated on students in further and higher education. Conducting research with adult dyslexics where they are not a captive audience is difficult, finding a representative sample being a particular problem. Volunteers are likely to be the 'most needy', others being reluctant to participate. Whatever the reason, dyslexia has remained an educational issue, rather than one which affects daily living, including employment. Eighty per cent of the population of the United Kingdom is over 16 years of age, and therefore there must be a correspondingly large percentage of adult dyslexics: the needs of this group, however, have been given far less attention than those of children still at school. Whilst this makes sense if one assumes that early intervention will minimize the impact of dyslexia on people's lives, it is unfortunate. Considering the nature of dyslexia as it is manifested across the lifespan should lead to a greater understanding of the needs of dyslexic children. It is only by taking a long-term view that we will develop a complete understanding of the nature of dyslexia and how it affects people, and be able to provide appropriate support and intervention. Furthermore, the persistence of dyslexia in the adult years raises important issues about definition, with consequent implications for practice. To take advantage of the provisions of the 1995 Disability Discrimination Act, for example, it is necessary to establish that a dyslexic's difficulties constitute a disability that has significant day-to-day effects. A narrow view based on the experiences of children will not protect dyslexic people from discrimination, nor will it allow them to access important resources.

In the absence of a large body of quantitative data we must rely on the small-scale studies which exist, as well as on the individual experiences of dyslexic people and those working with them. There are also several factors that should influence good practice in assessment, counselling, teaching, training and employment:

- the nature of dyslexia in adulthood
- psychological development across the lifespan
- the principles underlying education and training in the adult years
- the factors which research has shown to contribute to the success of dyslexic people
- the educational and legal context.

The first of these is described in this chapter, the following three are described in Chapter 2, and the last is discussed in Chapter 10.

Terminology

As dyslexia has been and continues to be regarded as an educational issue, much of the language surrounding it belongs to the world of learning and teaching. Viewed from the adult perspective, a good deal of the terminology is inappropriate. One should not, for example, suggest that the manager seeking to improve his report-writing skills is in need of 'remedial help'. Even 'dyslexia' is often incorrectly used interchangeably with specific learning difficulty or reading difficulty, the focus being on literacy. It is a specific learning difficulty but only one of a number – including dyspraxia, dyscalculia and attention deficit disorder – sometimes referred to as 'hidden disabilities'.

Even the generic term 'learning difficulty' is, however, inappropriate for many adult dyslexics since they have learned very well, albeit differently, but continue to have a 'performance difficulty'. We are using the word 'dyslexia' here in its very broadest sense, that is as 'a family of lifelong manifestations that show themselves in many other ways than poor reading' (Miles et al., 1998). Dyslexic people can find learning difficult but in the adult years their ability to 'perform' in social, family and work settings is of greater concern.

Further, it has been suggested that it is preferable to refer to 'people with dyslexia' rather than 'dyslexic people' or 'dyslexics'. Consistent with the theme of empowerment and the suggestion of Reiff et al. (1993), that adults with learning difficulties should participate in the process of description and definition, we continue to use phrases such as 'dyslexic people' or the word 'dyslexic'. We have met few who have described themselves as 'an adult with dyslexia'. Some of our clients have specifically disregarded phrases such as 'a person with dyslexia' because of its medical connotations.

The nature of dyslexia

Although in many countries dyslexia is still viewed as a reading difficulty, there does seem to be some agreement in the UK that the problems experienced by dyslexic people extend beyond literacy skills. There has yet to be a large-scale systematic survey of dyslexia in the adult population that attempts to identify the incidence, and more specifically, its nature. Miles (1993) has rightly described it as a syndrome which is typically characterized by 'an unusual balance of skills'. In our experience, and according to existing research, adults seeking advice and support manifest both primary and secondary characteristics.

Primary characteristics

The primary characteristics, or those that derive directly from the cognitive difference which constitutes dyslexia, include:

Organization – including personal organization, as well as organization for work and learning. Included here is time management and time-keeping.

> Organising my life is an arduous task.

Literacy – including word recognition, reading fluency and comprehension, spelling, written expression and writing fluency.

> Spelling and numeracy problems are still predominant but I now have strategies to cope with them – on the whole. Knowing left from right and reading the time prove to be problematic (because they tend to have to be performed quickly, removing the opportunity for using strategies). I am incapable of reading aloud and this is a problem when I try to read to my daughter.

Numeracy – this is not a conceptual difficulty but a problem with the procedural aspects, including symbol recognition, calculations and remembering the order in which operations should be undertaken. There can also be a problem with the language of maths. Some dyslexic people become very good mathematicians but continue to experience problems in areas such as mental arithmetic and have never been able to learn tables.

Social interaction – some dyslexic people do seem to experience social difficulties.

> You open your mouth to say something and then silence – only a blank space in your head.

The existence of problems with social functioning amongst dyslexics is not disputed. In reviewing the literature Vogel and Forness (1992) list:

- Word finding difficulties and problems with verbal fluency, which can lead to saying the wrong thing or the embarrassment of prolonged silences, e.g. 'an Indian winter' and 'let's not beat the bush around'.

- Slow rates of processing language or interpreting accompanying facial expressions and body language, which can lead to inappropriate verbal and non-verbal responses.
- Memory deficits that can, for example, lead to a fear of forgetting a question, resulting in poorly timed interruptions.
- Problems with eye contact. This can be too intense when an individual attempts to overcome poor auditory processing skills by gaining as much visual information as they can. Sometimes they might avoid eye contact so that they do not become too overloaded with information.

Secondary characteristics

The secondary or affective characteristics, that is, those which develop as a result of and in response to the above, are:

Lack of confidence – although many dyslexic people are very able, they do not perceive themselves in this way. Their achievements have often been below their own expectations and this has undermined their confidence in their abilities.

> Dyslexia affects people in different ways, personally it affected my self-confidence I was always made to feel lazy, stupid, ugly and sometimes even worthless. When I was diagnosed as dyslexic it was more a relief than anything else, so this is why my handwriting is like this and that's why I have problems with essays (putting information under the right section), that's why my maths is so bad that's why I always have problems with numbers, I remember once when I was at school someone asked me for my telephone number but I just got more confused and frustrated and couldn't remember it so I felt stupid.

Low self-esteem – dyslexic people often have a low opinion of themselves generally. They do not value their abilities or their achievements and can be inclined to apologize too much, having become used to getting things wrong. One could almost design a diagnostic test based on the number of times they say 'sorry' when unable to answer a question.

> It's never being sure you are right.

Anger and frustration – this can include anger about the way they have been treated in the past, as well as their current situation.

> I have a lot of anger still about all the failed tasks and why none of the professionals who taught me stopped to ask what was wrong with this child who couldn't produce the written work equal to her other skills. I wish they had.

Anxiety – including general anxiety, as well as a particular reaction to learning, examinations and testing.

> I feel completely out of control and unable to function. Others may tell me that I am not out of control, but that does not alter how I feel: I feel disorientated, I keep forgetting things – my short-term and working memories are terrible, I mislay things all the time – I can't concentrate for more than a few seconds – I can't make even the simplest decision about anything – silly little decisions hold me up for hours – I feel worn out and as if on another plant much of the time – terribly stressed and at the point of collapse – only I never do collapse! I just carry on laughing it off and covering it up – trying even harder to cope when I can't.

Social interaction – problems in this area can be both primary and secondary. That is, academic, learning and performance difficulties can lead to poor self-concept, rejection or isolation from peers, or other negative consequences that interfere with the development of social skills (Forness and Kavale 1991).

There is ample evidence of the existence of the secondary characteristics described above, both systematic and anecdotal (Miles and Varma 1995; Cohn 1998; Hughes and Dawson 1995; Gregg and Ferri 1998; Miles 1993; Riddick et al. 1999). Their origins are easier to understand; being put down, misunderstood and years of underachievement do little to enhance confidence or promote positive self-esteem. Gardner (1996) speculates that a child who has five negative experiences a day, be they physical, cognitive or emotional, will have experienced 10 300 such experiences by the time they are five years of age. If we project this into the adult years the total is staggering. People whose parents and teachers have held low expectations of them or who have jumped to 'obvious' conclusions about the reasons for their under-performance will have low expectations and jump to obvious conclusions about themselves. They will believe what they have been told even when this is inconsistent with the obvious truth. Dyslexics whose achievements indicate that they are far from idle will, for example, describe themselves as 'lazy'. There are dyslexic people who are 'victims of a poor education' – those whose difficulties were obvious but received little in the way of support, even if they were identified as dyslexic. There are also 'victims of a good education' – those who have been taught well, worked hard and whose problems were less obvious and were attributed to factors such as attitude, and who are left wondering why they are less efficient in learning and work settings than they would like to be.

> Being dyslexic obviously creates problems with study within 'normal' systems, as the majority of schooling and higher education is based entirely on the written word. So this alone leads to stress and frustration, but for me the secondary factors of being dyslexic, anxiety and lack of self confidence have had more of an impact on me. It was not until I started to research dyslexia, for this learning profile, that I realized how closely related they are.

Secondary characteristics are no less important than the primary ones, and are often more difficult to resolve. It can be easier to teach someone to read than it is to improve their confidence. Even highly successful dyslexic people express doubts about their ability. Their confidence always remains fragile and setbacks can be enormous. Further, there is a two-way interaction between primary and secondary factors, and this influences performance from day to day.

> On a good day, I imagine that I am a highly creative and intelligent (an original thinker), with amusing and endearing quirks. Work goes better than ever, I feel I'm moving forward in strides and that I am appreciated!
>
> On a bad day however, I feel overwhelmed, confused and worried about my ability to cope. If I have a lot of work or something I find difficult to do, trying to organize a plan or schedule can send me into a panic. Just the mental act of keeping numerous dates, names and important information in my head is tricky. I feel I'm moving at a snail's pace and at times like these my workroom can begin to resemble the chaos in my mind, with papers spread higgledy piggledy. If I am cold calling people for work/research, I have to do

> several mini rehearsals first, otherwise I risk sounding tongue tied.
>
> Often I am unable to hold on to the thoughts for long enough for me to form a sentence – either written or spoken. Using a computer helps, in that I can wipe out bits as I go along and keep the text neat and tidy. Hand written notes always end up in a terrible mess these days – although it used not to be so. But even when using a computer, it is still difficult and of course my eyes feel strained.

Positive characteristics

The problem with labels is that they refer to only one aspect of a person's life. Dyslexia refers to what people can't do, the risk being that what dyslexic people can do is overlooked.

> Dyslexics are usually very creative people they have to be to overcome some of the difficulties they are faced with. Because we think in pictures, dyslexics are usually artistic. They are lateral thinkers and overcome problems by thinking laterally. I would also say that people with Dyslexia are more articulate they say things verbally better than maybe in writing. Of course if you are speaking you don't need to bother with logical ordering or handwriting or spelling. To overcome Dyslexia you need to be efficient and more organized than if it did not affect you.

It has been argued that the neurological organization of a dyslexic person's brain leads to them having stronger functioning in some areas (Davis 1997; West 1997; Stein 2001) and that dyslexic people have a different 'cognitive style' (Morgan and Klein 2000). Amongst positive characteristics noted are:

- good powers of visualization
- artistic talents, particularly where good visual-spatial skills are required
- good practical and problem-solving skills
- creative thinking skills, including lateral thinking
- a holistic (big picture) approach to problem-solving
- an intuitive empathy with others.

I think dyslexia forces one to have a more individual viewpoint on life because evidence suggests we think more holistically. Numerous artists, musicians and actors are/have been dyslexic, as well as famous scientists/inventors etc. I would hope I am better able to empathize with people who experience difficulties in learning or life in general. I also hope I am more open to different learning approaches, even different philosophies, trends, etc. Some think that dyslexia can 'give you the edge' on your chosen field because you have to be more thorough in your study/practice by necessity.

Much of the so-called evidence for this is based on speculation about creative and gifted people, such as Einstein. This practice, because it can raise false expectations, is considered by some to be undesirable, as there is little evidence for such claims (Adelman and Adelman 1987; Thomas 2000; Kihl et al. 2000).

There are some systematic studies that have explored the notion that dyslexic people have visual strengths but the results have been contradictory. Everatt et al. (1999) established evidence of stronger creative abilities consistent with anecdotal reports, but were not able to attribute this to enhanced right hemisphere functioning. Shaywitz has written that dyslexia is 'an encapsulated deficit, often surrounded by significant strengths in reasoning, problem solving, concept formation, critical thinking and vocabulary' (1996: 104); that is, 'an unexpected weakness in a sea of strengths'. In contrast, Winner et al. (2000) found little support for the view of dyslexia as a deficit associated with 'compensatory visual-spatial talents', and suggested that the disproportionate number of dyslexic people in jobs requiring good spatial skills might be the result of them having chosen an occupation by default: that is, they have been channelled into it because of their difficulties with written language. It is perhaps inevitable that they thrive on courses and in jobs where there are fewer demands on language based activities.

We do need to be careful as the idea of 'dyslexia as a gift' can be misleading. In the same way that focusing on the 'disability' can lead to abilities being overlooked, too much emphasis on the talents can mean that the difficulties are not addressed which might prevent a person from capitalizing on such talents.

> I'd like to say yes there are loads of positive things about being
> dyslexic, unfortunately, I just see it as a pain in the arse. The way I
> tend to look at my situation is; It could be worse I could be stupid
> and there is no way back from that. To the best of my knowledge
> there isn't an operation that cures stupid. I'm fortunate, I have
> 'brains', it was just not immediately apparent, to the education
> system, nor myself, how to utilize them.

Dyslexic people are just the same as non-dyslexic people in the sense that
they have strengths and weaknesses. The latter, however, are not just 'things
they are not good at' like being unable to draw, but are such that they can
undermine effective performance in education and at work.

At an affective level, and in contrast to the secondary characteristics
described above, dyslexic people have also been found to be:

- persistent
- determined
- hard-working
- resilient.

They have needed to be, to become successful (Gerber et al. 1992; Spekman
et al. 1992).

Explaining primary characteristics

Defining dyslexia has, however, remained an elusive business. Traditional
definitions have focused on the discrepancy between ability and attainment
in literacy, particularly reading, but these are now considered unsatisfactory
for a variety of reasons (Stanovich 1991; Siegel 1992; Beaton et al. 1997). It has
been suggested that 'it is time to move away from the restricting definitions of
reading failure by reference to arbitrary cut off points on behavioural tests
and arbitrary discrepancies between test scores' (Frith 1999: 199). Mather has
put the case somewhat more strongly, writing that 'our knowledge of the
cognitive correlates of dyslexia has increased to the extent that the practice
of using aptitude–achievement discrepancy formulae as the sole or determining criterion for the identification of individuals must be discontinued'
(Mather 1998: 7).

Discrepancy definitions are particularly inappropriate for adults who
have been able to develop their literacy skills to a level at which the

discrepancy is no longer obvious. According to a discrepancy definition, such people would no longer be dyslexic, despite clearly continuing to experience difficulties that stem from the same cognitive difference responsible for their slower acquisition of literacy skills.

The Division of Educational and Child Psychology of the British Psychological Society produced a report which offered as a working definition: 'Dyslexia is evident when accurate and fluent word reading and/or spelling develops very incompletely or with great difficulty' (DECP 1999: 5). This is despite the fact that ten years ago Miles and Miles wrote that 'there is no contradiction in saying that a person is dyslexic while nevertheless being a competent reader; and indeed many dyslexic adults come into this category' (Miles and Miles 1990: ix). Some authors now refer to 'literate dyslexics', recognizing that there are problems that extend beyond literacy (Beaton et al. 1997). Dyslexia continues to undermine the performance of literate dyslexic adults. They are still dyslexic, regardless of whether they have learned to read, write and spell. Cooke is quite correct in writing that the DECP definition 'will cause serious concern to dyslexic adults - particularly those who are sometimes (inappropriately) called "compensated" dyslexics - those who have few problems with reading but have all kinds of other problems' (Cooke 2001: 49).

Much more is now known about the aetiology of dyslexia, and Frith (1995, 1999) has described a framework that provides a useful way of organizing what we do know, as follows:

Biological differences (genetics and neurology)

↓

Cognitive differences (information processing)

↓

Behavioural differences (primary characteristics, e.g. reading)

Biology and neurology

There is strong evidence for a heritable genetic factor being the initial cause of dyslexia. This is derived from family studies, where the relatives of children with reading problems perform less well on reading tasks than those whose children do not have such difficulties. More convincing evidence comes from twin studies (Pennington 1990; De Fries 1991; De Fries et al. 1997). As yet the process of transmission is not fully understood, although a link to Chromosome 6 has been identified (Fisher et al. 1999). Certainly the experience of interviewing dyslexic people provides much evidence of a family history of dyslexic-type difficulties, but this is by no means universal.

It has been established that dyslexics show significant neural organization differences to non-dyslexic people. These differences persist throughout the lifespan, and are regarded as the fundamental cause of the characteristics manifested by dyslexic people at a behavioural level (Bigler 1996): that is, they are dyslexic essentially because of their neurological make-up. The evidence comes from a variety of sources, including neuroanatomic and brain imaging studies.

Neuroanatomic studies have shown that whereas non-dyslexic people have an asymmetrical brain, the left being larger than the right, dyslexic people show symmetry, particularly in the planum temporale (Best and Demb 1999). Furthermore, nests (or clusters) of neurones which reflect 'altered neuronal migration' to the cortex have been identified where they do not exist in non-dyslexic people. Galaburda et al. hypothesized that 'the affected cortex is different in terms of its cellular and connectional archi-tecture, hence its functional architecture' (1985: 127). More recently, Galaburda (1999) has described dyslexia as a multi-level syndrome in which areas of the brain connected with perceptual processing, as well as those involved in metacognitive tasks, are anatomically affected, implying that dyslexia represents a complex interaction of both low and high level processing deficits.

The emphasis on 'interaction' is important as too much is made of the left/right or verbal/visual brain dichotomy: 'The brain is made up of anatomi-cally distinct regions, but these regions are not autonomous mini-brains; rather they constitute a cohesive and integrated system' (Greenfield 1997: 39). Skills such as reading rely on the interaction between visual, auditory and motor centres. Stein and Talcott (1999) have argued that the magnocellular pathways in the brain, particularly those which link the parts involved in reading and spelling, differ in dyslexic people. They suggest that dyslexia results from 'patchily abnormal development in magnocellular neurones' throughout the whole brain, contributing to visual instability, and like Fawcett et al. (1999), who have identified differences in the cerebellum, associate this with reduced phonological skills, and motor problems.

Brain-imaging techniques such as magnetic resonance imaging (MRI) and positron emission tomography (PET) scans, combined with blood-flow techniques, have allowed the further exploration of structural and functional differences in the brains of dyslexic people. The former have confirmed some of the structural differences, identified by autopsy studies, notably those relating to symmetry. PET scans and blood-flow techniques have provided support for functional differences (Hynd and Hiemenz 1997; Shaywitz 1996).

In the main, these differences are seen in areas relating to language skills (Zeffiro and Eden 2000). Flowers (1993), for example, found evidence of reduced blood flow in Wernicke's area when adults who had been diagnosed as dyslexic in childhood were presented with a verbal task.

Cognition

In order to explain how the observed differences in neurology may lead to differences in behaviour, researchers have considered their effects on cognitive processes. Cognitive processes are hypothetical constructs which can be tested as possible explanations for the differences between dyslexic and non-dyslexic people. This has resulted in an attempt to define dyslexia as a particular kind of deficit or faulty cognitive mechanism. There have been three main scientific approaches.

- Dyslexic people experience problems with phonological processing (Stanovich 1996; Shaywitz 1996; Snowling 2001; Frith 1999).
- Dyslexia is a problem with visual processing, including orthographical dyslexia, where there are specific deficits in the visual system or visual memory (Goulandris and Snowling 1991; Roberts and Mather 1997; Skottun and Parke 1999; Evans 1998; Stein and Talcott 1999).
- Dyslexic people fail to develop a number of skills to an automatic level (Nicolson and Fawcett 1995, 2001).

There is considerable evidence to support the notion that problems in phonological processing undermine the development of reading skills. These deficits are thought to persist into the adult years, even amongst people who have reached age-appropriate levels in reading (Wilson and Lesaux 2001). It has become the orthodox view that dyslexia is a phonological processing deficit, with even those who have concerned themselves with visual processing and automaticity making links to the phonological system (Stein and Talcott 1999; Nicolson and Fawcett 1999). The problem with this approach is that the focus has been on dyslexia as a reading and spelling difficulty. Problems in broader areas of functioning have not been addressed.

Research into automaticity (Nicolson and Fawcett 1995) was originally more descriptive than explanatory. It focused on the apparent failure of dyslexic people to develop a number of skills to an automatic level, including memory, motor skills and literacy, thus taking a wider perspective. Nicolson and Fawcett are not alone in suggesting that dyslexia is more than a phonological processing difficulty (Beaton et al. 1997; Frith 1999), and the different approaches to the study and understanding of dyslexia should not be perceived as contradictory, particularly as there now appears to be a consensus that phonological processing is involved. Rack (1997) has suggested that we should talk about narrowly and broadly defined dyslexia: the former can be defined as developmental phonological dyslexia, while the latter can be defined as being related to any underlying specific learning difficulty, not solely a phonological processing difficulty. This might, however, be less helpful than trying to bring together seemingly disparate views. If, as Frith (1999) suggests, 'a phonological processing deficit is persistent and universal', we should be endeavouring to explain its impact on the areas of functioning other than literacy with which dyslexics commonly report difficulties. That is, we should be asking whether such a deficit can account for the fact that dyslexic adults report difficulties with organization, including planning and time-keeping, concentration and dealing with distractions, as well as with all aspects of literacy and some features of numeracy.

Dyslexia: a pragmatic model

Enabling dyslexic people to deal effectively with both primary and secondary issues begins with promoting understanding, particularly self-understanding. They need a sensible and comprehensive model which they can understand and which:

- explains all their primary difficulties
- allows them to anticipate what might be difficult in the future
- enables them to see the relevance of specific strategies.

In turn, there should be a reduction in stress and automatic benefits for confidence and self-esteem.

The understanding we have of dyslexia derives from our professional training and background, but has been influenced enormously by what we learn from the dyslexic people we work with on a daily basis. Our experience is their experience! Reiff et al. (1993) have written:

> First-hand experience is vital for helping professionals in the field of learning disabilities to understand and appreciate the realities of living with learning disabilities. Such information provides a useful yardstick for measuring current conceptualizations, for one criterion of a definition's validity must be the ability to reflect or correlate with the experiences of those who receive a label based on

that definition. Furthermore, those insider's perspectives may provide a foundation
for formulating a new definition that blends current theoretical constructs with
first hand experience.

(Reiff et al. 1993:116)

Our practice in assessment, counselling teaching and training has for some
years been based on the assumption that all the primary difficulties experienced by dyslexic people stem from an inefficiency in their working memory
(McLoughlin et al. 1994). This view is based on the scientific literature, but
also on our practical experience. It is reinforced by the feedback provided by
our clients. We have refined the model we use according to the experiences
dyslexic people report, both in terms of the problems they encounter and the
solutions they find helpful.

Most human activities involve working memory at some level (Logie
1999), and most major information-processing models of skill acquisition and
learning include working memory as a component (Swanson 1994). The
typical tasks involving working memory are those:

> . . . in which the person must hold a small amount of material in mind for a short
> time while simultaneously carrying out further cognitive operations either on the
> material held or on other incoming materials.

(Morris et al. 1990:67)

More specifically, working memory is a dynamic system responsible for:

- holding on to information provided by the senses in the very short term
- entering information for effective storage and retrieval in long-term
  memory
- enabling the finding of information from long-term memory on demand
- allowing all three of the above to happen at the same time.

In the original model proposed by Baddeley and Hitch (1974) and revised by
Baddeley (1986), working memory was conceptualized as being made up of
three subsystems:

- The Central Executive: this controls what we attend to, and in this way
  determines what information is processed. It directs the ability to focus
  and switch attention, and combines information arriving via two
  temporary storage or 'slave' systems, which have larger memory capac-
  ities.
- The Phonological Loop: this deals with words in the broadest sense,
  remembering letters, words and numbers.

- The Visual-spatial Sketchpad: this is responsible for remembering visual images and spatial position.

Brain-imaging studies have found that these three components 'are echoed precisely in the activity seen when people carry out cognitive tasks' (Carter 1998: 189). Their functions and cortical location are shown in Figure 1.1.

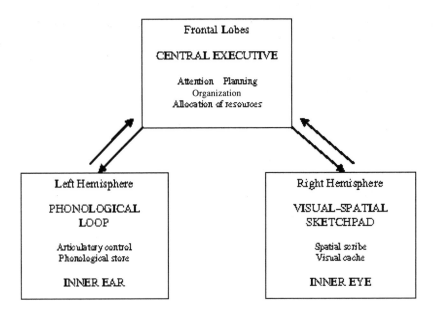

Figure 1.1 The components of working memory. (Adapted from Cohen et al. 1993)

The functions of the central executive have been described as:

> . . . a set of behavioural competencies which include planning, sequencing, the ability to sustain attention, resistance to interference, utilisation of feedback, the ability to co-ordinate simultaneous activity (i.e. the ability to change set), and more generally the ability to deal with novelty.
>
> (Crawford 1998: 209)

There is no doubt that dyslexic adults manifest difficulties with aspects of executive functioning, including planning, attention and 'changing set'. A good example of the last is the approach to reading comprehension often adopted by dyslexic people. Having developed good reading accuracy skills, they will use the same strategy, regardless of the purpose of reading. Ask them to read a poem and they will, appropriately, read all the words carefully. They will do the same with a novel, as well as with a reading comprehension task. In other words, they do not adopt a more suitable strategy. Likewise, they might well be organized in some aspects of their life but do not apply the techniques and strategies they use to other areas.

Executive functioning has been operationally defined as an individual spontaneously changing a control process as a reasonable response to an objective change in an information-processing task. That is:

1. An individual uses Strategy A with Task X.
2. Task Y is introduced.
3. The individual replaces Strategy A with Strategy B

or

During the course of problem solving, an individual finds Strategy A ineffective and replaces it with Strategy B.

(Borkowski and Burke 1996)

Dyslexic people do not seem to develop what are known as meta-cognitive skills automatically. In particular, they have difficulty with the generalization of newly acquired skills and strategies but whether or not this reflects a specific deficit in the central executive remains a subject for investigation.

The phonological loop has two components: the articulatory control system, which can hold information by articulating it subvocally; and the phonological store which holds speech-based information. Both components use phonological coding. As suggested earlier, the relationship between the phonological loop and the literacy difficulties experienced by dyslexic people has clearly been established. It is also thought to play a part in their difficulties with the procedural aspects of maths. Recent research (Venneri 2000; Vandierendonck and Franssen 2000) has also suggested a link between the phonological loop and temporal processing as well as time perception, which might explain why some dyslexic people have trouble with time management and time-keeping. It would also account for some of the difficulties they have with social interaction. A problem with the phonological loop can therefore explain some but not all of the problems they have with organization and planning.

The visual-spatial sketchpad processes visual imagery and spatial information, receiving both from visual perception or through retrieval from long-term memory in the form of images. It is less well understood than the phonological loop but is thought to store images of the visual appearance of objects and scenes. It has been suggested that, like the phonological loop, it might contain two systems – a visual cache and a spatial scribe – but this remains the subject of investigation. There seems to be little evidence for dyslexic people having a visual-spatial deficit.

Although it is mainly in the phonological loop component that dyslexic people manifest evidence of a weakness, it has been suggested that this leads to 'competitive dynamics' within the whole working memory system (Pennington et al. 1996). More specifically, Swanson et al. (1998) have written that:

> When storage demands exceed storage capacity in one of the specific store systems, however, some central executive capacity must be devoted to storage with the result that fewer resources are available for alternative activities.
>
> (Swanson et al. 1998)

It seems reasonable to hypothesize that the patterns of interaction in working memory are such that, because dyslexic people have a weakness with low order processing in the phonological loop, higher level processing such as executive functioning is disrupted when there is a heavy demand on speech and language. This would explain why dyslexic people do report problems with the behavioural competencies described as features of executive functions, including planning and organization. Further, it might work both ways in that, if the central executive is overburdened, lower level processing is less efficient. One of the phenomena reported by dyslexic people is 'good days/bad days' and an overload on either the phonological loop or the central executive might account for this. When there are 'too many words' to deal with it is hard to organize and plan. When there is too much planning and organization to be done it is hard to find the words.

The dynamics of the working memory system might also provide a further explanation as to why it seems some dyslexic people make a success of careers in occupations that rely on good visual-spatial skills. If they do not have a deficit in the visual-spatial sketchpad, perhaps when they are able to rely more on visual imagery than on verbal or written language, there is no interference with executive functioning, making tasks such as planning and organization less arduous.

When dyslexia is interpreted to clients in this way it allows one to provide answers to many of their questions. For example:

- their ability to recognize faces but not remember names can be explained in terms of the competence of the visual-spatial sketchpad, but weakness in the phonological loop
- their ability to recognize places and landmarks but not follow directions can also be explained as being the result of the competence of the visual-spatial sketchpad, but weakness in the phonological loop

- the 'good days/bad days' phenomenon can be explained as a result of the impact of a 'heavily loaded' central executive on the phonological loop
- such an interpretation also allows dyslexic people to see the relevance of using visual strategies such as mind maps to assist with planning and note-taking
- in general it enables dyslexic people to see the relevance of using particular types of strategies and also allows them to plan their time in appropriate ways. Knowing that on days when there are many demands on the behaviours influenced by executive functioning it will be very difficult to write allows them to consciously decide to leave the report to another day.

Tonnessen (1997) has suggested that proposed definitions of dyslexia should all be formulated and treated as hypotheses. On the basis of the above we propose the following definition:

Developmental dyslexia is a genetically inherited and neurologically determined inefficiency in working memory, the information-processing system fundamental to learning and performance in conventional educational and work settings. It has a particular impact on verbal and written communication as well as on organization, planning and adaptation to change.

The word 'conventional' has been added in acknowledgement of the fact that it is because we live in a world where the 'written word' has taken on such significance that life has become increasingly difficult for dyslexic people.

Dyslexia and other syndromes

Specific learning difficulties are not necessarily unitary and there is considerable overlap. It is possible to be dyslexic, dyspraxic and have Attention Deficit Disorder. Different neurological and cognitive processing problems can often produce the same behavioural characteristics, and descriptions of each syndrome include at least some of the primary characteristics listed earlier. Interventions designed to assist dyslexic people will have much in common with those directed to people with other learning difficulties, and many of the skills, compensations and accommodations outlined in subsequent chapters of this book will be relevant to all hidden disabilities. The 'label' sometimes gets in the way, and it can be more important to focus on specific needs and solutions. At the same time, professionals must recognize that labels can empower people by allowing them to identify with and learn from others through their shared experience.

There are also syndromes which, though not specific cognitive difficulties, can affect skills such as reading, and sometimes these are more prevalent amongst dyslexic people. One example is the 'visual discomfort' experienced by some people (Wilkins 1995). These are best dealt with by a specialist such as an optometrist, although adjustments can be made for them in learning and work settings.

Degrees of dyslexia

A common question asked by dyslexic people is, 'How dyslexic am I?'. The answer is not straightforward. Do we consider the difficulties with literacy or the processing problem? Furthermore, adults only need the literacy skills that they *need*. Some could have fairly basic literacy skills but this does not present them with a significant problem in terms of their daily and working lives. Others might have few problems with literacy and processing but be struggling to cope with the demands upon them. Perhaps the 'degree' should be based on the 'extent' of the disadvantage, rather than on the literacy or processing problem, especially since transitions in life are particularly difficult for dyslexic people. It is sometimes because they have been successful they seek advice. They gain promotion, for example, and suddenly there are increased demands for which they need to learn new skills and strategies quickly. Changes in circumstances at work can also have this effect. One man, for example, had resolved many of his difficulties with written expression by making good use of technological aids, such as a word processor. A new director of the firm he worked for was very keen on the use of information technology. Inter- and intra-office communication came through email. The system in his office did not allow him to spellcheck documents easily. He was also used to being able to read using a highlighter pen. Technology had provided him with solutions but had also created new difficulties. His dyslexia had not been a problem until it *became* a problem!

In commenting on a young dyslexic woman's personal account of the difficulties she experiences, Wehman (1996) wrote:

> ... it illustrates what it is like to go through life when one cannot rely on the accuracy of what one reads or expresses either in speech or in writing. It documents the anxiety and stress an individual with a learning difficulty experiences and the energy he or she must expend to cope with the tasks that most people perform automatically, accurately, and with minimal effort. Her story also points out that 'dyslexia' does not do justice to the complexity of the experience, the effort required to compensate and cope, or the many other aspects of life that are affected.
>
> (Wehman 1996: 347)

The extent to which being dyslexic affects a person is the result of a complex interaction between primary and secondary characteristics, as well as cultural factors.

There is also considerable variation in their performance: the 'good days and bad days' phenomenon referred to earlier means that 'the degree' is greater on one day than on another.

> Most Dyslexics report having good days and bad days.This is certainly true for me, tiredness often leads to a bad day, but it's a vicious circle as completing most day to day tasks takes a dyslexic person longer and more concentration is needed, therefore we are more likely to tire quicker. Reading this account many my think that my English is a lot better than the picture I have created. I would like you to bear in mind that this is the fifth rewrite after being proof read by three different people.

Frith (1999) has in fact suggested that it is the last of these that shapes the clinical picture and time-course of dyslexia, and determines the degree of 'handicap'. For some people, dyslexia is just a *difference*: they learn to work with it and find solutions, although they sometimes hide the extent of their difficulties by doing so. Being dyslexic is often a *disadvantage*, particularly in situations when there is a heavy demand on the tasks that tap the cognitive inefficiency, but these can be accommodated. Sometimes, however, the problems experienced are such that an individual is unable to perform at an expected level without considerable adjustments being made and without a high level of support. If people are to be afforded equal opportunities through current legislation, policy and provision, dyslexia has to be regarded as a *disability*.

An approach to this issue described elsewhere (McLoughlin et al. 1994) and which many people, particularly dyslexics themselves, seem to have found helpful is to describe four levels. These are:

- *Dyslexic people who are not aware of their weaknesses and have not developed skills and strategies to overcome them.* This might be someone for whom literacy has not been important until they are promoted at work. It could, for example, be the unskilled worker who gains promotion to foreman and suddenly has to deal with some paperwork.
- *Dyslexic people who are aware of their weaknesses but have not developed strategies to overcome them.* This could be someone who knows that they have problems with literacy, but they have attributed this

to other factors and have relied on friends, family and colleagues to help them deal with literacy tasks.

- *Dyslexic people who are aware of their weaknesses, and have developed their skills and strategies*, but have done so without a good understanding of what they have done or why they have done it.
- *Dyslexic people who are aware of and understand their difficulties*, and have deliberately developed skills and strategies to overcome them.

One of the purposes of any intervention should be to help people to move to level 4 – that is, to a stage where they understand the nature of their problems and can actively participate in skill development, and/or make sensible decisions about compensations and accommodations. As many are at level 3, they find it encouraging to learn they only have to get to level 4.

We have debated whether there might be a 'level 5': that is, one at which dyslexic people no longer need to work on strategy development. This rather depends upon the development of their lives and careers, as well as changes in their circumstances. If demands continue to increase, so will the need to develop new skills and strategies, but dyslexic people who understand themselves and know how to transfer the skills they have to new situations will be able to meet new challenges.

The incidence of dyslexia

Estimates of the incidence of dyslexia in the population have varied enormously over the years. They are based entirely on the child population and a variety of definitions of dyslexia. There does, however, appear to be some consensus on a figure of ten per cent of the total population, with four per cent severely dyslexic and six per cent being mildly to moderately dyslexic (Riddick 1996). As people do not 'grow out of it', it can be concluded that a significant minority of the adult population is affected to some extent, the matter of degree being contentious.

For many years it was believed that dyslexia is more prevalent amongst males than females, a ratio of 3:1 being advanced. This has been questioned, both because studies supporting such a difference have employed a variety of criteria (Miles et al. 1998) and in the light of more recent neurological studies. Shaywitz (1996) has, for example, suggested that the prevalence of dyslexia is nearly identical in the two sexes, many females not being identified because they tend more often than men to compensate as a result of essential differences in the neurological processing of language.

The cure!

Dyslexic people are vulnerable and are at risk of being attracted by 'easy solutions'. In commenting on the search for 'cures', Gardner (2000) writes:

> The popular literature of recent decades is littered with premature claims that dyslexia – or autism or depression – can be cured by a single intervention, a single treatment, a single drug. Perhaps reading disorders have an intimate relation with colours or shapes or elongated sounds or patterns of crawling, but perhaps they do not. While the misleading media personality suffers no penalties for having 'hyped' the cure prematurely, the student and her family often do suffer. Most disorders, be they physical or cognitive, are complex, and most do not lend themselves to an instant cure. Caution should be the order of the day, particularly where another person's welfare is concerned.
>
> (Gardner 2000: xiv)

Summary

- The study of and provision for dyslexic adults presents a number of challenges, including issues surrounding definition and terminology.
- The characteristics manifested by dyslexics during the adult years are such that existing attempts to explain their difficulties have been too narrow as to provide a complete understanding.
- A pragmatic model based on patterns of interaction within the working memory system can help dyslexic people to understand their difficulties, to predict what might be difficult, as well as to see the relevance of the development of specific strategies.
- Establishing levels or degrees of dyslexia requires consideration of the complex interaction between primary and secondary characteristics, as well as cultural factors such as the demands on the individual.

There is no quick fix. Helping dyslexic people overcome their difficulties can require correct intervention and hard work.

Chapter 2
Interventions

This chapter considers dyslexia within the context of lifespan development, particularly the challenges that face dyslexic people at times of transition. The chapter describes interventions that assist dyslexic people to adjust, and the fundamental principles that underlie working with them.

Introduction

Interventions designed to assist dyslexic people fulfil their potential can be categorized as those that:

- facilitate self-understanding
- enable people to function more effectively in learning, work and social settings.

There is inevitably some overlap. The professional activities involved in the former are:

- assessment
- counselling.

The activities involved in the second group are:

- skill development
- compensation
- accommodation.

Before describing these in detail, however, it is important to consider them in the context of lifespan developmental psychology, and the factors that research has shown to contribute to the success of dyslexic people, as well as the principles underlying education and training in the adult years.

Psychological development in the adult years

Although adulthood is the longest stage of development, it is the least studied and therefore not particularly well understood. Nevertheless, it has been suggested that placing dyslexia within a lifespan developmental perspective will provide a foundation for an understanding of the adjustment challenges faced by adults, and make the knowledge gained from research more meaningful (Gerber 1994).

Two overriding concepts are important when placing dyslexia within a lifespan perspective. The first is lifespan development, the basic assumptions of which Baltes et al. (1980) describe as follows:

- Development is an active lifelong process; the young adult is not the finished product. We do not just get older but continue to change, development being a process of gains and losses. As we get older, for example, we might become slower at particular tasks, but maturity and experience can make up for this.
- Development is the expression of biological and socialization processes. That is, maturation involves meeting biological and social needs, including the need to reproduce and be part of a close social network.
- Development in adulthood is multi-directional, the changes that occur involving a number of aspects, including intellectual, physical and social.

The second essential concept is that of the mediating factors which influence development. Patton and Polloway (1996) describe four main variables:

- biological and intellectual
- personal and social
- past experience
- feeling of control over life events.

The last two of these are particularly important when considering dyslexic people, as previous successes and failures have an enormous impact on them. Many will consider that they have not been successful in the past and will not have felt 'in charge'. This can have a major impact on their response to interventions.

There are several theories concerning lifespan development, but there are common themes to them all, summarized by Smith (1996) thus:

- There is a fundamental universality to human development; everyone passes through the life stages in basically the same manner.
- There is a basic sequentiality to the human experience, everyone passing through the life stages in the same order; most people leave school, secure a job, find a partner, start a family, and so on.
- The life sequence leads towards a goal; we all work towards goals, whether these be in academic achievement, job satisfaction, career development, or just general contentment.
- There are adaptive, or positive, ways and maladaptive, or negative, ways of passing through the sequence of life stages.

To those working with dyslexic people an awareness of the last of these is most important. Everyone faces a series of transitions, that is, life changes and adjustments. The transition from school to college or to work is only one. There are continual challenges, including the transition from work back to school, from in-service training to job redefinition, from lower to higher levels of a job, from one department to another, from job to job, from employment back to unemployment, from young adulthood to mid-life, and then to old age. Transitions demand energy that enables coping and adaptation and can therefore be stressful to a greater or lesser degree. Assisting individuals with adaptation at any one stage is not enough; it is as important to prepare them for what is ahead of them (Garnett 1985).

Transitions can be difficult for anyone but are particularly galling for dyslexic people, as they might not have the skills necessary to effect a positive adaptation. They may need counselling, teaching or training intermittently across all the developmental stages. Dyslexic people can be very successful in all aspects of their lives, but as they confront new demands, and discover that previously successful skills and strategies need adjustment for different situations, they might seek assistance. It is because they are in transition, often as a result of having been successful, that many dyslexic people seek an explanation of the problems they face and help with the development of their skills. Promotion, for example, can place increased demands on organizational skills as well as written language tasks such as report-writing. Adults face increasingly complex tasks, especially at work and in their social lives. It is perhaps unsurprising, therefore, that to some their difficulties seem to get worse (Gerber et al. 1990; White 1992).

Successful adjustment

A great deal of research has been devoted to identifying the factors that make life difficult for dyslexic people. There are, however, so many adult dyslexics who have achieved success in their working and personal lives that dyslexia cannot be perceived as a problem acquiring basic literacy skills which presents an insurmountable barrier to success in educational, occupational or personal contexts.

Success is not easily defined but, in strict psychological terms, it is 'goal achievement': realizing desired outcomes and avoiding undesired ones (Marsiske et al. 1995). Individual goals will inevitably be determined by expectations, including personal, familial and social demands. Essentially, working as a psychologist, counsellor, teacher or tutor with dyslexic people involves helping them to clarify their goals and assisting them in working towards achieving these.

Research that has focused on the success of people with learning difficulties, rather than the reasons they fail, has identified factors which contribute to their success (Gerber et al. 1992; Spekman et al. 1992). The overriding factor is the element to which they have been able to take control of their lives or feel in charge. Control was seen to involve two sets of distinct but interrelated factors:

- internal decisions, that is, conscious decisions about taking control of one's life
- external manifestations, that is, being able to adapt and shape oneself in order to be able to move ahead.

The internal factors identified by Gerber and his colleagues were:

- a desire to succeed
- goal orientation
- a process of re-framing.

Desire is often manifested in dyslexic people and is the reason they approach professionals for advice and guidance. The motivation to succeed is often very impressive. Many dyslexic people present as being highly motivated and this is often intrinsic rather than extrinsic. It will sometimes have developed in response to the disappointing experiences of the past.

Goal-setting is very important: dyslexic people need long-term and short-term goals. One of the roles of the professional is to assist in helping people establish clear and achievable goals. A long-term goal could be to enter a particular profession, a short-term goal to gain the necessary qualifications. It is important, however, to set even shorter-term goals, such as developing the literacy, learning and technological skills appropriate to a course of training. Addressing the short-term goals makes it easier to achieve the long-term goal. One of the main disadvantages of not being diagnosed and not understanding one's difficulties is that it is impossible to set the correct goals. When setting both short- and long-term goals it should be ensured that they are specific, realistic, measurable and have time limits so that they provide a focus (Nathan and Hill 1992).

Re-framing refers to the process of self-understanding but is more than this. It involves recognizing that there are difficulties, accepting that these exist and developing an understanding of their nature. It also refers to the process of re-interpreting dyslexia in more productive and positive ways. It is, for example, being able to say 'I do it this way', without apologizing.

> I thought you may like to have an update on (my daughter's) progress in the world of the workplace and which may serve as some encouragement to other dyslexics. She was fortunate to secure employment initially with (Company A) as a Geodata Analyst and worked for them, outsourced to (Company B) for a year. Her dyslexia was seen as a positive advantage in the interpretation of seismic data and her affinity with computers earned her a reputation which led to 'headhunters' getting on her trail!

The external factors identified by Gerber and his colleagues are:

- persistence
- learned creativity
- goodness of fit
- social ecologies.

Persistence refers to the quality of determination, often identified amongst dyslexic adults. Again this is very impressive. They are people who have experienced setbacks but have seen these as an opportunity for learning and got on with life.

Learned creativity refers to strategy development. In particular, it is important that dyslexic people become better at information processing, developing appropriate learning and memory skills. They also need to find alternative ways of dealing with tasks, and the use of technology can be a significant factor.

Goodness of fit is a reference to the notion of being in an environment where one is comfortable with the demands. A simple example would be undertaking a course of training or study where assessment is on the basis of coursework, produced on a word processor throughout the year, rather than final examinations. It is being on the right course, at the right college, or in the right job. It is here that being able to understand and therefore explain to others the nature of dyslexia and how it affects a particular individual is very important. Being able to say 'I am dyslexic, which means that I like to use my own laptop computer because I am familiar with the software' can only improve understanding.

> She has found her niche and is a highly successful young lady who flies everywhere at her employer's expense and is extremely well rewarded in terms of salary and 'perks'. More importantly she is aware of her worth without being arrogant and her self-confidence is superb to the extent of giving presentations to other professionals in her field without the least hint of any anxiety. She is a happy and fulfilled individual who takes pride in being not handicapped by dyslexia but gifted with special attributes because of it.

Social ecologies refers to the support systems people are able to take advantage of, including supportive parents, partners, supervisors and colleagues. It is, for example, having someone who will proofread pieces of work prepared by a dyslexic without being overly critical.

One of the interesting aspects of the work by Gerber et al. is its consistency with studies of 'extraordinariness'. Gardner (1996) summarizes the characteristics of extraordinary people as being:

- They stand out in the extent to which they reflect on the events of their lives, large as well as small.
- They are distinguished by their ability to identify their strengths and then exploit them.
- Extraordinary individuals fail often, and sometimes dramatically; rather than give up their challenge they learn from their setbacks and convert their defeats into opportunities.

Successful dyslexic people and extraordinary people have in common high levels of self-awareness, a good understanding of their abilities, and have been able to learn from positive and negative experiences.

The adult learner

There are six fundamental assumptions which underline the teaching and training of adults (Knowles 1990):

- the need to know
- the learner's self-concept
- the role of experience
- readiness to learn
- orientation to learn
- motivation.

These principles are especially important for dyslexic people as they transfer the control of learning to them. 'Teaching' and 'learning' are not always consistent, especially if the learner is dyslexic.

In most learning situations, the teacher makes the decisions about what will be learned, and how and when it will be learned. The teacher is the 'expert' and the student may learn and pass examinations. The student is passive and dependent; they do not know *why* it is important to learn and how knowledge can be applied to their lives. As a consequence many 'unsuccessful' adults, particularly those who are dyslexic, have a low opinion of their ability to learn. By allowing the student more control, there is less chance of failure, because learning is self-directed and task-centred.

The need to know

It is essential for adults to understand why they need to learn a skill as this increases their determination. If they can see the relationship between what they learn and the difference it will make, particularly as it relates to the achievement of their goals, they will be more focused.

Adults often do not realize that it is the underlying skills they are learning rather than the subject matter that is important in the long term. Those who have had extra help at school can suffer from 'remedial burnout'. It is particularly important therefore that they understand why they need to develop specific skills, as well as the process of learning.

The learner's self-concept

Most adults have become independent and are used to being responsible for their own lives. Once they return to a more formal learning/training situation, however, they can again feel dependent, and might resent having a teacher impose their ideas on them. They are capable and self-directing people in all other areas of their life, but are unable to be as directive in an educational setting. At the same time their experience of education and training has usually been passive and they expect to be led and taught. Dyslexic adults are likely to have had negative learning experiences at school. Positive experiences are likely to be attributed to having a 'brilliant teacher', rather than anything they have done themselves. Their self-image as a student/learner is often low. Because they learn in different ways, the need for a dyslexic person to be 'self-directed' is greater. This conflict between needs deriving from past experience and current needs must be carefully managed. In particular, a dyslexic person has to understand why they have to become independent and self-directed in learning situations.

The role of experience

Adults will have learned a great deal since leaving formal schooling, having had a wide range of experiences. They will have developed many learning strategies, but often do not recognize them. These are the best resources for dealing with new learning but dyslexic people do not value them, nor do they have the confidence to use them in a formal education setting. Individualized teaching/tutoring can draw out the strategies people have developed and allow them to capitalize on these.

Some adults, especially dyslexics, will have had negative learning experiences since leaving school and will have developed inappropriate strategies. These sometimes need to be unlearned – or at least modified – to make them more efficient before new learning can take place. Dyslexic people often hang on to what is 'safe' even when it is ineffective. Consequently, they find it hard to unlearn or be open to new approaches.

Often, people define themselves in terms of their experiences, particularly their work, e.g. I am a salesman, a computer expert, a teacher. Their identity comes from what they do, particularly if they have been successful. It is essential therefore that their experience is seen to be valued and they be encouraged to use this as a basis for dealing with new learning. Rejection of their experience means rejection of the person themselves.

Readiness to learn

Adults need to be ready to learn. People do become ready to learn the skills they need in order to cope with real-life situations. Handling money, budgeting, and so on, become very important when someone leaves home, for example. In an era of 'conspicuous achievement', when there are increasing pressures on people to have a formal qualification for whatever they do, many adults are forced into learning situations when they are not ready for it.

Orientation to learn

The desire to learn new things often increases when presented with real life situations. Transitions throughout life make different demands on people. Someone with a reading difficulty, for example, might not be motivated to learn to read until she has a child to whom she wants to read stories, or be able to help with homework.

It is important for the individual to be learning for their own reasons in the context of real life situations. That is, they should not be asked to learn something without knowing how it would be used. They need to know the purpose and how what they learn can be applied.

Motivation

The most important key to positive learning is the individual's motivation. It can be extrinsic; that is, geared to some kind of external reward, e.g. more money, a better job, etc. Intrinsic motivation is, however, more powerful; that is, when an individual wants to learn for himself, gaining satisfaction from just knowing that they can improve their performance.

Types of intervention

Interventions address the questions, 'Why is it difficult?' and 'What can be done about it?'. The specific methodologies are described in subsequent chapters but can be summarized thus:

Assessment – the purpose of this is to identify abilities, including strengths and weaknesses. The interpretation of results of an assessment should provide an explanation as to why an individual is finding certain tasks difficult and promote self-understanding. The assessment process is described in Chapter 3.

It is a strange thing to say that I felt a failure, it isn't that easy. I felt more of a freak, different, I felt that everyone believed it to be within my power to change things and I just couldn't do it. I was never tested for dyslexia but as I heard my first talk on it a few years ago I realized with relief that it fitted me. KNOWING WHAT IS WRONG HELPS.

Counselling – Counselling is the logical extension of the assessment process. The emphasis should be on the development of self-understanding, including the nature of dyslexia:

> The only thing I believe that has helped me is getting the long awaited help that I should have had as a child. Being told your dyslexic is one thing, but doing nothing to help you and explain what it is just leaving you for years thinking you were thick and stupid, and having no confidence at all. Is so very wrong. I know that I am not the only person who feels like this, which has helped me. I can read, write, but not as good as others. I am luckier than some. But the mental block I have is unbelievable at times, and when you do something wrong like make a mistake at work, you can feel the whole world falling around your feet, that's the bit I still find hard to deal with. I can smile more, I even at times can make myself feel 'better than you' because I am gifted. I can learn in al different way from the 'norms' I am different, but I am not bad or stupid, thick, lazy. I am me. I feel I can control better, and I think with age it will get better with time.

Contextualizing problems, in the sense of placing them in perspective, is important, as is helping people establish realistic and achievable goals. The issues for counselling are described in Chapter 4.

The interventions that address the question 'What can be done about it?' are skill development, compensation and accommodation. These need to be understood within the context of development across the lifespan, which is an adaptive process and is both proactive and reactive. That is, individuals can actively effect change but also react to changes such as physical and intellectual maturation, as well as changes in circumstances. There is a maxim in developmental psychology that states: 'There is no gain without loss and no loss without gain.' Successful adaptation to developmental changes has been described as involving *selection*, *optimization* and *compensation* (Marsiske et al. 1995).

Selection refers to the choice of areas for continued development. It can be specializing in a particular academic subject or job, as well as acquiring specific skills which allow one to pursue these. Selection is concerned with (a) creating and giving direction to development, and (b) managing the fundamental resource limitations inherent in all living systems. Selection acts to focus development and make the number of challenges and demands facing an individual manageable.

Optimization reflects the view that development is the internally and externally regulated search for higher levels of functioning, leading to an increase in 'adaptive fitness'. It means that individual competencies are acquired and maintained at desirable levels. Optimization is aimed at enhancing the strategies used in achieving goals.

Compensation results from internal and external limits. It relates only to those processes whereby new means are acquired or old means are reconstructed and used to counterbalance functional limits or losses. That is, compensation is an adjustment process by which the impact of internal and external limits are minimized through relying on other means. It is, however, insufficient on its own: just working harder, for example, can lead to negative consequences such as being too exhausted to do anything else (Marsiske et al. 1995).

Skill development

This is an exercise in selection and optimization. It is the process of the dyslexic person setting goals and developing the literacy, numeracy, learning, memory and technological skills necessary to achieve these. Skill is coordinated activity to achieve a goal, in terms of fluency, accuracy and speed. It involves knowing how to carry out a task, a key aspect being adaptability to new situations and changing task requirements (Chimel 1998).

> As time goes on, I get better at dealing with situations, largely because I'm that much more practised. Also faith in myself and my ability to get through grows. The first time one approaches something new one can put up a log of unconscious resistance due to fear. Once that hurdle is over things get easier. However, it is also good to acknowledge when you need help or feedback from people and not be afraid to seek it. Also, generally the more anal one can become (in terms of making notes, developing filing systems etc) the better.

Compensation

The term compensation is sometimes used in a negative way, and often suggests 'covering up'. Compensation should in fact be seen as a positive and deliberate approach to finding and applying immediate and alternative solutions. Examples would include the use of diaries and other aids such as a Filofax or an electronic device to assist with organization. The idea of compensation must be conveyed positively to dyslexic people as it can easily be perceived as 'cheating'. That is, if they have listened to the tape rather than read the book they feel they have cheated.

Working harder and investing more time or effort is regarded as compensation (Backman and Dixon 1992). It is, however, an affective factor related to the individual's personality. Often dyslexic people work far too hard because they are reluctant to find other ways of dealing with tasks or simply because this has not occurred to them. The term compensation is used here to describe deliberate efforts to find alternative and more efficient ways of dealing with tasks.

Perhaps the best example of compensation is the use of technology. This can

- augment an individual's strengths so that his or her abilities counterbalance the effects of any disabilities
- provide an alternative mode of performing a task so that the disabilities are compensated for or bypassed entirely (Lewis 1998).

Cavalier et al. (1994) have written that 'technology can act as a cognitive prosthesis replacing an ability that is missing or impaired, or as a cognitive scaffold, providing support needed to accomplish a task'. Wanderman (cited in Lewis 1998) distinguishes between 'low-tech' and 'high-tech' aids. The former include Post-It notes and flags, highlighter pens and tapes, and also digital and talking clocks and wristwatches, tape recorders and organizers. High-tech compensatory aids include the use of computers. Voice recognition software can compensate for writing difficulties, while Text to Speech software can compensate for reading difficulties. Planning software can assist with the organization of ideas on paper, as well as with note-taking, and specialist spellcheck packages can compensate for continuing problems with spelling, especially difficulties with irregular words and homophones.

The essential difference between skill development and compensation can be illustrated through action verbs (Howard and Howard 2000). Some examples are shown in Table 2.1.

Table 2.1 Different action verbs associated with skill development and compensation

Skill development	Compensation
Teach	Offset
Learn	Substitute
Train	Work around

Accommodations

These involve the adjustments made by others in work and learning settings. They include support from colleagues, supervisors, teachers and tutors, as well as provision which can be made in situations such as examinations and adjustments to work tasks and settings.

Dyslexic people should be encouraged to ask three questions: 'What can I do or what skills can I develop?'; 'What else can I do or what compensations are there?'; and 'What can others do for me or what accommodations might be available?' Some of the answers are shown in Table 2.2.

Table 2.2 Some useful approaches to problems faced by dyslexics

Task	Skill development	Compensations	Accommodations
Spelling	Over-learn key words Memory strategies Learn rules	Make lists of key words Use technology: • word processor • portable spellchecker	Ask for someone to proofread
Prioritizing workload	Develop concept of time and estimation	Use alarms and timers Use software	Seek assistance of supervisor or secretary
Filing	Sequencing skills	Colour-code and use highlighters Use technology	Delegate or seek administrative assistance
Proofreading	Develop systematic strategy	Use Text to Speech software Spellchecker and grammar checker	Delegate
Improving attention	Develop self-awareness Task analysis	Use timer and other electronic aids	Seek distraction free environment
Telephone work	Develop listening and note-taking skills Learn to control conversation	Use recording device such as answering machine Use personalized pro forma	Ask employer to provide equipment such as electronic aids and memo pads

The role of the tutor/trainer

Dyslexic people seeking help from a tutor or trainer during adulthood are lacking the skills they need to deal with the tasks before them. Assuming that they have spent the usual amount of time in formal education, it is clear that conventional teaching has not worked for them. Difficulties with executive functioning necessitate an approach to teaching which focuses on the process of learning, particularly the development of metacognitive skills. To address this, tutors and trainers who work with dyslexic people need to:

observe	body language, gestures, mannerisms, facial expressions and speech
listen to	what is said and how it is said
use	what is learned from behaviour, both verbal and non-verbal
be aware	of their need to 'unload'. If one can't help or is not seen to be helping, clients can become angry
question	Are expectations realistic? Are the strategies right? Is the programme suitable?

Tutors and trainers need to be flexible and have a good understanding of the nature of dyslexia. They also need an understanding of the task ahead. Packages or narrow courses are insufficient. The key skills required by a tutor/trainer working with a dyslexic person include:

* being able to read, understand and interpret assessment reports
* knowing how to plan a programme
* listening skills
* effective communication skills
* a knowledge of and ability to administer attainment tests
* knowing how to assess learning styles
* report and letter-writing skills
* a sense of humour
* knowing how to deal with anger and distress.

It is important to be able to relate to and empathize with each individual, developing a knowledge of how they process information. Making use of that is more important than knowing subject matter. A detailed knowledge of the client's job or the topic they are studying is not needed, as the emphasis should be on process rather than content. This addresses executive functioning and provides 'an important key to improved adaptation as students learn to structure and organize their behaviour and cognitive resources' (Eslinger 1996: 368).

Working with a dyslexic person is not just a matter of 'teaching strategies'. It is a partnership in learning, and an interactive process that should draw out the individual's learning skills. The client will refer to a task they find difficult, and provide clues as to how they deal with it and other related tasks. The tutor or trainer should then offer suggestions and solutions, providing an explanation of the underlying processes involved.

Summary

- Successful development across the lifespan involves adapting to transitions. It is a process of gains and losses. Transitions are particularly challenging for dyslexic people and it is at such times that they will need support and guidance.
- Interventions designed to assist dyslexic people should promote self-understanding and provide them with the skills they need to adapt. They should also provide alternative solutions through compensation and accommodation.
- Successful adjustment starts with the dyslexic person feeling in control and this involves internal and external factors.
- Tutors and trainers working with dyslexic people should be guided by the fundamental principles which underlie successful adult learning, particularly as these transfer control to the student/client.

Chapter 3
Identification and assessment

This chapter outlines the processes involved in the identification of dyslexia, from the initial interview to formal assessment. Appropriate measures of cognitive ability and attainment are described and the issue of reporting, both verbal and written, is addressed. Sample psychological reports are provided.

Introduction

Identification and assessment addresses the question, 'Why are tasks difficult?'. It is a process known as differential diagnosis, as it attempts to isolate aetiological factors associated with the syndrome of dyslexia from other potential explanations for difficulties. It involves several stages (see Table 3.1):

- information-gathering – interview
- screening – this formally identifies the existence of behavioural characteristics
- psychological testing – this endeavours to explain the existence of behavioural characteristics.

Table 3.1 Steps in assessment

STRUCTURED INTERVIEW
↓ positive
SCREENING
↓ positive
FORMAL PSYCHOLOGICAL ASSESSMENT

Information-gathering

Definitions that focus on the discrepancy between ability and attainment have been rejected but the word 'discrepancy' remains useful in the identification process. Many dyslexic people do display inconsistencies in their performance, the most obvious being when someone appears to be intelligent and has spent the usual amount of time in school but cannot read and write. There is also an inconsistency in a professionally trained person having difficulty with spelling. It is evidence of such discrepancies which leads to an initial evaluation. Adult dyslexics are often self-referred, recognizing inconsistencies in their performance themselves, but it is also friends, tutors or employers who notice these and suggest an assessment.

There are many ways of explaining such discrepancies and they should not automatically lead one to conclude that a person is dyslexic. They should not be dismissed either: one of the reasons so many dyslexic people have not been identified during their school years is that someone has jumped to an obvious and incorrect conclusion. Information should be gathered in a systematic way through interviews, screening and formal psychological evaluation.

The purpose of assessment is ultimately to explain why there are discrepancies in an individual's performance, not just to label them as being dyslexic. To be effective an assessment should be rigorous. It should distinguish between:

- People whose cognitive and language skills are adequate, but whose educational experience has been such that they leave school without having developed appropriate skills. There are also many intelligent people who, because of inadequate education, have poor literacy skills or who have underachieved in life generally.
- People whose overall levels of cognitive and language functioning are such as to predispose them towards finding the acquisition of literacy, numeracy, learning and work-related skills difficult. Many people of low intelligence, for example, exhibit behaviours, such as difficulties with literacy and working memory, which have typically been associated with dyslexia.
- People whose cognitive and language functioning is at an average or better than average level, but who have specific areas of weakness which undermine their acquisition of skills. Dyslexic people, for example, come into this category.

Before the process begins, it is *essential* to establish that an individual is ready to accept the conclusion to which it might lead. Some people are just content to know that they 'might' be dyslexic, and they should *never* be pressed into pursuing the matter beyond a level they are comfortable with.

> Before I knew I dealt with things. Now my entire world is in a whirlwind. Now I feel everything is too much. I used to know where everything was. Now everything is too complicated. I have got to deal with it. I just need to work out how.

Interviews

The assessment process should begin with an interview. The information of significance includes that relating to education, qualifications, work experience, present occupation and family history, including details of the incidence of dyslexia within the family, as well as health. This information is best collected using a structured interview. An example is provided in Appendix 1, but interview schedules are best designed for specific educational and work settings. There are particular issues which should be raised. These include:

- reason for referral
- goals
- understanding of dyslexia
- educational experience
- experience of learning and training
- medical information.

Reason for referral

There will be a reason as to why an explanation for difficulties experienced is important at a particular point in time. Knowing this will help establish a client's level of motivation. Those who are self-referred are likely to be more motivated to understand and address their difficulties than those who have been persuaded by others, for example, friends, relatives or employers, to seek advice.

Goals

A client might have difficulty identifying their goals and might talk in general terms. Helping them to be more specific can influence the assessment process, particularly the advice given on follow-up. It may transpire, for example, that they are required to work with numbers, to write reports quickly and under pressure, to use filing systems, to do tasks in certain sequences or to carry out instructions given verbally, all of which place heavy demands on working memory. Specific information such as this can lead to them being provided with a satisfactory explanation for all their difficulties, as well as advice on appropriate skills, compensations and accommodations.

Understanding of dyslexia

What people understand about their difficulties is helpful in determining the level of explanation they will require. Most will describe behavioural characteristics such as poor spelling and not see the relevance of other factors such as memory.

Educational experience

The client's achievements, failures and preferences for particular subjects should be explored in detail. Absence through illness or difficult family circumstances may offer an explanation for lack of academic success. More useful information can be gleaned from their answers to questions about specific difficulties they encountered and whether these were addressed by teachers. Inconsistencies in performance are especially relevant. 'My class work was good but I had trouble with examinations' is a common remark. Their own explanations for poor performance at school are also important as they can reveal something about their self-concept. 'I didn't do very well but then I am lazy' comes up time and time again. They have come to believe it because it is what their teachers and school reports said.

Experience of learning and training

Training or other learning situations that the client has been exposed to since leaving school should be explored. This enables one to determine if strategies for coping with learning have been developed. It also provides further insights into how they perceive themselves in learning contexts. It could be that they have low expectations of themselves or have become resigned to failure. Alternatively, they may be overcompensating by being very persistent and working much harder than others.

Medical information

As well as general health, any history of neurological disorder and/or head injury is of significance as one might be dealing with acquired dyslexia.

Sensory impairments may also have a bearing: impairments in hearing or vision can, for example, undermine the development of perceptual processes which underlie literacy skills. If there is any doubt concerning the integrity of hearing and vision then an investigation by an appropriately qualified person should be recommended.

The conduct of interviews and screening

Whilst conducting an interview it is important to note how clients answer questions and communicate information generally. A tendency to talk excessively, for example, may be a strategy for limiting the flow of information received. Alternatively, a reluctance to speak may be a way of hiding an inability to keep track of what is said. Word-finding difficulties will often be in evidence. Furthermore, it is not enough simply to ask an individual if they are well organized or if they have difficulty with remembering telephone numbers. They might have developed strategies for overcoming such difficulties and not really be aware of the fact that they are 'different' in the way they deal with such things. It is more important to ask *how* they deal with such tasks.

The information gathered in an interview is critical to identification. It might be sufficient to suggest that someone should not pursue the matter further but it is more likely that it will indicate that further investigation is warranted and a screening evaluation can be recommended.

Whether conducting a screening evaluation or a full psychological assessment there are several considerations those administering tests should take into account, shown in Table 3.2.

Table 3.2 Considerations in testing

1. Assessment should promote self-understanding and should be a positive rather than a negative experience.
2. Dyslexic people have been humiliated in the past and should be allowed their dignity.
3. Assessments are only as good as the information they yield and should focus on the information required for diagnosis, and the provision of advice.
4. Tests used should have a face validity for the client: that is, they should clearly relate to explanations for difficulties and advice on strategy development.
5. Feedback should be provided during the course of the assessment, as this reduces anxiety. Many people worry that the assessment will show them to be lacking intelligence and need reassurance that this is not the case early on in the process.

As I suppose you may have gathered, I was very nervous and appre-
hensive about the day and really expected the whole thing to be a
much more difficult and traumatic experience than in the end it
turned out to be. After the assessment, I felt a little 'mixed up', well,
for want of a better phrase, I really found it difficult to explain
exactly how I felt. As I explained to you, part of me felt relieved
because at last there was a legitimate label to explain why, yes, I may
make mistakes, but this doesn't mean that I'm 'thick'. On the other
hand, although part of me had accepted (from the original
assessment that I told you about) that I was dyslexic, another part
had always hope that if I worked hard enough and tried hard
enough, the problem would somehow magically disappear. Coming
to see you and taking part in the assessment meant letting go of that
part of myself. I locked myself away in my room for a few days afterwards, not because I felt particularly upset, but because I needed to
sort things out in my head – but I feel much better now and really
feel that coming to see you is probably one of the best and most
sensible things that I ever did. This visit, plus becoming registered as
a disabled adult, were quite symbolic for me in the sense that for me
it's the beginning of facing up to who and what I am, coping with it,
and indeed realizing that 'this is me' – and there's nothing to be
ashamed or embarrassed about. This will make it so much easier, I
feel, not only to cope with my dyslexia, but also to work in
partnership with my employers so that they can better support me.

Screening

One of the biggest improvements in identifying dyslexia during the adult
years has been in the development of relevant screening tests so that we no
longer need to rely on adapting those devised for use with children. There is
no excuse for using inappropriate tests although the practice continues –
perhaps the worst example being the 30-year-old who was complimented on
his very high non-verbal ability which had been evaluated by asking him to
draw a man!

Screening instruments range from the widely used and recently much
improved Adult Dyslexia Checklist (Everatt and Smythe 2001), reproduced in
Appendix B, to computer-based packages such as QuickScan, and tests
including the Dyslexia Adult Screening Test.

The principle of 'specificity', that is, the notion that dyslexic people have
an underlying neurological inefficiency, is central to the assessment process.

Even in screening some measurement of general ability as well as specific processes such as working memory is important. Any procedure that fails to incorporate appropriate cognitive tests is likely to produce false positives: that is, the incorrect identification of people who have low intelligence. This can raise their expectations and lead to further frustrations. One young woman who had been told she was dyslexic on the basis of a literacy assessment alone was trying to complete university level studies with an IQ of 60. Both StudyScan/QuickScan and the Dyslexia Adult Screening Test include relevant measures, but tutors and teachers can also use the Verbal and Spatial Reasoning Test – VESPAR (Langdon and Warrington 1995). This consists of three verbal subtests – 'Verbal odd one', 'Verbal Analogy' and 'Verbal Series'; and three non-verbal tests – 'Spatial odd one', 'Spatial Analogy' and 'Spatial Series'. It was designed as a measure of reasoning ability, but in such a way as to minimize the influence of motor, sensory and cognitive impairments.

StudyScan and QuickScan

The StudyScan Suite (Zdzienski 1997) is a package of computer programs including QuickScan, a questionnaire designed for adults who want to find out about the way they learn. QuickScan outlines individual learning preferences and study styles, and produces a printed report on personalized study guidelines. It also indicates whether the student shows any signs of dyslexia and may result in a recommendation to go on to complete the full assessment in StudyScan.

StudyScan is a comprehensive battery of tests that covers most aspects of a full educational assessment. It will give an indication of general levels of attainment and highlight specific areas of strengths and weakness. It will automatically analyse the individual performance of students in different tests and produce a printed diagnostic report. StudyScan contains the following tests:

- memory (auditory and visual) and coding
- literacy (including reading and listening comprehension, spelling and punctuation)
- numeracy (including calculations and applications)
- cognitive abilities (including verbal and non-verbal reasoning, as well as vocabulary)
- proficiency tests (speed of reading and speed of copying)
- free writing.

Computerized packages can meet the need for quick and low cost screening and StudyScan is being used in the further and higher education sectors. It has been suggested that it has the potential for a wider application, and that one of the advantages of such a package is that it minimizes the need for clinical judgement (Reid and Kirk 2000). One of the major flaws of computerized assessment is, however, that it does not allow for behavioural observation and clinical judgement, and it is often the latter which is crucial in diagnosis.

Dyslexia Adult Screening Test (DAST)

The Dyslexia Adult Screening Test (Fawcett and Nicolson 1998) consists of eleven individual subtests, including:

- rapid naming
- one minute reading
- postural stability
- phonemic segmentation
- two minute spelling
- backwards digit span
- nonsense passage reading
- non-verbal reasoning
- one minute writing
- verbal fluency
- semantic fluency.

The DAST is soundly based in the authors' research into automaticity and several of the subtests are derived from existing established tests. The DAST provides an 'at risk' score and can be a useful first step in formal identification but it is not without its faults. Gunn suggests that use of the DAST 'raises underlying issues that cause more problems than it solves' (2000: 42). These include the need for a clear distinction between dyslexia and general learning difficulties at the screening stage; the use of psychological tests by non-psychologists; and the need for clarity as to its purpose. Certainly some of the suggestions for the application of the results it yields are questionable. Recommending that a student be allowed extra time in examinations on the basis of their performance on the 'One Minute Reading' and/or 'One Minute Writing' tests would seem inappropriate given that it is the rate of silent reading for comprehension which is important in an examination, and that the writing task is essentially a copying test.

Scholastic Abilities Test for Adults (SATA)

Another test worthy of mention here is the Scholastic Abilities Test for Adults developed in the USA. It is based on the discrepancy model and does not include tests of specific processing skills, but some of the achievement tests are quite useful for the measurement of attainment.

The SATA (Bryant et al. 1991) is designed to be a general measure of scholastic accomplishment. It can be administered as an individual or group test, and either timed or untimed, although the former is recommended for group testing. The SATA consists of nine subtests. Subtests 1 to 3 measure aptitudes, and are:

- Verbal Reasoning
- Non-verbal Reasoning
- Quantitative Reasoning.

The achievement tests are:

- Reading Vocabulary: a measure of word understanding. Four words are presented in a column and examinees have to decide if two of them are semantically related in some way and why.
- Reading Comprehension: measures an individual's ability to answer questions about passages that have been read silently. There are ten passages, each of which is followed by six questions in multiple choice format.
- Maths Calculations: assesses knowledge of the basic arithmetic facts and algorithms of addition, subtraction, multiplication and division, as well as their application in decimal and fractional forms.
- Maths Application: assesses the ability to apply fundamental mathematical facts and algorithms to solve word problems.
- Writing Mechanics: assesses skills in spelling, capitalization and punctuation. The examinee has an unpunctuated sentence with one word missing in front of them: a word is read aloud, they have to spell it correctly and amend the punctuation.
- Writing Composition: the examinee has a set of four pictures in front of them: these relate to job advancement and are used as a theme of a story which they have to write. The work is checked for vocabulary and thematic content.

Formal diagnosis

It is formal diagnosis which can best answer the question: 'Why are tasks difficult?' As well as provide an answer to this question, it should identify abilities and strengths. A thorough assessment should identify what a dyslexic person can do as well as what they can't do.

Formal diagnosis involves psychological testing, careful observation and clinical judgement. It is carried out by a psychologist because it requires the interpretation of 'closed tests' which are only available to qualified psychologists, as well as the exercise of judgements that require psychological understanding and knowledge. The steps leading to formal diagnosis are shown in Table 3.3.

Table 3.3 Steps in diagnosis

Intelligence (WAIS-III)

↓

Analysis of WAIS-III Profile

↓

Testing of Specific Cognitive Abilities
(e.g. Memory, Executive Functioning)

↓

Achievement:
Reading
Writing
Spelling
Numeracy

Testing intelligence

There is considerable debate and much disagreement concerning the measurement of intelligence. In the context of dyslexia, however, the issue is quite clear. The concern is to distinguish between the second and third groups of people described earlier, namely:

- people whose overall level of cognitive and language functioning are such as to predispose them towards finding the acquisition of literacy, numeracy, learning and work-related skills difficult, i.e. people who have problems learning most things
- people whose cognitive and language functioning is at an average or better than average level but who have specific areas of weakness which undermine their acquisition of some skills.

It is the latter group who constitute the population of people who have specific learning and performance difficulties such as dyslexia.

> As a first step in rebuilding my confidence, my assessment to identify if I had any specific cognitive skills and weaknesses has helped a great deal. While the assessment identified that I was dyslexic it also showed that I was far from unintelligent; importantly, the assessment has given me tangible evidence of this fact. Further explanation made me realize that it is something I should now use to constructively develop an awareness of my skills and abilities.

To eliminate ' general' learning problems, a comprehensive measure of intellectual ability or intelligence is administered. Usually this is the Wechsler Adult Intelligence Scale (III). This can be used as a normative test, allowing comparison with others of the same age, as an ipsative test, allowing comparison of some of an individual's abilities with other abilities, and as a measure of competencies.

WAIS-III as a normative test

The WAIS-III consists of 11 subtests, six forming a verbal scale and five forming a performance scale. It yields separate scores for verbal, performance and full scale IQs, the last being calculated on the basis of all 11 subtests. There are also three supplementary tests: Letter Number Sequencing on the Verbal Scale; Object Assembly; and Symbol Search on the Performance Scale. The subtests and the abilities they purport to measure are as follows.

Verbal tests
- Information: this measures the ability to access long-term memory by focusing on general knowledge.
- Digit Span: this subtest is designed to measure auditory sequential

memory. It has two components, digits forwards and digits reversed. The former is thought to measure short-term memory; the latter is a test of working memory – particularly important in the diagnosis of dyslexia.

- Vocabulary: this subtest, which requires the examinee to define words, involves word knowledge and the ability to express ideas.
- Arithmetic: this is a test of mental arithmetic, and requires an understanding of basic mathematical concepts: it also taps memory and attention.
- Comprehension: this subtest is designed to measure 'common sense', and the ability to understand social situations, as well as use practical reasoning.
- Similarities: this measures verbal concept formation and verbal reasoning. It requires the individual to consider the relationship between objects and concepts by explaining what they have in common. It is regarded as a good test of general intellectual ability, since it is virtually independent of any memory component and it is not unduly influenced by social and educational background.
- Letter Number Sequencing: this involves the recall of combinations of letters and numbers, and is a measure of working memory.

Performance tests

- Picture Completion: a measure of visual recognition and discrimination.
- Picture Arrangement: this subtest measures a number of skills including sequential thinking ability.
- Block Design: this measures visuospatial organization.
- Matrix Reasoning: this measures non-verbal abstract reasoning ability.
- Digit Symbol – Coding: requires the individual to associate an abstract symbol with a number and write it down. It is a strictly timed test that requires speed and accuracy. It can also be administered as a measure of incidental learning, i.e. the extent to which the symbols can be remembered without someone having tried to learn them.
- Symbol Search: a symbol checking task, involving memory and visual motor speed.
- Object Assembly: this subtest is a measure of visuospatial organization or spatial ability. It requires the individual to assemble some jigsaw puzzles of familiar objects.

Although designed as a measure of intelligence, originally defined by Wechsler as the 'capacity of the individual to act purposefully, to think rationally, and to deal effectively with his environment' (Wechsler 1944: 3), in the context of identifying dyslexia the WAIS-III is at its least useful as a measure of IQ. It will distinguish between the 'unable' and those who have specific difficulties, but because some of the subtests tap the areas of cognitive weakness associated with dyslexia, the overall scores can be an underestimate of potential. Miles (1996), for example, has questioned the value of calculating a global IQ. This was rectified to some extent by the development of the scale revised as a neurological instrument (WAIS-RNI) which provided multiple choice formats for subtests such as 'Information', but this has yet to be made compatible with the latest version of the WAIS.

In situations where a quick measure of intelligence is helpful, a four subtest version of the WAIS-III is available. Known as WASI (Wechsler Abbreviated Scale of Intelligence), it provides a verbal IQ based on 'Vocabulary' and 'Similarities', a performance IQ based on 'Block Design' and 'Matrix Reasoning', as well as a full scale IQ based on all four. A two subtest full scale IQ can be calculated on the basis of 'Vocabulary' and 'Matrix Reasoning'.

The WAIS-III as an ipsative test

The WAIS-III measures a wide range of abilities and dyslexic people often show an uneven profile, reflecting contrasting strengths and weaknesses. Ipsative testing refers to considerations of the potential implications of such contrasts.

A considerable amount of research has been devoted to identifying 'typical' dyslexic profiles of Wechsler subtest scores. Bannatyne (1974), for example, has proposed four groups of subtest combinations on which dyslexics and non-dyslexics are presumed to differ. They are 'Spatial' ('Picture Completion', 'Block Design' and 'Object Assembly'), 'Verbal Conceptualization' ('Comprehension', 'Similarities', 'Vocabulary'), 'Sequential' ('Digit Span', 'Arithmetic', 'Digit Symbol – Coding') and 'Acquired Knowledge' ('Information', 'Arithmetic', 'Vocabulary'). Dyslexics have been found to be equal to, or better than, non-dyslexics in spatial ability and conceptual ability but they do less well in sequencing ability and acquired knowledge.

A large number of studies have identified what is known as the ACID profile of Wechsler subtest scores and this has been used as a basis for diagnosing dyslexia. That is, 'Arithmetic', 'Digit Symbol – Coding', 'Information' and 'Digit Span' have been shown to be the subtests on which dyslexics typically do less well than non-dyslexics (Thomson 1990). Much of this research has involved children but there are several studies of adults which have provided support both for Bannatyne's clusters and the ACID profile (Cordoni and O'Donnell 1981; Salvia and Gajar 1988; Katz et al. 1993). A typical ACID profile is shown in Table 3.4.

Table 3.4 A typical ACID profile

WAIS-III PROFILE – Verbal Scale

		Inf	DS	Vocab	Arithmetic	Comp	Sim	LNS	
H	19								19
I	18								18
G	17								17
H	16								16
	15								15
	14								14
	13								13
	12					X	X		12
AV-	11			X					11
ER-	10								10
AGE	9								9
	8	X			X				8
	7		X					X	7
	6								6
	5								5
	4								4
L	3								3
O	2								2
W	1								1

WAIS-III PROFILE – Performance Scale

		PC	PA	Block Design	Matrix Reasoning	Digit Symbol	Symbol Search	
H	19							19
I	18							18
G	17							17
H	16							16
	15							15
	14							14
	13				X			13
	12			X				12
AV-	11							11
ER-	10	–X—					—X–	10
AGE	9		X					9
	8							8
	7					X		7
	6							6
	5							5
	4							4
L	3							3
O	2							2
W	1							1

The diagnostic utility of the ACID profile has been called into question (Frederickson 1999). However, the problem is not with the profile as such but that it has taken on a life of its own: the presence of an ACID profile being interpreted as definitive when there might be other explanations for some of the low scores; and the absence of an ACID profile leading to dyslexia being dismissed although behavioural observation suggests that the examinee might have had difficulty with some of the ACID subtests.

Critics of the reliance on the ACID profile as an indicator have failed to adequately address the issue of why it is so often a feature of the performance on the WAIS amongst people who have experienced problems with literacy. One way of interpreting it is that it reflects an inefficiency in working memory, 'Information', 'Arithmetic', 'Digit Span' and 'Digit Symbol – Coding' all tapping this to a greater or lesser extent. Frith (1999) is more specific, regarding the profile as evidence of a phonological deficit. At the very least, it should lead to hypotheses about why tasks are difficult, which can then be explored through further testing.

When interpreting the WAIS, psychologists should not just examine the subtest scores with a view to determining if the ACID profile exists. They should, during the course of administration, make behavioural observations such as those listed in Table 3.5.

Table 3.5 What to look for when testing

1. General confidence
2. Problems with 'word finding'
3. WAIS-III
   Information
       – problems with labels:
       e.g. names of people;
       directions
   Arithmetic
       – use of fingers
       – sub-vocalization
       – asking for pen and paper
   Digit Span
       – difference between forwards and reversed
   Digit Span and Letter Number Sequencing
       – use of fingers
       – sub-vocalization
       – chunking
   Digit Symbol and Symbol Search
       – use of finger as a guide
       – sub-vocalization
       – selection

The WAIS-III as a measure of competencies

As well as IQ scores the WAIS-III allows for the calculation of Index Scores: Verbal Comprehension, Perceptual Organization, Working Memory and Processing Speed, calculated on the basis of Scale scores as follows:

Verbal Comprehension	*Perceptual Organization*
Vocabulary	Picture Completion
Similarities	Block Design
Information	Matrix Reasoning

Working Memory	*Processing Speed*
Arithmetic	Digit Symbol – Coding
Digit Span	Symbol Search
Letter Number Sequencing	

The index scores provide useful diagnostic information, the discrepancies amongst them being regarded as a better guide to evidence of a learning difficulty than the ACID profile (Kaufman and Lichtenberger 1999). They also provide measures of competencies and this enables the psychologist to inform clients of what they can do, as well as explain why some things are difficult for them. Further, whilst the relevance of IQ might be questioned, identifying particular abilities – notably, language skills such as vocabulary, verbal reasoning and comprehension – is important as they underlie the development of reading skills. Without an adequate vocabulary, for example, skills such as reading comprehension will be impaired.

Knowing about competencies is helpful in providing academic and career guidance. Individuals who have an average or better than average Perceptual Organization Index score are likely to be suited to occupations involving visual perceptual skills. Abilities such as verbal comprehension have been identified as good predictors of success at college (Leonard 1991) and in making the transition from school to employment (Faas and D'Alonzo 1990).

The WAIS and multilingualism

The WAIS is available in many languages and ideally people should always be tested in their first language. This does not mean, however, that it cannot be used to assess those who are working in an English-speaking environment but, therefore, in a second language. In a study of overseas students attending a university in the United Kingdom, McLoughlin and Beard (2000) found that those experiencing more difficulty than anticipated with the development of their literacy and learning skills gained low scores on the subtests associated with the ACID profile. 'Digit Span', 'Digit Symbol – Coding' and 'Symbol Search' can be regarded as culture-free, and provided the language is understood the 'Arithmetic' test is also culture-free. Information is culturally biased but there are a number of items that can be considered as universals. The sun rises in the east wherever one comes from, for example. The main difference between the profiles of students from the UK and those from overseas was that the latter had more difficulty with the Vocabulary subtest, although there was considerable variation. Similarities and Comprehension posed fewer difficulties, the former requiring only one or two word answers and the latter 'common sense' responses.

Further psychological testing

Administration of the WAIS-III will have provided insights into cognitive testing and clues about areas of weaknesses which can be pursued. Specific tests of phonological processing could be administered, but there are few of these available for adults and using tests designed for children is inappropriate. Furthermore, it is important in helping adults understand why tasks are difficult that they are able to see the relationship between tests and the difficulties they experience. Yet another consideration is that test results can have implications for training and teaching: knowing strengths is as important as identifying weaknesses.

The Wechsler Memory Scales (third edition – WMS-III: Wechsler 1999b) provide a very comprehensive measure of memory skills, including:

- Immediate Memory: auditory and visual: specific auditory subtests are 'Logical Memory' and 'Paired Associate Learning', while visual subtests are 'Memory for Faces' and 'Family Pictures'.
- General (Delayed) Memory: auditory and visual: specific auditory subtests include alternative forms of 'Logical Memory' and 'Paired Associates', as well as 'Auditory Recognition': the visual tests are alternative forms of 'Memory for Faces' and 'Family Pictures'.
- Working Memory: auditory and visual: the auditory subtest is the 'Letter Number Sequencing' test included in the WAIS-III and the visual subtest is 'Spatial Span', described as a visual equivalent to 'Digit Span'.

Like the WAIS-III, it provides individual subtest scores as well as Index scores. Both sets of scores are useful diagnostically, as well as in programme planning. Low scores clarify the specific areas of weakness, and average or better than average scores provide clues as to the strategies that might help circumvent these.

The WMS-III is only available to psychologists but teachers and tutors can use the Learning Efficiency Test II (Webster 1997) to good effect. This test has norms for adult populations and provides measures of auditory immediate, short-term and long-term recall, as well as visual equivalents. It is designed to identify preferred learning styles (auditory or visual), global and specific weaknesses, and the strategies individuals use when learning.

Executive functioning

The adequacy of the executive system is measured by transfer or generalization tests. The most commonly used instrument is the Wisconsin Card Sort Test (Heaton et al. 1993). It measures the ability to shift cognitive strategies in response to changing environmental contingencies. It has, however, been suggested that the Wisconsin Card Sort Test is insufficiently sensitive in the detection of executive problems, and has been concluded that the test should not be used for clinical purposes in its present form (Bowden et al. 1998). A more recently developed British test is the Behavioural Assessment of Dysexecutive Syndrome (BADS). The authors of this test (Wilson et al. 1996) argue that most conventional neuropsychological tests fail to capture the core difficulties faced by someone with executive dysfunction as they are typically highly structured, deal with circumscribed material and the criteria for success are clearly specified.

Executive functioning is often difficult to assess because although the individual components are intact, people may be unable to use these skills. Clients are asked to tackle a single explicit problem, one at a time. In contrast, many everyday activities involving executive abilities require people to organize or plan their behaviour over long time periods, or to set priorities in the face of two or more competing tasks. If the pragmatic model of dyslexia described in Chapter 1 is correct it is also likely that dyslexic people will not show executive functioning problems unless there are heavy demands on the phonological loop.

The BADS test consists of the following subtests:

- Rule Shift cards: these examine the subject's ability to respond correctly to a rule and to shift from one rule to another.
- Action Programme: a practical problem-solving task, which requires five steps for its solution. The steps involve simple skills but one has to work backwards: that is, it is necessary to work out what needs to be done

before concentrating on how to achieve that end.

- Key Search: subjects are asked to show how they would find a lost key in a field. It is analogous to a real-life situation and also measures the ability to plan an efficient course of action.
- Temporal Judgement: this involves the estimation of answers to questions, e.g. How long does a dog live for?
- Zoo Map: a test of planning in which subjects are required to show they would visit a series of designated locations in a zoo.
- Modified Six Elements: this measures the ability to plan, organize and monitor behaviour. It also taps prospective memory, that is the ability to carry out an intention at a future time. Clients are asked to complete three tasks in ten minutes. The tasks include dictation, arithmetic and picture naming.
- Dysexecutive Questionnaire: a 20 item questionnaire constructed to sample the range of problems commonly associated with Dysexecutive Syndrome. There is one form for the subject and one for someone who has close contact with them.

The BADS provides standardized scores which allow ratings from impaired to very superior. Limited experience of using it with dyslexic people suggests that it can be of value, tests such as Temporal Judgement being particularly revealing.

Achievements in literacy and numeracy

Reading

There are essentially three aims in assessing an adult's reading skills:

- establishing whether the reader has sufficient competence in all aspects of reading as to enable them to deal with the tasks they face on a daily basis, in a particular occupation, or at least the programme of study leading to that occupation
- diagnosing reading difficulties and establishing a starting point for instruction
- measuring progress on reading programmes.

Reading levels

Where standardized tests have been used to assess reading levels scores have often been expressed as reading ages. This practice must be abandoned when working with adults. It is not helpful for an adult to know they have a reading age of 10 years, for example, and is demoralizing as they relate it to their chronological age. Self-esteem can be damaged and there are people who have lost their jobs because employers do not know what it means in real terms. We only need the reading skills we *need*, that is the skills which enable us to deal with the demands placed upon us by our educational, work and social programmes. The most enduring and important situation in which adults need reading skills is their work environment. Criteria for establishing levels of attainment amongst adults are, therefore, best derived from work tasks.

Adult literacy and numeracy skills can be rated as being at one of four levels. These are professional, technical, vocational and functional. For those who are more familiar with reading in an educational setting these levels are set out in Table 3.6 with their equivalent educational levels.

Table 3.6 Levels of reading

Level	Education level	Age
Professional	GCE A-level and above	Over 16 years
Technical	Beginning of secondary school to GCSE level	13–16 years
Vocational	Primary school	9–12 years
Functional	Infant school	Up to 9 years

Professional reading skills are those required by GCE A-level courses as well as by university studies and a professional occupation. Someone who has reached this level is capable of independent reading, has a wide reading vocabulary and the ability to understand sophisticated material.

Individuals who read at the technical level have sufficient competence in decoding and comprehension as to enable them to complete GCSE courses and a programme of further education. They would be able to work in occupations such as sales, secretarial work and computing. Those who are at the vocational level in all aspects of reading would have difficulty completing secondary education but should be able to understand the fundamental needs of many jobs that require a moderate amount of reading. They should be capable of undertaking semi-skilled work which only requires a minimum amount of reading.

Adults who read only at the functional level will show considerable variation but it can be expected that they will find jobs that require even a moderate amount of reading difficult. Those at the upper end of the functional level may have sufficient reading survival skills as to enable them to deal with jobs which place minimal demands upon reading skills but those at the lower end may not be able to deal with any type of job which requires some reading.

Within these four levels individuals can be identified as being at an independent, instructional or frustrational stage. The first reflects a stage at which the reader demonstrates excellent proficiency and is able to deal with material without assistance. The instructional stage indicates that the reader requires minimal assistance. Performance at this stage suggests that the reader would benefit from tuition to bring up their skills within this level. Once this stage has been established it is assumed someone can be given materials that are written at the particular reading level. Individuals who score at the frustrational stage cannot deal with reading material at that particular level and should be provided with materials at a lower level.

The components of reading assessment

Reading is a very complex skill, however. For the purpose of assessment, Aaron and Baker (1991) have suggested that it can be regarded as having two major components:

- decoding: the ability to pronounce the word, either overtly or covertly
- comprehension: the ability to understand the word and the text.

It is important to add to the first of these the ability to correctly pronounce the word covertly at an acceptable rate, as being able to read to oneself quickly is important in the adult years. To the second should be added 'when listening'. Listening comprehension underlies many adult activities including working, learning and socializing.

The assessment of adult reading skills should therefore include measures of decoding, reading and listening comprehension, as well as reading rate. Each subskill should be evaluated separately, particularly when the aim of an assessment is to diagnose reading difficulties and plan remedial instruction.

Decoding

Decoding skill has been measured typically by the use of single word reading and prose reading tests. There have been many examples of the first and they are much the same. They consist of lists of words graded in order of difficulty. The New Adult Reading Test (Nelson and Willison 1991), although sometimes listed as a single word reading test, was designed to estimate intelligence retrospectively, i.e. prior to deterioration through physical or psychiatric illness. The Wide Range Achievement Test (third edition – WRAT-3: Jastak and Wilkinson 1993) is normed for the adult population. It consists of tests with 42 words on a card. Spreen and Strauss (1991) questioned the use of earlier versions outside the USA because of a lack of correspondence with academic curricula in other English-speaking countries. They also argued that, due to a lack of availability of technical data regarding the properties of the test, 'as well as shortcomings in the standardization procedures the test should not be used as a diagnostic measure of academic difficulties' (Spreen and Strauss 1991: 109). The latest version has overcome some of these criticisms, in that more recent technical data have been provided. It is still, however, culturally specific and might not therefore 'travel well'.

The Spadafore Diagnostic Reading Test (Spadafore 1983) includes tests of single word reading which are better presented than they are on most individual reading tests: i.e. there are 20 words on a page for each grade level. This is far less threatening for the adult who has experienced problems with literacy than being presented with a large number of words all at once. It does have grade norms but is criterion-referenced, indicating whether an individual has reached the independent, instructional or frustrational stage for each of the four levels of reading described above.

Although they do have a place in the assessment of decoding skill, single word reading tests are of a limited value. When assessing an adult's reading skills, one is really attempting to determine how well they can function in everyday life, as well as in academic and work settings. Most people have to deal with prose rather than individual words. Prose reading tests usually consist of a set of passages graded in order of difficulty, which the examinee has to read aloud. The Spadafore Diagnostic Reading Test does have a prose or oral reading component and consists of passages up to the professional level of reading.

Two other prose reading tasks have become quite widely used in the assessment of adult reading skills. These are cloze tests, favoured by organizations such as the Adult Literacy and Basic Skills Unit (ALBSU 1995) and miscue analysis (Klein 1993). The former involves passages of a particular readability from which words have been deleted. The person being assessed is expected to supply these. Usually every fifth, seventh or tenth word is replaced by a blank space. Although it can be used as a measure of reading level, and decoding must be involved in successful completion of a cloze task, the procedure is of limited diagnostic value because it does not separate individual subskills.

Miscue analysis measures how well a reader is able to use language clues, their own expectations and decoding skills to derive meaning. That is, when the reader encounters the printed page they use a variety of language clues or cues, individual expectations about the message, and decoding cues to make rapid guesses about the words. Sometimes a reader makes wrong guesses and reads words different from those in print. These are not counted as errors but miscues. By careful examination of these one is able to draw conclusions about strengths and weaknesses in the reading process. The examiner is looking for indications of how well a reader is interacting with the language. One of the main problems with miscue analysis is that it is an oral reading task and the assumption is made that miscues in the silent reading process are reflected in oral reading. The precise relationship between the two is, in fact, unknown (Quandt 1977). A further criticism is that, when asked to read material which is unfamiliar in content and difficult, even the best readers will make errors that do not fit the context.

Comprehension

Measures of reading comprehension take a number of forms. In general they involve answering questions about material which has been read aloud or silently. Measures of silent reading comprehension are much more important. It is silent reading comprehension which is fundamental to being able to pursue formal education and most occupations. If one were to choose a particular aspect of reading which would predict success in an occupation it would be silent reading comprehension.

Tests of silent reading comprehension usually involve asking individuals to read a passage to themselves within a prescribed time and then answer questions about them. There are no British tests of this skill designed for adults but the silent reading comprehension tests from the Spadafore and the Scholastic Abilities Test for Adults (Bryant et al. 1991) have much to commend them. The former consists of passages graded up to the professional level. The reader is given a prescribed amount of time in which to read the passage, and is then asked questions about them which require a verbal response. Furthermore, it provides information about the level of reading skill required for specific occupations, so can be useful in career counselling. The latter also has a set of graded passages but questions are presented in written form and the response is in multiple choice format.

When examining people who, on the basis of their educational background, are likely to be at a functional or vocational level, Skillscape (Smith and Whetton 2000) is quite useful. These tests were designed for use in occupational rather than educational settings. The reading section, which focuses on silent reading comprehension, requires an examinee to answer questions about articles and advertisements in a specially prepared mock local newspaper. It has good face validity as its relevance is obvious to examinees.

The greatest strength of both cloze procedure and miscue analysis lies in the fact that what they do best is measure reading comprehension. It has been suggested that cloze tests only measure reading comprehension. Passages can be selected and analysed for readability, relevant to factors such as age and occupation. Miscue analysis suffers from the same problem as other oral reading tests; that is, the process of reading aloud can interfere with comprehension.

Listening comprehension

Listening comprehension is an important skill. It is the ability to analyse and understand what is presented aurally. A great amount of new knowledge is acquired through listening. Listening comprehension underlies performance in learning situations such as seminars, tutorials and work training programmes, as well as underpinning skills such as note-taking. Adults with poor listening comprehension skills can have difficulty functioning in learning and work settings. At the professional level, reading is more efficient than listening, but below that people are heavily reliant on listening comprehension. Measures of listening comprehension consist mainly of the examiner reading passages to the person being tested and then asking questions about what the examinee has heard. The Spadafore Diagnostic Reading Test provides a measure of listening comprehension up to the professional level.

Speed of reading

There are adults who can decode words quite well but do so very slowly. Being able to decode words at the professional level does suggest that an adult might be able to tackle courses of advanced study or undertake a professional occupation, but if the process is very slow there will be limitations. Being able to read quickly is also important to comprehension. Unless a person can read at a good rate they cannot keep the content in memory long enough to comprehend it.

Reading aloud is not a particularly important skill for most adults. The appropriate measure of reading speed or rate is based on silent reading, particularly when reading for meaning. Reading rates tend to increase in predictable increments across the age span. Average expected reading rates for the four levels of reading are set out in Table 3.7.

Table 3.7 Expected rate of silent reading

Reading level	Words per minute
Functional	100
Vocational	150–175
Technical	200–250
Professional	250+

Reading rate can be tested by asking the examinee to read a passage silently, with a view to answering questions about the material. 'Mark' is called after one minute has elapsed, and the number of words read is counted. The average for several passages at the same level of difficulty provides the most reliable measure (Manzo and Manzo 1993).

Metacognition

An additional area which should be considered, particularly when working with readers operating at an advanced level, is metacognitive skills, i.e. people's own thinking about the way they learn and work. Brown (1980) first applied the concept of metacognition to reading and underscored its crucial role in effective reading. Metacognitive skills related to reading can be described as reading for meaning (comprehension monitoring) and reading for remembering (studying or learning). A good reader possesses metacognitive skills in reading, is aware of the purpose of reading and differentiates between task demands. When reading text for a study assignment, for example, or reading a magazine for pleasure, the reader actively seeks to clarify the task demands through self-questioning prior to reading material. This awareness leads to the use of suitable reading strategies. Good readers vary their reading rate and comprehension level as a function of materials being read. The altering of reading rate according to the purpose of reading and the difficulty of the text is known as flexibility. This can be tested by calculating and comparing rates of reading for simple and difficult materials (Manzo and Manzo 1993).

Awareness can also lead readers to monitor their reading comprehension. When good readers encounter a comprehension difficulty they use 'debugging' strategies. These attempts at problem-solving reflect self-regulation. Good readers evaluate their own comprehension of material and this has important consequences. If readers do not realize that they have not understood a particular part of given material, they will not employ suitable 'debugging' strategies such as back-tracking or scanning ahead for possible cues to solve the difficulties. Fluent or mature readers are rarely conscious of their overall comprehension monitoring. When a comprehension failure arises the fluent reader immediately slows down in reading and either reviews the difficult sections or reads on, seeking clues in subsequent text. Metacognition therefore has two components: one is online monitoring of comprehension; the other is taking corrective action when encountering difficulty (Wray 1994). The assessment of metacognition in reading involves investigating two sub-skills:

- whether someone has a reasonably correct estimate of their own abilities
- whether or not they are comprehending what is read or heard.

Readers should be encouraged to ask questions such as:

- When I read a book how often do I go back to a passage or sentence and reread it so as to clarify things?
- How often do I ask a fellow student or tutor for clarification of ideas?
- How often am I unable to get the main idea of a passage that I have read?
- How often after an examination do I feel I have done well but find the results are disappointing?

If the answer is 'rarely' to the first three and 'often' to the last, it might be that the reader is not good at comprehension monitoring (Wong 1986).

Writing and spelling

A sample of the client's writing should also be examined. A simple topic can be suggested or they can choose one of their own. Many dyslexics find this difficult and it is important to suggest something that they do not have to think too much about. Something such as their journey to the assessment centre or a description of hobbies minimizes thinking time. Skillscape includes specific tasks – writing a postcard and writing a letter – and the writing tests from the SATA described earlier can also be useful.

There has been a dearth of information regarding the average writing speed for particular groups of adults, but this situation is changing. Hedderly (1996), for example, cites research which shows that the writing rate for an average adult not in education is 20 words per minute but 25 words per minute for an adult in education. Dyslexics can be slow to produce written work. Sterling et al. (1997) found that dyslexic undergraduates wrote significantly shorter essays than their non-dyslexic peers, the difference being approximately 100 words over a half-hour period. The mean rate of writing for the dyslexic was 16 words per minute whilst it was 19 words per minute for the non-dyslexics. A measure of writing speed can be established by calculating the number of words produced per minute. It can be difficult to separate out writing and thinking speed but one can make a judgement about the contrast with the individual's verbal fluency.

The quality of the written work in terms of legibility, structure, syntax and punctuation should be evaluated. Again, one is interested in the contrast between this and verbal ability. Dyslexics will make characteristic errors such as omitting words, including prepositions and pronouns they intended to include, as well as have difficulty with spelling (Gregg 1983). Spelling errors can be analysed for characteristic errors such as letter order confusion and it can be helpful to administer a single word spelling test. One of the few that provides adult norms is the WRAT(3). Although knowing a spelling age or grade level can be helpful to a teacher, these are relatively meaningless to the client and can in fact be depressing. What is often more important is to go through the words on the spelling test with them and point out how close they were to getting a particular word correct. The dyslexic who has benefited from a good education will often make only minor errors but this would still result in a very low score on a spelling test. Further, writing and spelling place a very heavy load on working memory. There are individuals whose score on a standardized spelling test will not be significantly outside average limits. However, their skills can deteriorate markedly when they are writing prose, particularly under pressure. Often these errors can be construed as carelessness, so it is important to look at their nature. For example, confusion of letter order, omission of letters and phonic spelling or words spelled as they sound are characteristic of a dyslexic person. Problems with homophones persist.

Numeracy

The testing of arithmetic skills can be helpful, particularly when difficulties with these have been raised by a client or an employer. Dyslexic people do not usually have a conceptual problem with mathematics and the specific difficulty with mathematics known as dyscalculia is rare. This does not, however, mean that dyslexic people find mathematics easy, but that their difficulties are 'manifestations of the same limitations which also affect their reading and spelling' (Miles and Miles 1992).

Some of the potential areas of difficulty described by Chinn and Ashcroft (1993) include:

- directional confusion
- sequencing problems
- problems arising from weak working memory skills
- the language of mathematics
- problems arising from reading difficulties.

A poor background in maths, as well as an overwhelming lack of confidence in one's ability to deal with the subject, will inevitably be contributing factors.

Arithmetic tests are usually just measures of attainment and a low overall score might only reflect gaps in knowledge of mathematical operations due to poor teaching. Appropriate tests include:

- the arithmetic section from the Wide Range Achievement Tests (third edition: Jastak and Wilkinson 1993), described as 'a measure of number computations', which covers basic counting tasks to elementary algebra
- the Numeracy test from Skillscape (Smith and Whetton 2000), which includes three sections: calculations (the four basic rules of number), approximations (working out rough answers to difficult calculations) and problems (interpreting graphic displays and verbally described problems as found in everyday life)
- the Scholastic Abilities Test for Adults (Bryant et al. 1981), which includes two maths tests: 'Calculations', which assesses knowledge of the four basic rules of number, as well as their application in decimal and fractional form; and 'Applications' which assesses the ability to apply the same rules when presented in written problem form.

All of the above can be of diagnostic value when responses are analysed carefully; that is, an examination of the kinds of error made can determine whether they reflect underlying processing problems or poor learning. Chinn (2000) has produced The Informal Assessment of Numeracy Skills, to be used alongside standardized tests as a way of providing a comprehensive diagnosis.

Measuring secondary characteristics

The secondary characteristics manifested by dyslexic people – i.e. problems with confidence, anxiety and self-esteem – will usually be evidenced by their behaviour and verbal responses at interview. Quantification can, however, be valuable in some situations and two examples are given here.

Self-esteem

Self-esteem refers to the perception an individual has of their own worth. It is a composite of their feelings, hopes, fears, thoughts and views of who they are, what they are, what they have been and what they might become (Battle 1990). The Culture-Free Self-Esteem Inventories (Battle 1992) provide a measurement of three dimensions in adults: General, Social and Personal. Clients are asked to provide a yes/no response to questions such as 'Are you as intelligent as most people?' There are 40 such items, which can be read by the client or administered either verbally or via a tape recording. Scores are expressed as centile rankings and the results can be used to identify those people in need of counselling or psychotherapy. The results can also be used to support clinical judgement in a more objective fashion. In a litigation case where an adult was seeking financial compensation from their former local education authority, it allowed the conclusion that 'although X had made up much lost ground in terms of her literacy skills, her self-esteem was so low that it might take years for her to recover'.

Anxiety

The Beck Anxiety Inventory (Beck 1990) provides a quick and easily administered measurement of anxiety levels experienced by individuals. It evaluates both physiological and cognitive symptoms of anxiety. Clients are asked to indicate the extent to which they have been troubled by 21 symptoms (e.g. 'unable to relax'), using a four point scale. Total scores are rated as indicating 'normal', 'mild to moderate', 'moderate to severe' or 'severe' levels of anxiety.

Again, this can be useful for planning or recommending further counselling or therapeutic intervention. Another example of its use with a dyslexic adult was in supporting a request for accommodations in examinations. A dyslexic who had developed most of his literacy/learning skills to an advanced level experienced extreme examination anxiety. His 'severe' rating on the Beck Scale successfully supported an application for extra time in examinations.

Re-assessment

There will be times when dyslexic people need a re-assessment. This can be for several purposes, including:

- monitoring progress
- determining need with regard to adjustments and accommodations
- determining need with regard to provision.

The purpose of the re-assessment should establish its content. Complete diagnostic assessments should be unnecessary if dyslexia is recognized as a syndrome which is intrinsic to the individual and persists across the lifespan. One of our clients was forced to undergo three complete diagnostic assessments during the course of her undergraduate studies. Her comment was that each time she thought, 'This is where I discover that I am not really dyslexic but just stupid'.

Re-assessments directed towards monitoring progress should include measurement of the skills being taught, and ideally should employ the same tests as were administered initially.

When needs regarding accommodations and provision are being determined it is important to establish what a dyslexic person is able to do, as well as what he or she is not able to do. Persisting reading difficulties can be compensated for by the use of audio tapes and 'Text to Speech' software but their use requires adequate listening comprehension skills. Slow and untidy handwriting can be accommodated by allowing someone to use a word processor. It is, however, necessary to establish that the latter has become the main way in which someone communicates in writing and that their typing skills are automatic. Without ensuring this a dyslexic person can be even more disadvantaged.

Feedback to clients

Acceptance and understanding have been identified as essential factors in determining whether dyslexics are able to take control and overcome their difficulties. Providing feedback is therefore the most important part of an assessment. The goal is to enable individuals to understand their difficulties in order that they can take appropriate action. It is through proper explanations that clients will be able to start developing their awareness and understanding. If, following an assessment, clients leave without a greater understanding of the nature of their difficulties and what can be done to overcome them, then it has been a waste of their time.

Too often one meets teenagers and adults who have known that they are dyslexic for years but, when asked what it means, can only describe symptoms such as poor spelling. Professionals conducting assessments should spend time explaining the nature of dyslexia to their clients. It is particularly important for adult dyslexics to know that their main weakness is in working memory and that their problems with reading and spelling are only signs of this.

Feedback should take two forms. Immediately after testing, it should involve a careful explanation of the test results and their implications. A simple operational model, preferably one which is illustrated graphically, can be a useful aid to understanding. The client's strengths and weaknesses should be described and strategies for dealing with the latter outlined. It is important to be positive. Many adult dyslexics will have already developed their own strategies and the way these can be applied constructively to deal with other areas of difficulty can be explained. Practical information about sources of further help, including agencies and appropriate literature, tapes and videos should be provided. It can be helpful to include partners, colleagues or employers in the feedback session so that they too develop a better understanding of the client and his or her needs.

Written reports of assessments are only as good as the information they generate, and reports are useful only to the extent that they convey information clearly to the client, as well as to tutors and employers. In writing the report the author should consider whether it will help the dyslexic understand and address individual difficulties, and whether it will help tutors and employers support the dyslexic person. Essentially the report should reiterate what the client was told at the end of the assessment session. It should be as 'jargon free' as possible, because the language can be misinterpreted. The negative consequences of reporting age scores have been mentioned earlier, but terms such as 'statistical significance' can also create problems. It is confused with real-life significance when it might in fact be of no practical importance.

Too many assessment reports written about adults are based on the format used by psychologists when describing their assessments of children. It should be remembered that they are being written for quite a different audience. A dyslexic adult should feel comfortable about showing it to people such as their personnel manager, who will not necessarily be trained in test interpretation. Test scores are best provided in an appendix so that the client can make them available at their own discretion. Sample reports follow in Case Studies A and B.

Case Study A

REPORT OF ASSESSMENT

Name: Male A   **Age:** 31 years

Introduction

I interviewed and assessed A with a view to determining if any specific cognitive weaknesses might account for the difficulties he is experiencing with the development of written language skills.

A told me that he experienced problems during his school years and that his achievements when he left were modest. He did best in practical subjects, failing English. On leaving school he joined the Armed Forces and has remained in the service ever since. A has reached the rank of Corporal, passing promotion tests. He did, however, tell me that he needed to rely on practical work to balance out his poor performance on written papers and this enabled him to 'scrape through'.

A's general health has been sound. The acuity of his vision and his hearing are within normal limits. He did, however, suffer from glue-ear as a child and had consequent speech difficulties. I understand that one of his own children is finding academic work difficult.

A is keen to gain further promotion and has therefore been seeking a solution to his ongoing problems with written language. He also reported difficulties in areas such as taking telephone messages. His completion of the Adult Dyslexia Checklist proved positive.

Behaviour in test setting

A was initially rather nervous and self-conscious in an assessment setting. He did, however, relax as he met with success. He is lacking in confidence in his ability. Although in terms of content his language skills are quite good he is inclined to mumble when nervous.

Cognitive ability

Administration of the Wechsler Adult Intelligence Scale (III) showed there to be considerable variation amongst A's cognitive abilities.

On the verbal scale A gained above average scores on Comprehension and Verbal Reasoning, the best predictors of academic success. His score on Vocabulary was within average limits, although weaker. He does, however, have sufficient competence in spoken English as to suggest that ordinarily one could expect him to have at least average reading, writing and spelling skills.

On the performance or non-verbal scale A gained high scores on perceptual reasoning (Block Design) and Matrix Reasoning. His scores on visual discrimination and visual sequencing were within average limits.

A had more difficulty on tests which placed demands on working memory. That is, his scores on Digit Span (auditory memory), Arithmetic (mental) and Digit Symbol (copying symbols at speed) were all below average. Although his overall score on Information (recalling factual material) was at an average level I noted that he had trouble with items involving the 'labelling process'.

These lower scores render the profile of A's subtest scores typical of that of a dyslexic person, in that they reflect the inefficiency in working memory which characterizes the syndrome.

Memory skills

Auditory memory

A's score on the Working Memory Index from the Wechsler Intelligence Scale was below average indicating that he has trouble processing aurally presented material in working memory.

Visual memory

A's ability to recall visually presented material was tested by the administration of the Wechsler Memory Scales (III) Spatial Span Test. He gained a low score. His memory problem does therefore affect his ability to process both aurally and visually presented material.

Literacy skills

Reading

A's reading skills were assessed by the administration of the Spadafore Diagnostic Reading Test. He read prose accurately at the technical level, the third of four levels of reading. This is equivalent to GCSE standard and indicates that A does have the word recognition skills which should enable him to work at a more advanced level. He performed at the instructional stage, making a number of pronunciation errors. There is a need for him to expand his reading vocabulary. A had more difficulty with a test of silent reading comprehension. He scored at the vocational level, indicating that his ability to assimilate and retain material is not good. He read prose to himself very slowly (100 words per minute). A scored at the technical level on a test of listening comprehension.

Writing and spelling

A writes legibly but untidily in a mixture of print and cursive script. He writes slowly (12 words per minute). He expresses ideas clearly in simple sentences and punctuates these appropriately. He is, however, hampered by the limits of his spelling skills. On the Wide Range Achievement Spelling Test (Third Edition) he gained a score which placed him at the 2nd centile. This exaggerates his difficulty with spelling to some extent as a number of his incorrect attempts were close to being right. Other efforts bore little resemblance to the word he was endeavouring to spell. He does not yet have sufficient competence in spelling as to enable him to take advantage of conventional electronic spellcheck devices and packages.

Conclusion

A presents as being of average general intelligence. He does, however, have strengths in verbal and non-verbal areas. He has particularly good non-verbal reasoning skills. Diagnostic testing does indicate that he is dyslexic, in that his working memory skills are inefficient. He has a marked difficulty processing both aurally and visually presented material in working memory. A has obviously persevered and has been able to develop some of his skills to a reasonable level. He does, however, continue to experience difficulties with all aspects of reading but particularly with silent reading fluency and comprehension. He also writes slowly and his ability to express ideas on paper is hampered by his spelling skills.

Enabling A to become more efficient and effective at work and on courses of training involves three processes which can be described as *Skill development*, *Compensations* and *Accommodations*.

Skill development

A can improve his skills. The emphasis should be on the following:

- A should not find it too difficult to expand his reading vocabulary. This is now largely a matter of practice but he requires feedback of the correct pronunciation of words. Activities such as listening to tapes of printed material whilst following the text and CD-ROM based reading material would enable him to do this independently.

- A's spelling skills are still quite weak. He would benefit from working with one of the structured phonetically-based programmes designed for dyslexic students, modified to meet the needs of an adult. In both reading and spelling it is important that A focuses on developing a technical vocabulary so that he can deal with his job more effectively.
- A should learn how to use a word processor. This will reduce the load on working memory significantly and allow him to deal with written tasks more effectively.
- A should learn how to plan pieces of written work so as to reduce the load on memory further.
- With regard to taking tests and examinations it is important that A be taught effective techniques and strategies. He needs to learn how to revise properly.
- A would find it difficult to take notes in learning and work settings. He needs to develop a minimalist technique, focusing on writing down headings and key words. Wherever possible he should use a tape recorder as a back up.
- A does report difficulties with general memory tasks. Memory improvement is about the development of strategies. These should always suit A and be 'task-specific'. That is, he will need particular techniques for dealing with specific activities.
- A will find it difficult to proofread his own work accurately. When he is not in a position to adopt the best solution, that is, to have someone else check over his work for him, he should take a step by step approach, focusing on grammar, punctuation and spelling individually. Reading from right to left when checking for spelling errors can help as this prevents anticipation.
- Above all, A should be more confident about his ability as well as his own way of learning and working. He is an intelligent young man who has obviously persevered and has developed techniques and strategies which work for him. Identifying these and applying them to ongoing areas of weakness should enable him to become more effective at work as well as on courses of training.

Compensations

Compensation provides immediate as well as long-term solutions. In A's case this could include:

- A could take advantage of some of the more specialized software when using a computer. Voice-activated word processing, for example, would enable him to achieve a direct match between his verbal skills and his written work. It would also circumvent his spelling problem.

- Having a portable scanner would allow A to deal with tasks such as note-taking more effectively. Using Text to Speech software would allow him to read by listening, his listening comprehension skills being better than his reading comprehension.
- A would benefit from having a tape recorder or memo device to help him deal with notes, as well as general memory tasks.
- A should recognize that learning does not necessarily involve reading. He could use video and audio tapes to good effect.
- A might find it useful to have a portable electronic spellcheck device and/or electronic organizer.

Accommodations

Accommodations can be made for A at work as well as on courses of training. These could include:

- Ensuring that he has appropriate technological aids to hand.
- Allowing him to participate in a relevant training programme.
- Designating someone to proofread work for him.
- Modifying expectations with regard to the achievement of targets in performance appraisals.
- Whenever A takes tests and examinations for academic purposes or for promotion it would be appropriate to make special arrangements for him. These could include allowing him extra time to do them so that he is less disadvantaged by his reading difficulty, as well as his slow rate of writing. In the evaluation of his written work an allowance should be made for poor spelling. In some situations the best way of determining A's knowledge and understanding might be through a verbal examination.

Appendix

Name: Male A

Age: 30 years

WAIS-III PROFILE – Verbal Scale

		Inf	DS	Vocab	Arithmetic	Comp	Sim	LNS	
H	19								19
I	18								18
G	17								17
H	16								16
	15								15
	14								14
	13								13
	12					X	X		12
AV-	11	X							11
ER-	10								10
AGE	9			X					9
	8								8
	7								7
	6		X		X			X	6
	5								5
	4								4
L	3								3
O	2								2
W	1								1

WAIS-III PROFILE – Performance Scale

		PC	PA	Block Design	Matrix Reasoning	Digit Symbol	Symbol Search	
H	19							19
I	18							18
G	17							17
H	16							16
	15							15
	14			X				14
	13				X			13
	12							12
AV-	11							11
ER-	10	—X—						10
AGE	9		X					9
	8					X		8
	7							7
	6						X	6
	5							5
	4							4
L	3							3
O	2							2
W	1							1

Index Scores	Centile
Verbal Comprehension	58
Perceptual Organization	82
Working Memory	4
Processing Speed	18

Memory Skills	Centile
Auditory Memory	
WAIS-III Working Memory Index	4
Visual Memory	
WMS (III) Spatial Span	20

Reading

Spadafore Diagnostic Reading Test
Accuracy

– Prose Reading	Technical level

Comprehension

– Silent Reading	Vocational level
– Listening	Technical level

Speed

– Silent Reading	100 words per minute

Writing and Spelling

Rate of Writing	12 words per minute
WRAT-3 Spelling Test	2nd centile

Case Study B

Name: Male B   Age: 30 years

Introduction

I interviewed and assessed B with a view to determining if any specific cognitive weaknesses might account for discrepancies in his performance.

B experienced difficulties with learning during his primary and early secondary school years. I understand that he was evaluated by an educational psychologist but this did not lead to him being given any help. He was identified as 'lazy'. He needed to re-take most of his O-level subjects and did improve his grades. He was much more successful at GCE A-level. B has since completed both undergraduate and postgraduate studies successfully. He has worked in Policy Research but believes that he has reached a 'plateau'. Completion of a screening test suggested some positive indicators of dyslexia so he decided to pursue this further.

B's general health has been sound. His hearing is within normal limits. He is short-sighted and wears glasses to correct this.

Behaviour in test setting

B presented as a very articulate young man. Although somewhat self-conscious he worked well in an assessment setting. He was keen to understand his difficulties as well as learn how he might improve his performance.

Cognitive ability

Administration of the Wechsler Adult Intelligence Scale (Third Edition) showed there to be a good deal of variation amongst B's cognitive abilities.

B gained very high scores on Information (recalling factual material), Vocabulary Comprehension and Verbal Reasoning, reflecting excellent spoken language skills. It is verbal ability which predicts achievements in written language as well as academic performance generally. The fact that he is placed in the top 1% for the population on the Verbal Scale suggests that he is someone who should have sophisticated written language skills. It is consistent with him having being able to gain high-level qualifications.

B's scores on non-verbal tests such as visual discrimination and two-dimensional problem-solving were quite good, and his score on matrix reasoning was average. In contrast B had difficulty with tasks which placed demands upon working memory and processing speed. Although he did well on Digit Span he used a grouping technique. He had more difficulty with the Letter Number Sequencing Test, gaining an average score. His score on Arithmetic (mental) was below average. His Working Memory Index Score (55) is average. This is markedly discrepant with his other verbal abilities and his performance on mental arithmetic alone would suggest that he has trouble processing auditory material in working memory.

B gained below average scores on Digit Symbol (copying symbols at speed), as well as Symbol Search, gaining a Processing Speed Index Score at the 21st centile, which is well below average.

The contrast between B's verbal ability and his performance on tests of Working Memory and his Processing Speed indicates that he is dyslexic.

Memory skills

Auditory memory

That B has trouble processing auditory material in working memory was established by his performance on tests such as mental arithmetic and letter number sequencing.

Visual memory

B had difficulty with the Wechsler Memory Scales Spatial Span Test, which measures visual sequential memory. He gained a below average score. He does therefore have trouble processing both auditory and visual material in working memory.

Literacy skills

Reading

B's reading skills were tested via the administration of the Spadafore Diagnostic Reading Test. He read prose accurately at the professional level, the highest level of reading. He had more difficulty with a test of silent reading comprehension. He read slowly, his rate of silent reading (180 words per minute) being below an expected level (250 words per minute). He then had some trouble answering questions, scoring at the instructional stage of the professional level.

Writing and spelling

Examination of some of B's written work showed that he writes untidily in cursive script. His rate of writing (15 words per minute) is slow. He does not structure, organize or punctuate written work in a manner which reflects his verbal ability and his spelling skills are erratic. On the Wide Range Achievement Spelling Test (Third Edition) he gained a score which placed him within the average range (47th centile). In general his errors were only minor in nature and included the omission and addition of letters. He has sufficient competence in spelling as to enable him to take advantage of technological aids.

Conclusion

B presents as being of very high verbal ability. He is dyslexic, having trouble processing auditory and visual material in working memory. This is having an impact on his ability to process symbolic material quickly. He has obviously worked hard over the years and developed many of his skills to an advanced level. He does, however, manifest residual difficulties in literacy, particularly in areas such as silent reading fluency/comprehension, as well as writing fluency, spelling and written expression generally. He is someone who would find tasks such as proofreading and note-taking onerous.

Enabling B to become more efficient and effective at work involves three processes which can be described as *Skill development, Compensations* and *Accommodations.*

Skill development

B has been able to develop many of his skills to an advanced level but this has been without understanding the nature of his difficulty. Improved self-understanding should enable him to work more deliberately on skill and strategy development. He should pay particular attention to the following:

- At present and like most mature dyslexic people, B enhances comprehension by reading all the words carefully. He needs to develop 'speed comprehension' techniques. That is he needs to learn how to focus his reading so that he concentrates on extracting only important information.
- In spelling the emphasis should be on overlearning, important job or course related words being targeted. B can also learn how to use memory devices such as mnemonics and visual imagery to facilitate recall. It is important that these tap his excellent reasoning skills, rather than his weaker automatic recall.

- B should be making maximum use of technological aids. Using a word processor to complete written tasks reduces the load on working memory significantly. He could experiment with voice-recognition software as a way of allowing a direct match between his verbal ability and his written work.
- B could consider using dictation as a way of dealing with written tasks, provided he has access to the services of an audio typist.
- Whether producing written work by hand, giving dictation or using a word processor, B should plan carefully. Written expression places a heavy load on working memory but a step by step approach will reduce this.
- Dyslexia is most easily understood as an inefficiency, the implication being that B is someone who needs to learn how to learn and work in more efficient ways. He should deliberately focus attention for short periods at a time as this will facilitate concentration. When learning new material it will enable him to remember more.
- The most effective way of dealing with note/minute-taking is to focus on listening and understanding whilst jotting down headings and key words or using a visual strategy such as mind-mapping. B should have a tape recorder with him as a back-up. Ideally the machine he uses should have a counting device on it, so that he can note the times at which important points were made, as this will mean he does not have to listen to a whole session twice.
- The most effective way of proofreading material is to have someone else check over one's work. When this is not possible B should take a step by step approach, focusing on grammar, punctuation and spelling individually. Reading from right to left when checking for spelling errors can help as this prevents anticipation.
- B raised concerns about his ability to speak in public. Some general coaching in this area would be helpful but it is essential that he makes sure that when giving a presentation he can focus on speaking, rather than worrying about visual aids too much. That is, he should rely on computer-based packages such as PowerPoint and designate someone to write on a flip-chart for him.
- Memory improvement is just a question of developing strategies. There are many of these and B needs to experiment with different ones and choose those with which he is the most comfortable. I reiterate that strategies will be effective if he can rely on his good reasoning skills, rather than automatic recall.
- B's difficulty with aspects of arithmetic has always caused him some concern. He needs to recognize that this is a result of him being dyslexic and just accept that he needs to rely on strategies, including the use of electronic aids.

- Above all, B should be very confident about his ability as well as his own way of learning and working. He is a highly intelligent young man who has done well, without support. This means he has acquired techniques and strategies which work for him. Identifying these and applying them to ongoing areas of weakness should ensure that he is able to become more effective in learning and work settings.

Compensations

Compensation provides immediate as well as long-term solutions. In the main, this involves taking good advantage of technological aids including the following:

- As suggested above, B should make maximum use of technological aids such as a word processor. Voice recognition software might allow a direct match between his verbal ability and his written work.
- B could use a scanner to allow direct entry of material into a computer. This would compensate for his slow rates of reading and writing. One of the pen scanners would be useful for library and research work.
- B could use text to speech software as a way of reading and proofreading by listening.
- B should equip himself with an electronic memo/recording device as a way of dealing with notes and minutes, as well as general memory tasks.
- B should acknowledge that learning and becoming better read through the use of video and audio tapes, as well as CD-ROMs, is perfectly acceptable.
- Dyslexic people are often reluctant to delegate, believing that they should be able to deal with everything themselves. B does need to acknowledge that he has strengths and weaknesses, and that he should focus on the former.

Accommodations

Adjustments can be made for B in the workplace and on courses of training. Appropriate adjustments would include:

- Ensuring that he has appropriate technological aids to hand. His employers could seek funding through the Department for Employment's Access to Work Scheme.
- Allowing B to participate in a skills development programme. Again funding might be available for this through the Department for Employment.

- Designating someone to proofread work for him and perhaps highlight the important parts of documents he needs to read.
- Providing him with secretarial support where this is appropriate, including the services of an audio-typist so that he can dictate.
- B will find it difficult to cope with distractions and it would be best if he could work in an office on his own, rather than in an open-plan situation, or at least be able to withdraw to a quiet room when he is dealing with complex literacy tasks.
- Should B be in a position where he has to take tests or examinations for academic purposes or for selection/promotion, it would be appropriate to allow him extra time to complete them so that he is less disadvantaged by his slow rates of reading and writing.

Appendix

Name: Male B

Age: 30 years

WAIS-III (Wechsler Adult Intelligence Scale - Third Edition) – PROFILE

		Recall of Facts	Digit Span	Vocabulary	Mental Arithmetic	Comprehension	Verbal Reasoning	LNS	
H	19								19
I	18								18
G	17			X		X	X		17
H	16								16
	15								15
	14	X							14
	13		X						13
	12								12
AV-	11								11
ER-	10							X—	10
AGE	9								9
	8				X				8
	7								7
	6								6
	5								5
	4								4
L	3								3
O	2								2
W	1								1

Block Design 12, Matrix Reasoning 10; Symbol Search 8; Picture Completion 12, Digit Symbol 8

Index Scores	Centile
Verbal Comprehension	99
Perceptual Organization	64
Working Memory	55
Processing Speed	21

Memory Skills

Visual

WMS (III) Spatial Span	37th centile

Attainments in Literacy Skills

Reading
Spadafore Diagnostic Reading Test
Accuracy

– Prose Reading	Professional level

Comprehension

– Silent Reading	Professional level (Instructional stage)

Speed

– Silent Reading	180 words per minute

Writing and Spelling

WRAT-3 Spelling Test	47th centile
Rate of Writing	15 words per minute

Summary

- The identification of dyslexia involves three stages: information-gathering, screening and psychological testing. The last of these is an exercise in differential diagnosis, which attempts to isolate factors that answer the question: 'Why are tasks difficult?'
- The concept of 'specificity' is essential to identification; that is, it should distinguish between those who have trouble learning most things because they are of low general ability, and those who have difficulty learning some things because they have specific cognitive weaknesses.
- The assessment of attainment should be comprehensive and include reading accuracy, fluency and comprehension, as well as listening compre-

hension. Measures of writing fluency, single word spelling, and spelling in context are important. The testing of maths can sometimes be helpful.

- Secondary characteristics can be measured objectively by the use of Anxiety and Self-esteem scales.
- The correct reporting of assessment findings is fundamental to the development of self-understanding.

Chapter 4
Counselling

This chapter outlines the issues that arise when counselling dyslexic people. Appropriate models for counselling, as well as suitable techniques, are described. The emphasis is on an educational rather than psychotherapeutic approach.

Introduction

When an adult has been identified as dyslexic and starts to work with an appropriately trained person it is often the first time in their life that they have felt properly understood. It is inevitable, therefore, that the relationship which develops is such that dyslexic people will feel that they can unburden themselves. They will wish to talk about their anxieties and frustrations, as well as other personal problems.

> It is perhaps easier to tackle the learning difficulties than it is to pursue the emotional back-log which resides in you. I have a lot of anger still about all the failed tasks and why none of the professionals who taught me stopped to ask what was wrong with this child who couldn't produce the written work equal to her other skills. I wish I had been diagnosed as a child and never blamed for what is wrong.

It is not necessary for tutors, psychologists and trainers to become counsellors, but they can engage in what Sanders (1994) has termed 'informed helping', and it is therefore useful for them to understand and adopt some of the fundamental principles and practices of counselling. Likewise, professional counsellors working with dyslexic people need to understand the nature of dyslexia, as well as its manifestations and consequences. Without this, inappropriate interpretations and interventions can occur. One psychodynamically orientated psychotherapist, for example, interpreted an adolescent's problem with organization as being 'an over-dependence on his mother'. He was perhaps overly reliant but this was because, being dyslexic, he was so disorganized.

Aims of counselling

The aims of counselling are:

- that the client will feel empowered or have a greater sense of personal autonomy
- the client has a greater sense of self-understanding
- to enable the client to live in a more satisfying resourceful way
- that the client has a greater sense of well-being
- that the above gains should be enduring (Sanders 1994).

Issues in counselling dyslexic people

In meeting the aims described above, the issues to be addressed when working with dyslexic people are quite clear. Firstly, counselling or informed helping should be an extension of the assessment process in promoting self-understanding, including:

- what dyslexia is and how it affects people
- 'normalizing' primary characteristics, that is, putting them in context, e.g. 'We all forget sometimes'
- helping establish long- and short-term goals
- advising on strategies and sources of help.

> For me being dyslexic has caused me much upset and still does. I can't seem to function properly, don't understand anything first or third time around. I cry a lot. I don't like myself. I have no confidence and this is very noticeable to others. I hate being dyslexic. I have known since the age of ten. Dyslexia is to me – panic, anxiety, waiting for things to go wrong. When they do you give you such a hard time. Frustration when you can't understand anything, I forget things all the time, I have a bad memory. I don't trust anybody. I can't believe anything I am told, as the trust is not there. I am negative. I

have no confidence. I can't understand numbers in my head, they do not mean anything, i.e. I can read them for the price of things, but more than one thing, I can't add up or even see the sum my brain goes black inside, and that panic starts up again. I hated maths at school; no one would help me. This made me feel unworthy and so I did not bother going to maths!

The second function of counselling is in dealing with the secondary characteristics which have developed. Barton and Fuhrmann (1994) have described four issues:

- stress and anxiety resulting from being overwhelmed by the complexity of life's demands
- low self-esteem and feelings of incompetence
- grief or a feeling of loss over what might have been
- helplessness, resulting from a limited understanding of learning abilities and disabilities.

My first session with you last week shattered the way I have been able to live previously. I have always blocked off a great deal. I have always thought I have been unable to do a lot of things. I always knew there was some reason for this but I didn't know what it was. I actually thought I wasn't entitled to anything or to be able to do very much and as long as I believed that, it was all OK, but now, having spoken to you, and seen the graph that you produced, I realize what I could have done and perhaps what I could have achieved and how different things might have been. I don't know what to do with the feelings of loss and anger that I have now. I am also dealing with my mother's guilt. I have found this book that I keep reading wonderful. I have read it over and over again. All the others talk about reading and spelling. This one talks about the memory being part of the problem and it is this that has pervaded the whole of my life. It has been so insidious because I have never understood what it is all about. Now I don't know where to go, what job to do. I can't cope with my present job any more. I feel completely unable to do anything. I hate my job and I seem to be getting less and less confident and more and more dyslexic. Is that possible? My mother's guilt is very difficult. I feel I should try and make it better for her, but she told me that when I told her, she didn't help. I am hurting so much. I don't know how to deal with

> this. Through my life I have had a lot of therapy and a nervous breakdown, but I now strongly believe that being dyslexic has been the reason and cause of most of it.

To some extent, these are addressed by dealing with the primary problems, but they might also bring about a need for specific counselling.

Approaches to counselling

There are numerous different theoretical approaches to counselling – Nelson-Jones (1995) lists 13 under six general headings. All these different approaches might have something to offer when working with adult dyslexics but since they all involve an explanation of behaviour according to a particular theory some are likely to be more helpful than others. A major review of the outcome of different approaches to counselling or therapy led to the conclusion that there is little evidence to show that one approach is necessarily better than another, non-specific factors such as the relationship between client and counsellor being more important (Roth and Fonagy 1996).

One way of defining counselling is in fact to stipulate the central qualities of good helping relationships which are both *necessary* in that change will not occur if they are not present, and *sufficient* in that, if they exist, change will occur. Rogers (1951) has defined the qualities or core conditions as:

Empathy – seeing the world of another from their point of view. This involves:

- listening sensitively
- trying to make sense of what is heard
- understanding the other person in their own terms
- checking to see if the meaning, with all the subtleties, has been interpreted properly.

Genuineness – this involves the helper being open to their own feelings, being fallible, vulnerable, imperfect, not knowing all the answers.

Non-judgemental acceptance – described as 'unconditional positive regard'. This involves accepting the other person as being a worthwhile human being, regardless of their faults and failings.

Egan (1994) has elaborated on Rogers's work, arguing that the core conditions are necessary but not sufficient. In particular he focused on the skills needed by helpers during the different stages in the process of change. Egan identified three stages and the skills required as follows.

Stage 1 Building a relationship and exploration: that is, developing empathy, genuineness and non-judgemental acceptance.

Skills
Developing a trusting relationship:

- making and maintaining contact
- structuring
- communicating non-judgemental warmth
- communicating genuineness
- active listening and communicating empathy
- identifying, acknowledging and reflecting thoughts, behaviours and feelings
- paraphrasing
- clarifying.

Stage 2 Changing the clients' perceptions of themselves.

Skills
Linking and integrating individual issues and problems into themes:

- showing deeper understanding and empathy
- helping the client focus on specific issues.

Challenging the clients' views:

- offering new perspectives
- sharing experiences and feelings
- helping the client move on.

Goal-setting:

- helping the client identify what they want to achieve.

Stage 3 Considering ways of acting to help resolve the problem, including risk assessment and possible outcomes.

Skills
Helping the client move on to considering action, as well as developing and choosing action plans.

Developing and choosing action plans:

- brain-storming
- creative thinking
- problem-solving
- decision-making
- planning.

Evaluating consequences of actions:

- recording events
- evaluation
- reviewing plans.

An approach to counselling which seems relevant to working with dyslexic people is known as the psychoeducation model (Authier 1977; Hornby 1990). This adopts the view that the client's problems are skill deficits rather than abnormality (or illness). The sequence 'Illness – diagnosis – prescription – therapy – cure' is replaced by 'Dissatisfaction – goal-setting – skill teaching – satisfaction (or goal achievement)'. The model further elaborates on the work of Rogers and Egan, there being a three-stage approach, as shown in Table 4.1.

The skills required by counsellors at Stage I according to both the Egan and Hornby models are very much the same as those needed by tutors working with dyslexic people. It is the relationship with the tutor that will allow the dyslexic person to disclose the issues that require further intervention. Tutors do need, however, to recognize the limits of their skills and be prepared to refer on when issues are beyond their own expertise.

Central to Stage II is changing self-perceptions. It is here that the reframing process identified by Gerber et al. (1992, 1996) as being essential to success is important. Reframing refers to:

> A set of decisions relating to reinterpreting the learning disability experience in a more productive and positive manner. It clearly allows for one to identify strengths and parlay them into successful experiences, while still being aware of weaknesses that have to be mitigated or bypassed.
>
> (Gerber et al. 1996: 98)

Reframing is a dynamic process, consisting of the four stages shown in Table 4.2.

In facilitating reframing, 'cognitive restructuring' approaches can be helpful. Rational-emotive therapy – as developed by Ellis (1962), for example –

Table 4.1 Psychoeducation: the three stages – exploration, intervention, empowering. (Adapted from Hornby 1990)

Stage	Exploration I	Intervention II	Empowering III
Aims	Relationship-building Clarifying concerns/patterns Assessment	Developing new perspectives Increasing experiential awareness Developing new behaviours	Consolidating changes Supporting action programmes Enabling self-actualization
Skills	For example: • empathic responding • respect • genuineness • probing • immediacy • specificity • self-disclosure • linking • circular questioning *Assessment:* • intrapersonal • interpersonal	*Psychoeducation –* focused on: *Affect:* for example: • focusing • evocative responding • active listening *Behaviour:* for example: • teaching life skills: goal-setting; communication skills; family living skills; vocational skills, etc. *Cognition:* for example: • active listening • reframing and metaphors • cognitive restructuring • interpretation and confrontation	For example: • identifying changes • elaborating action programmes • affirming strengths • developing skill deficit areas • increasing self-esteem and self-control • expanding options • referring on • promoting self-help strategies • developing personal and social responsibility *Termination:* • evaluation • follow-up

Table 4.2 Reframing stages

Stages	
1. Recognition	– that one is dyslexic
2. Understanding	– the nature and implications of dyslexia
3. Acceptance	– that there are issues to be dealt with
4. Action/Plan of Action	– to achieve goals

assumes that maladaptive feelings are caused by irrational beliefs. Ellis argues that through mistaken assumptions people place excessive demands upon themselves. The adult dyslexic who assumes, incorrectly, that most people are very skilled in spelling, and who consequently thinks that his or her own spelling skills are much worse than they really are, is a typical example. Counselling involves challenging such assumptions. Likewise, Beck et al. (1979) attribute numerous psychological problems to the negative ways in which individuals think about themselves. Their approach to counselling involves questioning clients so that they can discover for themselves the distortions in their thinking and can then make changes that are consistent with reality.

> The sessions have also helped restore my confidence, which has – over the years – been eroded by the fact that I have associated the problems that dyslexia causes me with my being unintelligent and partly lazy. This loss of confidence has been compounded by feelings of inadequacy caused by my modest academic achievements at school and my lack of further education. It has been important for me to address in my development sessions why I failed nearly all my formal school examinations despite being motivated and highly determined to succeed.

A cognitive-behavioural assessment attempts to identify the typical distorted cognitive processes of the client. Scott and Dryden (1996) cite Burns's (1980) list of the ten most common self-defeating thought processes, adapted here for dyslexic people:

- All or nothing thinking: seeing everything as black and white, e.g. 'If I am not in complete control, I will lose all control'
- Over-generalization: where it is concluded from one negative event that other negative events are thereby likely, e.g. 'I wasn't successful at that and now everything is probably going to fall apart'
- Mental filter: seizing on a negative fragment of a situation and dwelling on it, omitting any consideration of any positive feature, e.g. 'The boss didn't like my report, it was awful'
- Automatic discounting: a sensitivity to absorbing negative information and summarily discounting positive information, e.g. 'My boss said my presentation was good, but he always says that'
- Jumping to conclusions: where a conclusion is inferred from irrelevant evidence, e.g. 'I won't get the job because of my poor handwriting'

- Magnification and minimization: magnifying imperfections and minimizing positive attributes, e.g. 'I can't spell so I am hopeless'
- Emotional reasoning: using feeling as evidence of the truth of a situation, e.g. 'I didn't do very well at school so I can't have worked hard enough'
- 'Should' statements: an overdose of moral imperatives, 'shoulds', 'musts', 'have to's' and 'oughts', e.g. 'I should be able to spell (remember names, etc.) better'
- Labelling and mislabelling: emotional reactions are in large measure a product of the label a person attaches to a phenomenon. An inappropriate label can produce a distressing reaction, e.g. 'I forgot his name so I am stupid'
- Personalization: egocentric interpretation of interpersonal events relating to the self, e.g. 'Two people laughed and whispered something to each other when I walked by, they were probably talking about me being dyslexic.'

> I don't think I have ever come across anything positive about being dyslexic. I am a very negative person. I think it is all due to the unnecessary and horrible experiences I have had since a small child to date. It is very hard to be positive when nothing you do is right.

By addressing such distortions dyslexic people can be helped to reframe and move on to find solutions. Some of the skills described at Stage III can address specific issues described by Barton and Fuhrmann (1994), such as that of stress and anxiety, which can undermine a person's ability to function effectively in learning and work situations. It can therefore be beneficial for dyslexic people to be taught relaxation techniques. These are well documented and include the following:

- progressive relaxation: focusing on the major muscle groups of the body, group by group
- visualization: producing feelings of calm and well-being by training people to use the right hemisphere of their brain to produce pictures in their minds of themselves in safe, warm and comforting environments
- deep breathing: which stimulates relaxation and reduces stress and anxiety.

Practitioners trained in hypnotherapy and neurolinguistic programming have worked successfully in treating the stress and anxiety experienced by dyslexic people. They are never enough on their own, however. Symptom removal without addressing the underlying problem can only lead to short-term gains. This is well illustrated by the college student who was suffering from panic attacks to the extent that she was no longer able to attend classes. She had tried hypnosis with only limited success. It was only when a diagnostic assessment conducted by an educational psychologist revealed poor working memory that the source of her panic was understood. She had been struggling with increased demands on her learning and organizational skills, and this had led to feelings of being out of control. A programme of skills development combined with hypnosis enabled her to deal more effectively with both primary and secondary issues.

In building up confidence and self-esteem, techniques such as assertiveness and social skills training can be useful. Learning to advocate for themselves with tutors, employers and socially is very important for dyslexic adults. They have often not learned to negotiate for their rights and for appropriate accommodations at college or in the workplace. Some, because of their inefficient information-processing system, have not intuitively learned appropriate social skills. These need to be directly taught and treatment of problems with social skills has focused on educational rather than therapeutic interventions (Forness and Kavale 1991). Assertiveness training can also be of value in helping deal with their anger. Many dyslexic people are justifiably angry about the way they have been treated. This should be acknowledged, but they must be helped to manage their anger and learn how to respond appropriately when put on the defensive.

As we have learned from our dyslexic clients, dyslexic people can learn from each other. There is no doubt that they can benefit from formal and informal support groups. Group therapy has in fact been utilized with college level students. Rosenblum (1987), for example, describes a group which was directed towards raising self-esteem. This allowed the members to share:

- past experiences
- feelings of being misunderstood
- ideas on the development of strategies.

It was considered that there were not only direct benefits in terms of the development of skills but also indirect ones, in that the group members were accepting and supportive of one another, providing comfort and strength which allowed for the development and maintenance of improved self-esteem.

Referring on

Professionals working closely with dyslexic people need to be aware of the possibility of their clients becoming more dependent rather than independent. Further, one of the characteristics of a mature professional is knowing when they are out of their depth and other expertise is required. There are dyslexic people whose life experience has been such that they need in-depth counselling. Rogan and Hartman (1990) reported that amongst a sample of 68 adults with learning disabilities, 75 per cent of college graduates and 62 per cent of high school graduates had experienced some type of psychotherapy or counselling in their lives and considered this a significant factor in determining a successful outcome.

Counsellors do not need to be experts in dyslexia but it is necessary to recognize that a dyslexic person has constitutional difficulties that make certain tasks more difficult for them than they are for people who are not dyslexic. They need to be aware of how these difficulties have operated to produce further complications in a person's life and behaviour. The complex interaction of the psychological difficulties and the constitutional difference must be fully acknowledged if the individual is to make progress. That is, the relationship between primary and secondary difficulties needs to be acknowledged and understood. Further, counsellors need to adapt their approach to take into account the unique processing style of each individual.

Couple counselling

As well as gaining better self-understanding, dyslexic people need also to be understood by others, especially those close to them. It can be helpful to include partners in counselling sessions as this can improve the way they perceive and support the dyslexic person. Living with someone who is disorganized and forgetful, for example, can place stress on a relationship. Understanding that this is 'can't' rather than 'won't' can ease the situation and lead to the non-dyslexic person supporting their partner in constructive ways.

Further, following diagnosis and effective training there can be quite dramatic changes in confidence and motivation. As the dyslexic person becomes more competent they are less dependent and this can change the balance in a relationship, leaving their partner feeling threatened. Including them in counselling can help them understand and adapt to the changes taking place.

Summary

- Counselling dyslexic people should promote self-understanding, assist in goal-setting and include advice on strategy development.
- Counselling should also address secondary issues such as confidence, self-esteem, anxiety and stress.
- Educational models for counselling are more suitable for dyslexic people than psychotherapeutic models.
- Dyslexic people can help each other through participating in group counselling.
- Partners of dyslexic people should be involved in the counselling process so that their understanding of issues that arise is improved.

Chapter 5
Personal development

This chapter addresses the issues facing dyslexic people in their personal development, including memory, organization, goal-setting and social skills. The importance of the development of metacognitive skills is emphasized, as is the role of the professional working in partnership with dyslexic people.

Introduction

All interventions directed towards assisting dyslexic people, regardless of the issues or skills addressed, should contribute to their personal development. Dyslexic people need to be able to access the expertise of professionals, but they also need to tap and enhance their own experience as a learner, as a worker and as a dyslexic person. Everyone has their own individual skills and abilities, and enabling dyslexic individuals to capitalize on their strengths allows them to deal more effectively with both primary and secondary problems.

Self-understanding

One of the keys to becoming a successful dyslexic person is self-understanding. This has several dimensions:

- understanding the nature of the difficulty
- understanding what one can do about it
- understanding one's strengths and abilities.

However, it involves more than just knowing the above. Dyslexic people need to be able to focus on their abilities and what they can do if they are to feel more in charge of every aspect of their lives.

> The main fear that I had to face was working with and coming to terms with being dyslexic. The revelation that I had to start working with my dyslexia did not appear overnight, more something that went hand in hand with knowing it was time for change. I realized that I had to stop fighting against being dyslexic and start working with it. The critical turning point came for me when I visited a dyslexia centre. Guidance and help was what I was looking for but I left the building knowing that I could achieve anything I want to, for at last someone totally understood me. They were there to point me in all the right directions, give me sound advice to what I was entitled to and where to get it, and also to offer tutoring and counselling. I can clearly remember sitting on the train going home, thinking this is the first day of the rest of my life, I can achieve my goals if I want to, for at last there is the kind of help that I had longed for.

The nature of the difficulty

When trying to understand dyslexia there are several facts people should know:

* It is genetic in origin and they are not therefore to blame
* It is part of their make up and will always be
* It is not an insurmountable barrier to educational or occupational success
* They need to acknowledge that it is there and they might need to make more adjustments than most when faced with new challenges.

Interpreting dyslexia

Before dyslexic people begin to actively work towards seeking effective solutions they need to understand why tasks are difficult for them. We use a simple model of working memory as a way of interpreting their difficulties as inefficiency in the processing of information. Working memory is described as a system that allows performance of several tasks at once and is illustrated graphically in Figure 5.1.

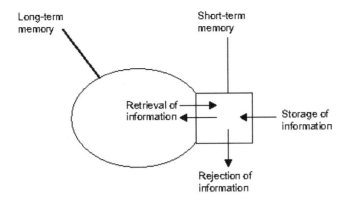

Figure 5.1 A model of working memory

The way in which specific skills are affected is explained. A problem with reading comprehension, for example, would be described as a result of the overload resulting from recognizing words, finding their meaning, and making sense of the material simultaneously. Difficulties with written expressions are explained as the result of overload which comes from thinking of an idea, finding words to express it, spelling the words correctly, and putting them in the appropriate order, with proper regard for grammar and punctuation:

> Dyslexia affects people in different ways, personally it affected my self-confidence. I was always made to feel lazy, stupid, ugly and sometimes even worthless. When I was diagnosed as dyslexic it was more a relief than anything else. So this is why my handwriting is like this and that is why I have a problem with essays, that's why maths is so bad, that's why I always have problems with numbers.

This model is one that we find dyslexic people can identify with. Once they have adopted it, they are provided with a method of interpreting their difficulties themselves. It enables them to make sense of the problems they have experienced in the past and their current difficulties, and enables them also to predict what might be challenging in the future. We encourage them to make it relevant to their situation and some have taken the model further, providing their own analogies. One young man, for example, explained his difficulties in an examination setting as follows:

> The main effect of my dyslexia in the examination setting has been that I read and write more slowly as my word recognition and retrieval is not as automatic (i.e. efficient). I find it takes me longer to assimilate longer questions. To use a computing analogy, if the mind is like a computer running Windows, the working memory is like RAM where the processing is done and the long-term memory is like the hard disk. If a computer has more data to process than can be stored in RAM, it stores it temporarily on the hard disk in 'virtual memory' and has to constantly refer to it. This is comparatively much slower than holding it in RAM, thus the task is accomplished, but takes longer than would be achieved by a computer with more RAM. Being dyslexic is like a computer with insufficient RAM, you can accomplish as much but take longer to get there.

A further advantage of this approach is that it enables dyslexic people to explain their difficulties to others in a way that can be understood. They are therefore in a better position to advocate for themselves. People do need to know that dyslexia can be recognized as a disability and that this means they can access resources. They already know that being dyslexic is a disadvantage, it is why they are seeking help. In interpreting it to them, however, the emphasis should be on 'difference'. We describe dyslexia as an 'inefficiency', the implication being that they can become more efficient by being confident in their own different way of learning:

> My results prove what you and my parents always told me, and I might just be starting to truly believe, and that is that I can do almost anything if I set my mind on it. What next, I do not know but I plan on setting myself a high standard so that I finish off one level higher than I would have done if I had set no standards at all. Thank you very much for helping me to Believe in myself.

Dyslexic people will of course want to know more and what follows are some common questions asked and suggested responses.

What is dyslexia?

Dyslexia is very complex and we still don't know everything about it. It is best described as an information processing difference that affects all aspects of life, including organization, literacy skills, time-keeping and remembering things. It could be described simply as an inefficiency within the working memory system which, when overloaded, crashes. When talking about literacy skills, it is often simplest to say that dyslexia means that you have a problem with remembering sequences of things, studying and reading.

How did I get it?

It is genetic so therefore some member of the family must be dyslexic. However, the actual genetic link is, at this stage, unclear. Some families have one dyslexic person, in others all members are dyslexic.

Will my children have it?

It is quite possible – the answer is as above really, but it is important to say that dyslexic children of dyslexic parents are not necessarily going to experience the same learning difficulties as their dyslexic parent. This is partly because they are likely to be identified sooner and partly because each dyslexic person has their own pattern of difficulties.

Why wasn't it found out earlier?

There are often many reasons for this. Sometimes it is due to lack of awareness in schools. There might have been other reasons that have prevented identification, and it may indeed be that the dyslexic person has been 'a victim of their own success'. That is, they have either worked hard and overcome many of the more obvious difficulties, or alternatively they have just worked hard and sat quietly in the classroom and been passed over. Dyslexia is very complex and therefore unless the indicators really are quite pronounced during the school years, it quite often does go unnoticed. It could be said that dyslexia is only a problem when it *becomes* one and it is usually at transition stages that it becomes evident.

Is the fact that I muddle up my words because I am dyslexic?

Yes, muddling up words or not being able to find the right word at the right time is one of the characteristics of dyslexia. It occurs as a result of the overload in the working memory system. It is not that the person does not know what the word is. For example, being unable to tell left from right is simply being unable to find the label at the right time.

Why do I forget?

A poor memory is characteristic of dyslexia because again, the short-term or working memory system is inefficient. If it is overloaded, the information does not go in effectively, and what is stored is harder to retrieve.

How do I tell people?

To disclose is a difficult matter and it is a very personal one. Some people feel that they don't want to say anything, but if they want to access resources and accommodations, they need to disclose that they are dyslexic. People need to think carefully about what they are going to say. It is better to keep the explanation as simple as possible and to say how it affects them, but it is very important to say what they can do rather than what they can't. The emphasis should be on solutions.

Will I ever be cured?

People with dyslexia will always be dyslexic but if they develop the right skills and strategies, this should not prevent them from being successful.

Why is my dyslexia not the same as others'?

Dyslexia can be described as a pattern of strengths and weaknesses. It affects each person differently: some people can be very articulate, others have a word-finding difficulty. Some can read well, others always find it hard. Some people can spell and write well, others find these impossible tasks. This is why understanding the nature of dyslexia and 'self-understanding' are so important.

Abilities and strengths

Identifying abilities is as important as understanding the 'disability'. Dyslexic people should be encouraged to be confident in their own way of doing things, and reassured that they already have many of the skills, strategies and solutions they need. Often they do not recognize their strengths and do not use them automatically when it is appropriate to do so. Most will have been actively discouraged from approaching tasks in a way that suits them, and some believe that it is wrong to do so. An example is the man who, having employed someone to read material to him when studying, used the word 'cheating' to describe how he managed to gain a university degree. It is common to find that, when told one way of enhancing reading comprehension is to read the questions before the material, a dyslexic person will admit with embarrassment that they already do it that way, despite having been told not to do so when at school. Some have been discouraged from their preferred way of taking notes, e.g. drawing pictures. They have therefore unsuccessfully attempted to deal with it in a more conventional way:

> I had the feeling that knowing would be enough but once you know that you are dyslexic, you want to go back and learn all the things you couldn't learn the first time.

Hopefully, a dyslexic will have gained insights into their abilities from their diagnostic assessment. They might, for example, have learned that their memory for images is better than their auditory memory. Further information about their abilities and learning style can be elicited in a number of ways, mainly asking the right questions. One of the simplest examples is asking a dyslexic person how they find their way about. The usual response is that they rely on landmarks (the pub) rather than labels (left and right or north and south). This is an indication that they process visual information better than auditory information. Appropriate questions can be included during an initial diagnostic interview.

There are systematic approaches to evaluating learning styles, mainly questionnaires (Dunn et al. 1996; Lashley 1995; Hopson et al. 1998). QuickScan (Zdzienski 1997), referred to in Chapter 3, is a computer-based approach to analysing an individual's learning profile. These are only starting points, however, and should always be followed up by a discussion about how the individual does things automatically. Do they, for example, talk to or argue with themselves, visualize, or role-play? Do they make plans, write lists, draw pictures? Questionnaires have good face validity, that is, they seem like an objective test, but the insights of individuals into their own ways of learning and working can be just as revealing.

We referred earlier to the literature that focuses on the visual strengths of dyslexic people. It has been suggested that they are more 'right-brained' than 'left-brained'. We have also written that it is misleading to talk about the hemispheres of the brain as independent entities, it being the interactions between them that are important. In general, however, the right hemisphere of the brain has the ability to manipulate space, to generate mental maps, to rotate images and to conceptualize visually. It has been suggested that learning is most effective when the two hemispheres work cooperatively, but that the demand on verbal left hemisphere activities is greatest in most academic settings. Those with a strong preference for right hemisphere functioning are therefore at a disadvantage.

These dyslexic people need to be encouraged to be comfortable with and confident about the use of visual imagery. This will often have been discouraged during their school years. They can, for example, be encouraged to use visual strategies, such as mind-mapping, for the planning of pieces of written work and then translate their ideas into language. They can also be encouraged to use visual information, such as graphs and pictures, to locate information.

Personality is also a factor in effective learning and performance. This can be illustrated by analogy through reference to fictional detectives such as Poirot and Sherlock Holmes. They both gather information in order to make sense of or find a solution to a specific problem but they each use a different approach. The same can be said for someone learning. Some people are very methodical in the way in which they approach a situation, some are very logical and rational, and some are much more intuitive. Some people have leaps of cognition and a variety of ideas, and others absorb the information in a step by step approach. Those people who make 'cognitive leaps' need to be able to track back their thinking process so they can explain it to the more methodical learner. Cottrell (1999) suggests that there is a 'range of approaches to learning': the 'diver' jumps in and has a go working in short bursts of activity; the 'logician' needs to know the reasons behind things; the 'dreamer' thinks a lot about a subject and has no idea where times goes; the 'searchlight' finds everything interesting and has difficulty selecting what is relevant. This model is useful because it can encourage dyslexics to realize that there is more than one way in which to learn. A greater understanding of thinking skills and abilities and a recognition of their own preferred learning style allows dyslexics to become creative problem-solvers and to develop their skills and abilities.

In Figure 5.2, which follows, a sample can be seen from an essay a student had been trying to write with great difficulty.

During the course of the interview it was noted that he 'doodled' a lot. This was discussed and it was suggested that he try to use drawings for both planning and note-taking. He brought the following notes (Figure 5.3) to the next session. They contain some pictures and quite a lot of words.

At the next session he demonstrated that he had developed the use of pictures further, and ultimately he was able to plan and record everything in pictorial form, the example in Figure 5.4 being some more of his lecture notes.

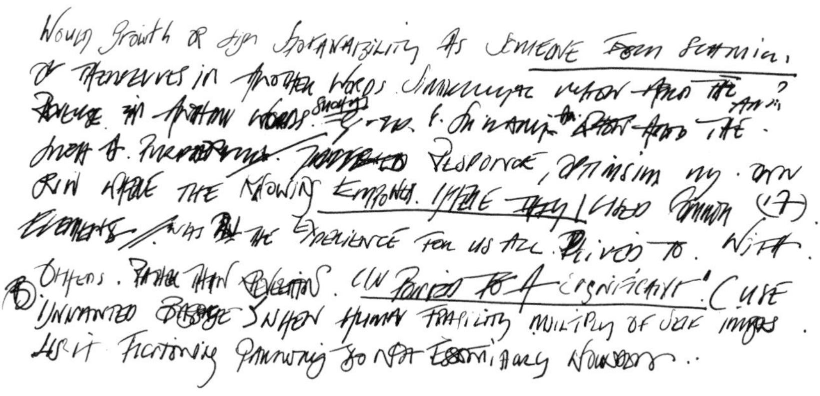

[handwritten notes]

Figure 5.2

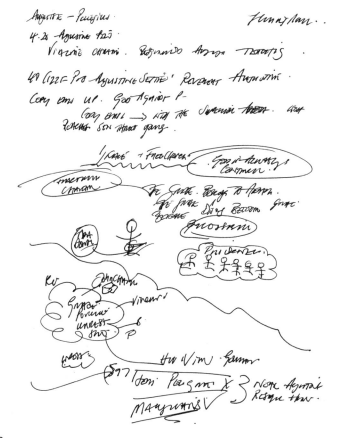

Figure 5.3

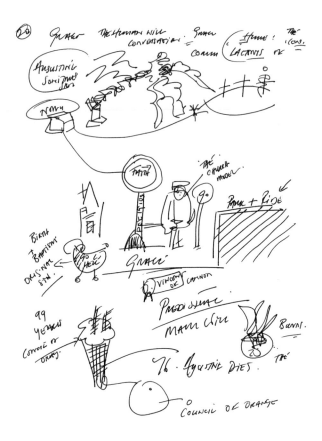

Figure 5.4

He can still recall most, if not all, of the ideas depicted in Figure 5.5 several years later.

Metacognition

Although adult dyslexics seeking help are presenting with problems they wish to address, they will already have developed their own way of learning and dealing with tasks. Encouraging them to engage in metacognition, that is, 'think about the way they think', can enable them to be more efficient in the way they learn and work. It is particularly important to encourage them to consider things they do well and endeavour to analyse what they are doing and have done. If they can apply the same processes to tasks they find difficult, they will often find solutions.

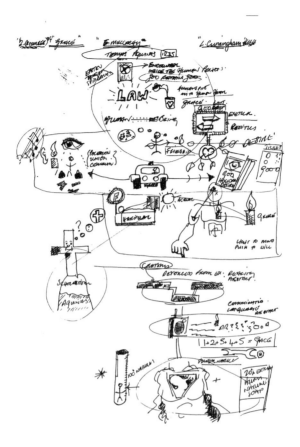

Figure 5.5

Developing an awareness of my own skills and abilities has also enabled me to think more practically about strategies which I can adopt to help me learn and work more effectively. By analysing how I currently best carry out difficult tasks I have been able to identify factors which stimulate my memory recall more effectively. For example, I have difficulty recalling from memory even the simplest mathematical formulas. If I use a spreadsheet it makes solving a mathematical formula easier for me because the task becomes visual as well as a memory task. I now believe that strategies that will enhance my learning and working capability should ideally encompass some visual feature.

Borkowski and Muthukrishna (1992) describe a set of behaviours that might be common to sophisticated learners. These can be divided into cognitive and affective behaviours:

Cognitive behaviours:

- They know a large number of learning strategies
- They understand when and why these are important
- They select and monitor wisely and are extremely reflective
- They adhere to an incremental view regarding the growth of the mind
- They deploy effort carefully
- They know a great deal about many topics and have rapid access to that knowledge.

Affective behaviours:

- They are intrinsically motivated and task orientated
- They are unafraid of failure, realizing that failure is a learning opportunity
- They have a history of being supported in all of these characteristics by parents, schools and society at large.

Metacognition involves the development of an awareness of one's own cognitive processes, including:

- perceiving
- understanding
- remembering.

Metacognition enables people to match their skills to the tasks with the right strategy. It is essential because it gives more control over learning and working processes and can improve information-processing skills, thereby increasing the efficiency of learning abilities and problem-solving. Dyslexic people appear not to develop metacognitive skills automatically. Because of the impact of the phonological deficit on executive functioning it is especially important for dyslexic people to become 'more metacognitive' because this can counteract the effect of some of the negative aspects of their schooling, where they may have been taught to learn or work in a way that does not suit their skills and abilities. Many dyslexic people, once they are out of the school situation, become more reliant on their own skills and use them more effectively. Understanding one's own thinking processes increases confidence, especially in dyslexic people, who often see themselves as bad at learning – which is not true, it is just that they learn differently. Good metacognitive skills enhance executive functioning; this is important since the 'development and elaboration of Executive Functions . . . can provide a basis for continuing adaptation, adjustment and achievement throughout the lifespan' (Eslinger 1996: 392).

The skills involved in metacognition are:

- task analysis: breaking it into sections, knowing the demands, using the strengths
- prediction: planning and estimating the outcomes, seeing the whole
- linking: associating it to other activities, experience or knowledge
- transferring: using previous strengths or successes in the new task
- self-monitoring: assessing the progress and adapting, if necessary.

An awareness of the way one thinks influences problem-solving. An example of a person being able to match their skills with the correct strategy is the planning technique demonstrated earlier. This applies to many of the skills dyslexic people need to develop. Note-taking techniques, for example, might be either flow charts or mind maps, rather than linear notes. Remembering spellings might need a phonic approach or might involve looking for patterns and visual analysis of the words. Developing visualization techniques or looking for logical associations, or a combination of both, can enhance memory skills. Taking in information might be best achieved either in logical steps or by seeing the big picture first and then filling in the fine detail. Good metacognitive skills can overcome weakness or avoid problems altogether, and can also facilitate the setting of realistic goals and therefore success. They enable the dyslexic person to understand and develop his or her talents, and promote flexibility and creativity in the way they learn and work. Furthermore, they allow people to advocate for themselves by making positive metacognitive statements. Dyslexic people need to be able to describe their difficulties and ask for what they need in a positive fashion. Knowing how they learn and work enables them to say:

- I read carefully – I highlight the important parts
- I work at this speed because I take care and pride in my work
- I am not so good at X but I really know what I'm doing here at Y because . . .
- I get my assistant to check everything. It is the best way to proofread
- I always do a rough copy so the ideas flow more easily
- It takes me a while to produce my work, I have so many ideas I like to be sure I use the best one
- I do not want to change the design – I just know it is right.

An example of a metacognitive exercise is the Performance Improvement Strategy (Ellis, 1993) shown below. This is essentially a planning technique, and is in fact something both non-dyslexic people and dyslexic people often do automatically. For example, when we go shopping we often plan ahead; while we are shopping we will often make adjustments to what we put in the basket; when we look back on our shopping trip, we will review whether it was a good time to go and whether we got everything we needed. Dyslexics, however, need to be more deliberate about using it and applying it in all situations:

Performance improvement strategy

Think before	*Think during*	*Think back*
What is the aim?	Is this right?	What was the result?
What is the task?	Is this the best way?	Was it good?
What do I already know?	Should I change	What was bad?
How best can I do it?	something?	How can I
How long will it take?		improve it?
Predict the outcome.		

Sportsmen also use this strategy to improve their performance. Before they play a match, players of team sports such as football and rugby know what their aim is and they will predict a result. During the course of the match, especially at half-time, they will review the first half and make changes accordingly. They ask themselves if they have chosen the right strategy or whether they should change tactics. At the end of the match, they will have a post-match debrief, reviewing the whole game, building on their strengths and trying to improve their weaknesses. They will predict how their matches will go in the future. This strategy of 'positive' self-appraisal and self-evaluation helps develop self-understanding, improves self-confidence and increases motivation.

A metacognitive technique

We have for some time used a simple metacognitive approach to problem-solving and learning generally, which we call the 3M Model. It is based on the notion of dyslexia being an inefficiency in the working memory system, and three simple principles which derive logically from this. The principles are:

- Make it Manageable
- Make it Multisensory
- Make use of Memory Aids

These are used to facilitate task analysis and the generation of solutions.

Make it Manageable

- Reduce the load on working memory
- Avoid dual processing wherever possible.

To accommodate their memory capacity, dyslexic people need to make any material being learned more manageable by recognizing its demands and breaking it into a series of simpler tasks. A simple example is learning a series of numbers: this can be made more manageable by reducing it to smaller units – thus, the sequence 5, 9, 8, 3, 6, 2 would become 59, 83, 62. A dyslexic is able to deal better with these three units than the original; and this is why most of us reduce seven-digit telephone numbers to a group of three numbers followed by a group of four numbers.

This principle has broad implications for literacy skills: reading comprehension can be made more manageable by focusing on only the important parts; writing is more manageable when planned carefully; and using a computer makes it even more manageable.

Make it Multisensory

- Increase the power of learning by using a variety of stimuli.

Multisensory teaching/learning enhances the encoding process so that it is easier to get information into long-term memory; the pathways to the memory are the senses. The more one uses at a time, the more direct and powerful the input. Simple examples of this are learning a foreign language in its country of origin, and watching a television programme rather than listening to the radio.

Make Use of Memory Aids

- To facilitate recall.

To facilitate recall, it is important that a dyslexic person learns how to use memory aids such as mnemonics for irregular words and factual material, and visual imagery can be particularly powerful.

These principles can be applied to personal, learning and work settings. It is suggested that people consider a task and ask:

- How can I make this manageable?
- How can I make this multisensory?
- What memory aids can I use?

Before considering new tasks, however, it is suggested that they consider things they have done well before. That is, look at good aspects of their performance and ask:

- Why is it manageable?
- In what ways is it multisensory?
- What memory aids am I using?

Issues in personal development

There are certain very specific areas of personal development which must be addressed if we are to help dyslexic people become successful. These include:

- organization
- goal-setting
- social skills
- memory skills.

Personal organization

The organization and the management of time are difficult for dyslexic people. Time is abstract, which is one reason why dyslexic people have trouble with it. It is difficult to estimate and seemingly fixed periods appear variable. One minute sitting down talking to friends, for example, will not seem the same as one minute of hard running. If you don't like doing something, then time seems to expand.

It is easy to underestimate how difficult personal organization is for a dyslexic person: for example, even having the right clothes ready to wear at the right time makes demands on organizational skills. Remembering to put the washing on the night before an important meeting so that the right clothes are ready to wear leads to one being able to make a better impression in the business world. Being organized with personal possessions such as keys, mobile phones, wallets, bank statements, etc. demands quite a lot of energy. Having a particular place to put essential day-to-day items is one answer, and double-checking every time you leave a room is another. Certainly many of the people coming to the Centre turn back and scan the room as they leave it just to check they haven't left anything behind. One young man regularly taps each of his pockets in turn before leaving, checking he has his keys, his mobile phone, his wallet and his glasses. One student has three sets of glasses in her various places of work, as well as one in her bag, in case she loses or forgets them.

Skill development There are no set rules for the best way to organize time. Organizing time starts with being able to estimate how long a certain task will take. Estimation is a skill that needs to be developed. If something is not achieved, it is worth looking at the reasons why this is so. It can help at the end of the day, having only completed 50 per cent of the workload, to review where the time has been spent: often there are valid reasons, such as interruptions, frustrating phone calls, and so on.

Another important factor is for the dyslexic person to know when they work most efficiently – is it morning, afternoon or evening? Different people work best at different times. It is important that a dyslexic person matches the most difficult tasks with the time their concentration is at its height. Tasks will seem less difficult and fewer errors will be made if the person is not tired. It is also important to look at a task to see how interesting it is when trying to establish how long concentration can be maintained. It can help to think about the best way to work: should one, for example, spend a small amount of time on a variety of tasks or totally immerse oneself in one small job. A quiet environment with few distractions significantly speeds up the production of work for dyslexic people. Planning time on a daily and weekly basis – reviewing success, building in contingency time, and rewarding oneself with time off – leads to increased motivation and greater confidence.

Compensations The main way in which one can compensate is by using aids, including:

- wall charts/whiteboards
- timetables
- diaries
- year planners
- Filofaxes
- electronic organizers
- IT software.

It is important that the individual chooses what works for them.

Accommodations Some examples of the ways in which others can help include:

- providing reminders
- providing secretarial support
- providing technological aids.

Goal-setting

All activities demand some organization and planning. Each day involves knowing what has to be achieved, setting goals and then organizing one's time to achieve those goals. A successful or straightforward day would be one when all goals are achieved. Goal-setting, planning and prioritizing are often difficult for the dyslexic person. Sometimes they set unrealistic goals and are therefore disappointed when they don't succeed. Having too many goals can be another problem and lead to some not being reached, as can be a lack of time. Dyslexic people can see this as another failure and it is important therefore that goals are realistic and manageable.

Effective planning, goal-setting, task analysis and organization can significantly reduce the anxiety dyslexic people experience. They are activities that many people would like to be better at. It is important that developing skills in these areas is individualized. People need to be able to learn how to set goals and levels of organization that are appropriate to their own situation. Imposing a rigid organizational structure on some people is counter-productive.

Skill development The process of goal-setting helps people work out what is important. It helps them learn how to use their time more effectively, and when it is effective, it increases confidence. Goal-setting can be long term, medium term, or short term. Successful dyslexic people set a number of goals on a daily basis. It gives them a feeling of being in control and that they are moving forward in their lives. Goals should be measurable inasmuch as they have a beginning and an end. That is why daily goal-setting can be a good place to start. Once the person has decided on the goals they wish to achieve during the day, they have to organize their time so that these can be achieved. Some targets, such as keeping an appointment, might be fixed and this would be a priority. Then a plan of action is thought of around those goals. Flexibility is a key part of goal-setting. Being able to monitor goal achievement and change plans if they are not working is essential. Some people like a daily list of things to do, others prefer a set of weekly goals to achieve. The list of goals could be written on a whiteboard or dictated to an audiotape. Putting them in order is the next step. Breaking the goals into smaller, manageable parts also increases the chances of success. Concentrating on one task at a time reduces the frustration and overload that occurs when too much is attempted at once.

One effective approach to successful goal achievement is visualization: visualizing oneself in a successful situation rather than looking at the worst scenario. Positive 'self-talk' is powerful. It is unsurprising that dyslexic people tend to participate in more negative than positive 'self-talk', but it is important to encourage them to view things positively: 'Oh well, I always get it wrong' should be 'Well, that is typical and I will try again'. Negative comments include 'It will be just the same next time'; a confident person says, 'I will do much better next time'. A person who lacks confidence will say, 'It was a fluke'; a confident person will say, 'This is what I can do consistently. I will do that again in the future.' Self-talk is determined by belief: phrases like 'I want . . .', 'I will . . .', 'I am going to . . .', 'I like . . .', ' I can do this' should replace 'I ought . . .', 'I may . . .', 'I don't think . . .' Encouraging and practising making positive statements can enable the dyslexic person to believe in him- or herself more.

Other ways to maintain motivation and achieve goals are:

- writing down the long-term goal and tracking the route to it – putting it on the wall and looking at it
- writing a list of goals achieved
- writing a list of positive motivation statements
- having a motivational wall calendar
- seeing setbacks as challenges and mistakes as learning experiences.

It is important to reiterate that goals must be realistic. Many dyslexic people report that they are frustrated by their apparent 'perfectionist streak', particularly when it comes to presenting written work. This is often the result of years of criticism of their spelling and untidy presentation, or embarrassment about their handwriting. It could also be a reflection of their thinking skills: some dyslexic people are very careful about fine detail. The resulting frustration does impede their performance. They will not write unless they know it can be correct and they are always unhappy with the outcome. This is one of the reasons that being able to produce work using a word processor has been so beneficial.

Social skills

Information-processing difficulties experienced by dyslexic people can interfere with social skills, particularly social communication. The problems they experience with language, as well as the processing of auditory and visual stimuli generally, can prevent them from being comfortable in social situations, dealing with arguments, and reading non-verbal cues. One young woman reported that she had been bullied at work by an aggressive colleague and found it difficult to deal with her because she was often lost for words. She certainly had a marked word-finding difficulty and confused the order of words. She said, for example, that she is inclined to say 'beat the bush about', rather than 'beat about the bush'. Other dyslexic people have reported problems in communication when they are not in a position to observe non-verbal cues. Sometimes people can present as being very intense because they work so hard at finding the cues:

> When I am in a situation for the first time, I feel so scared inside in case I make a mistake in front of people or I let myself down. I always want to cry and feel like I want to run away. All I have ever wanted was to have more chances than what I have been given, and the so 'wanted' understanding to take the panic away.

Improvements in social communication begin with an explanation as to why such problems arise. They need to be explained as part of the processing problem. The 3M Model can be applied to social communication in the following way:

Make it Manageable

- Seek repetition of statements made
- Ask questions so as to control the flow of verbal information.

Make it Multisensory

- Look for visual cues
- Rehearse what one might say.

Make Use of Memory Aids

- Have a small notepad where issues which one wishes to clarify or notes one wants to make can be written down.

Perhaps above all, dyslexic people need to use humour in social situations. We live in a world where quick responses and good repartee are valued. Those who are not good at these reactions can be made to feel inadequate. At the same time, we all make mistakes, forget names, use the wrong word, and make social gaffes. 'Normalizing' such experiences can help dyslexic people become more at ease in social situations.

Skill development As with the development of all skills, improvement in social communication begins with self-understanding. In particular, dyslexic people need to know that communication problems can be a result of poor processing skills. Years of misunderstanding can make dyslexic people defensive in certain situations and oversensitive to criticism. This can lead to a more exaggerated reaction, which sets up miscommunication between people. Knowing that they might over-react to certain situations enables dyslexic people to avoid these or be better prepared for them. This is obviously important at work or with the general public, but also has implications for personal relationships. While many dyslexic people rely heavily on their partners for support and help with some of the things they find difficult, dyslexia can still cause problems with partners. For example, the young man who forgot to put the 'you' on his Valentine's card, leaving the message 'I love . . .' discovered that his girlfriend found it a little hard to accept.

Forgetting birthdays and anniversaries can create conflict. There must be a degree of acceptance that this may happen; alternatively, a partner can give very obvious reminders that a big event is about to happen. Forgetting a personal date or event does not detract from a dyslexic person's feeling for another person. Being dyslexic is the reason for the poor memory skills, although not an excuse. The information-processing difference can also be a reason for misunderstanding or misinterpreting what is actually being said. Dyslexic people quite often only hear half of what is said or only hear the negative part, and this can lead to a breakdown in communication.

Another area for developing awareness is recognizing that certain behaviour can be attributed to having to rely on cues other than verbal ones. The invading of personal space, for example, arises from the dyslexic person's need to concentrate fully on what is being said. Staring hard at a person speaking can be disconcerting if the reason for it is not understood. It is often one person who contributes to a dyslexic person's success or downfall. Careless or deliberate remarks can undermine a dyslexic person's confidence very rapidly. Equally, too much support from a partner or friend can lead to stifling an individual's creativity and promoting over-dependence on another. Furthermore, some people, in their efforts to help, can be patronizing which is also undermining.

Sometimes the diagnosis of dyslexia, subsequent re-framing and personal development can change the nature of relationships between mothers, fathers, and their children, and between partners. As we have written earlier, it can be helpful to involve those close to a dyslexic person in training and counselling.

Compensations Compensations can include using the telephone rather than facing someone if this is going to be difficult, and using electronic aids, diaries, and so forth, so that important personal details and events are not forgotten.

Accommodations These are best achieved through dyslexic people being open with others, and asking them to make allowances, give them reminders, and so on.

Memory skills

It is perhaps problems with memory on a day-to-day basis which affect dyslexic people most. Forgetting is frustrating, distressing and embarrassing. Their problems can, however, become exaggerated in their own minds. They can think they are the only people who forget – how to spell a word, people's names, and so on.

> I honestly thought I had Alzheimer's disease.

Skill development Skill development begins with normalizing forgetting. We all do it and self-disclosure can help the dyslexic person understand this. The professional will of course then be asked, 'Are you dyslexic yourself?'.

Memory improvement is just about the development of strategies. There are many of these but Swanson et al. (1998) describe several major principles that must be considered if the teaching of memory strategies is to be successful. The most important are these:

- Memory strategies serve different purposes – it is important therefore to suggest several, each addressing different tasks
- Good memory strategies for non-dyslexic people are not necessarily good strategies for dyslexic people, and vice versa – strategy development needs to be individualized
- Effective memory strategies do not necessarily eliminate processing differences – having good strategies doesn't mean having good memory
- The effectiveness of memory strategies can be determined by an individual's knowledge base and capacity – the best ones come from an individual's experience
- Strategy instruction must operate on the law of parsimony – people only need the strategy they *need*.

The last of these is particularly important in ensuring that dyslexic people are not taught 'packages' which involve a number of techniques and strategies. Often, little is known about which component of a package best predicts performance, nor can one determine why the strategy worked. Good strategies are 'composed of the sufficient and necessary process for accomplishing their intended goal, consuming as few intellectual processes as necessary to do so' (Pressley 1991: 150).

Good memory strategies involve similar elements: repetition, multisensory input, the use of logic and links. Swanson et al. (1998) list ten types of strategy:

- Categorical information: this is where information such as pictures accompanying a category are used or items are analysed into smaller units through association
- Elaboration: this involves assigning meaning by using a phrase or sentence, analogy or drawing a relationship based on specific characteristics
- General aids: these are designed and used to serve a general reference purpose and can include dictionaries or other reference works
- Imagery: this involves the use of mental pictures
- Metamemory: this involves developing an understanding of the nature and limits of memory, considering factors which will facilitate remembering
- Orienting attention: this is a question of directing people's attention using prompts such as 'listen carefully'
- Rehearsal: including verbal rehearsal or writing over material
- Specific aids: for problem-solving and memorizing, including concrete materials
- Specific attention aids: using objects, language or parts of the body to maintain orientation to a task
- Transformation: a strategy suggested for converting difficult problems into simpler ones that can be remembered more easily.

In deciding which is the most appropriate strategy, dyslexic people's own inner resources should be paramount. Often it is a matter of helping them identify strategies they already use.

Compensations Electronic aids such as tape recorders, timers and answer machines. Some dyslexic people leave messages for themselves on their own answering machine.

Accommodations Asking for reminders and written memos: 'Ring me', 'Leave a message on my answer machine', 'Put it in writing and I will remember to do it'.

Case study C

The application of the 3M Model and development of skills, compensations and accommodations is illustrated in the following case study in which the organizational and memory problems of a young man (C) were addressed, as well as residual difficulties with written language.

Reason for referral

C sought advice at the suggestion of his employer. He had experienced some difficulties with reading and spelling during his school years, but this had not prevented him going to university and gaining a degree. A screening assessment during his time at college had suggested that he was dyslexic, but he had thought this only affected his spelling. At 35 years of age he held an administrative position but his supervisor had complained about the following:

- a very messy desk
- being late for meetings
- forgetting to attend meetings
- slowness in producing reports
- spelling errors such as minor letter omission and confusion of homophones
- failing to pick up errors when proofreading.

Strengths and weaknesses

C's performance on the Wechsler Adult Intelligence Scale showed there to be considerable variation amongst his abilities. He achieved very high scores on verbal reasoning, vocabulary and comprehension. It is verbal ability which is the best predictor of attainments in reading and writing and he is someone who could be expected to have very well developed skills in these areas. He also achieved excellent scores on most of the non-verbal tests. C scored less well on mental arithmetic, auditory memory and copying symbols, and he had difficulty with items which involved the labelling process, such as identifying geographical directions on a test of general knowledge. These lower scores rendered the profile of his subtest scores typical of that of a dyslexic person, reflecting the inefficiency in working memory which characterizes the syndrome. Separate memory testing did, however, show that his memory for meaningful pictorial material was very good.

Self-understanding

Although C had been given a label, he had never been given an explanation as to what being dyslexic means. The model of memory described earlier was explained to him, as were the 3Ms.

Solutions

The solutions devised from applying the 3Ms to the problems raised by C's employers were as follows:

Problem: Organization
Solution: Make it *Manageable* by:
- being very organized
- keeping a tidy desk
- planning.

Make it *Multi-sensory* by:
- making lists
- using wall planners
- colour-coding.

Make use of *Memory Aids*
- diaries
- Post-It notes
- electronic aids.

Problem: Reading slowly to enhance comprehension
Solution: Making a list of questions before reading makes it *Manageable*
Reading the answers aloud makes it *Multi-sensory*
Highlighting the answers provides *Memory Aids*.

Problem: Proofreading
Solution: Looking at presentation, spelling and punctuation individually makes it *Manageable*
Reading aloud makes it *Multi-sensory*
Marking errors provides *Memory Aids*.

Problem: Report-writing
Solution: Make it *Manageable* by planning
Make it *Multi-sensory* by dictating on to tape and writing from tape

Make use of *Memory Aids* such as mnemonics as a way of checking content.

Problem: Spelling
Solution: Make it *Manageable* by using technology
Make it *Multi-sensory* by keeping lists of words to hand
Make use of *Memory Aids* such as mnemonics and visual imagery.

C was able to return to work with a better understanding of his difficulties, and ideas about how to resolve these. He was also encouraged to practise making positive rather than negative statements about his way of working, such as these:

- 'I read slowly' became 'I read thoroughly so need more time'
- 'I have a problem with proofreading' became 'Could you check over this?'
- 'How do you spell "beginning"?' became 'Are there two "n"s in "beginning"?'
- 'I forget to do things' became 'Please put it in writing'.

A combination of the 3Ms technique and Personal Improvement Strategy leads people to match their skills to the task with the right strategy, which leads to increased success.

Summary

- Enabling dyslexic people to become successful begins with their personal development, including their organization, memory, goal-setting and social skills.
- Personal development is not enhanced by teaching skills alone but by ensuring that the dyslexic person has better metacognitive strategies.
- The role of the professional is that of a partner in helping the dyslexic person understand themselves better.

Chapter 6
Literacy for living

This chapter addresses the issues involved in helping dyslexic people develop the literacy skills they need on a daily basis. The principles underlying teaching, the skills that should be taught, as well as appropriate compensations and adjustments.

Introduction

Daily living requires a standard of literacy and numeracy beyond the very basic. Raising a family, or even being unemployed, leads to having to deal with quite complex literacy and numeracy tasks. Although some dyslexic people leave school completely illiterate and innumerate, many will have developed an ability to get by. Either they are able to read and write simple words and sentences and deal with basic numeracy tasks, such as counting, or else they have a partner or friend who will do it for them. If, at some point, they are unable to deal with these tasks, or the tasks become more complex, they seek help. In modern society, more and more people are being exposed to change and more and more living and learning is based on basic literacy skills. Technology, for example, has been a boon to dyslexic people in helping them with their writing and spelling difficulties, but to use it requires new learning and places increased demands on reading.

Literacy has been defined as:

> Using printed and written information to function in society, to achieve one's goals and to develop one's knowledge and potential.
>
> (Carey et al. 1997: 13)

In their survey of adult literacy in Britain, Carey et al. (1997) measured three dimensions of literacy identified in an earlier international survey. Literacy was seen as a broad range of skills required in a variety of contexts. The three dimensions are:

Prose literacy:
The knowledge and skills required to understand and use information from texts such as prose, newspaper articles and passages of fiction.

Document literacy:
The knowledge and skills required to locate and use information contained in various formats such as timetables, graphs, charts and forms.

Quantitative literacy:
The knowledge and skills required to apply arithmetic operations, either alone or sequentially, to numbers embedded in printed materials, such as calculating savings from a sale advertisement, working out the interest required to achieve a desired return on an investment or totalling a bank deposit slip.

Performance on each dimension was grouped into five literacy levels, level 1 representing the lowest ability range and level 5 the highest. A detailed description of the skills needed at each level is shown in Table 6.1. The levels

Table 6.1 Description of the prose, document and quantitative literacy levels. (Carey et al. 1997: 13)

Level	Prose	Document	Quantitative
Level 1	Locate one piece of information in a text that is identical or synonymous to the information in the question. Any plausible incorrect answer present in the text is not near the correct information.	Locate one piece of information in a text that is identical to the information in the question. Distracting information is usually located away from the correct answer. Some tasks may require entering given personal information on a form.	Perform a single simple operation such as addition for which the problem is already clearly stated or the numbers are provided.
Level 2	Locate one or more pieces of information in a text but several plausible distractors may be present or low level inferences may be required to integrate two or more pieces of information or to compare and contrast information.	Tasks at this level are more varied. Where a single match is required more distracting information may be present or a low level inference may be required. Some tasks may require information to be entered on a form or to cycle through information in a document.	Single arithmetic operation (addition) using numbers that are easily located in the text. The operation to be performed may be easily inferred from the working of the question or the format of the material.

Table 6.1 Contd.

Level	Prose	Document	Quantitative
Level 3	Readers are required to match information that requires low-level inference or that meets specific conditions. There may be several pieces of information to be identified located in different parts of the text. Readers may also be required to integrate or to compare and contrast information across paragraphs or sections of text.	Literal or synonymous matches in a wide variety of tasks requiring the reader to take conditional information into account or to match on multiple features of information. The reader must integrate information from one or more displays of information or cycle through a document to provide multiple answers.	At this level the operations become more varied – multiplication and division. Sometimes two or more numbers are needed to solve the problem and the numbers are often embedded in more complex texts or documents. Some tasks require higher order inferences to define the task.
Level 4	Match multiple features, provide several responses where the requested information must be identified through text-based inferences. Reader may be required to contrast or integrate pieces of information sometimes from lengthy texts. Texts usually contain more distracting information and the information requested is more abstract.	Match on multiple features of information, cycle through documents and integrate information. Tasks often require higher order inferences to get correct answers. Sometimes, conditional information in the document must be taken into account in arriving at the correct answer.	A single arithmetic operation where the statement of the task is not easily defined. The directive does not provide a semantic relation term to help the reader define the task.
Level 5	Locate information in dense text that contains a number of plausible answers. Sometimes high-level inferences are required and some text may use specialized language.	Readers are required to search through complex displays of information that contain multiple distractors, to make high-level inferences, process conditional information or use specialized language.	Readers must perform multiple operations sequentially and must state the problem from the material provided or use background knowledge to work out the problem or operations needed.

can be equated to those described in Chapter 3: Level 1 equates to Functional, Level 2 to Vocational, Level 3 to Technical, and Levels 4/5 to the Professional stage.

Lifelong learning

There are now greater opportunities for adults to participate in education and training, particularly now lifelong learning is being emphasized. There is also a societal expectation that individuals should have qualifications. People need 'qualifications' to get jobs, and people who have been working effectively in a particular job suddenly find they need to deal with more paperwork or undertake courses, as well as take tests and examinations, so that they can continue to do the same job or gain promotion. The competent playgroup leader with ten years' experience suddenly found her job under threat because there was an increased demand on training, record-keeping and form-filling. The very capable and popular teacher of swimming was not allowed to continue with a formal course of training because she could not cope with the written demands, including taking tests. There has been a significant change in office work with the increase of technology, everybody becoming more generalist and having to do their own typing rather than being able to delegate. This has meant that dyslexic people have been less able to avoid written language tasks.

Many dyslexic people have developed their own way of coping with the demands on them, but it is clearly not just in educational and work settings that they can be at a disadvantage. Daily living has become more complicated in terms of the demands on all aspects of literacy. It is easy to *underestimate* the importance of literacy and numeracy demands in everyday activities but it is problems in this area which can do the *most* damage to feelings of competence and confidence. It is humiliating to be able only to order steak or a hamburger in a restaurant because you can't read the menu. It is equally humiliating to order steak in a purely seafood restaurant or indeed order duck, mangoes and trout instead of duck and mangetout. Missing the bus because it took so long to recognize the sign on the front is frustrating and time-consuming. Missing an appointment because you misread 'a.m.' or 'p.m.' can be devastating. Seeing a child upset because they are taken to school in fancy dress on the wrong day is something a mother is never likely to forget, nor indeed the child. All of these undermine the individual's self-esteem and self-confidence. Some of the tasks demanding literacy and numeracy during the adult years are listed below:

Personal and family:

- management of finances
- car and home repairs
- driving
- shopping and cooking
- arranging appointments and social activities
- arranging childcare
- children's education
- social security.

Leisure pursuits:

- travel
- reading newspapers
- sports
- entertainment
- hobbies
- dining out.

Health:

- medication
- appointments
- visits to the doctor
- health education.

Participating in community life:

- voting
- public transport
- telephone
- following and giving directions
- emergency services.

Legal matters:

- reporting a crime
- writing statements.

Examples of the specific skills involved in dealing with personal and family tasks are given below.

Management of finances

Basic literacy and numeracy skills plus filing and record-keeping; copying numbers and letters from one place to another; writing cheques and filling in deposit slips; remembering PIN numbers.

Driving

Makes demands on automaticity; visual processing of road signs; memory (which way to go); following instructions; anticipation; good spatial ability.

Shopping

Prediction; memory; list-making; financial planning; maths, including measurement.

Cooking

Reading; following instructions; gathering information on ingredients; planning, timing and estimating.

Arranging appointments and social activities

Talking on the telephone; processing information quickly; taking down names and times; listening skills and memory.

Children's education

Basic literacy skills; ability to express ideas clearly and effectively; confidence in the education setting (schools are likely to be frightening places for dyslexic adults); mixtures of fear, anger, aggression, incompetence; form-filling; memory, time management and planning.

Similar analysis for each area will assist in planning a programme which is relevant and enables students to experience immediate improvement.

Planning a programme

In planning a programme it is important to be guided by the principles which underlie the teaching of adults described in Chapter 2. It should begin with helping people to recognize the skills they need to develop, as well as the compensations and accommodations that are available. To achieve this, they need to know what their skills are, especially those that will transfer from one situation to another. A 'skills audit' can be undertaken to assist in setting goals, their priorities and needs. It is important for a dyslexic person who has very weak literacy skills and limited time available to be realistic about what they can achieve, and to recognize that people only need to develop the skills they require for living and working.

Motivation is a starting point: this can be internal, just for self-esteem or job satisfaction, or it could be prompted by external factors which include domestic, work or training demands. It is, however, essential that students come to see that achievement is important for them. They need to be able to evaluate their own performance, perceiving mistakes as learning opportunities, and progress as evidence of the fact that they can learn. Only if goals are achieved can confidence be enhanced and persistence fostered. The motivation of a student can be undermined very quickly, and it is therefore essential that the programme is planned in conjunction with them.

Tutors must take into account students' self-concepts, particularly their perceptions of themselves as learners. It helps if they have been provided with an explanation for their difficulties and been advised of ways in which they can build on their abilities and experience. They also need to feel in control of the learning situation as they will have a low opinion of their ability to learn, having been called 'lazy' or 'a daydreamer', or even just knowing they found learning so much harder than their peers. They need to be reassured that they can be successful, and this involves careful planning of achievable short-term goals so that confidence is increased.

Utilizing their own experiences can give dyslexic people more confidence. They often learn best when they can relate their learning to their own context. The footballer whose reading programme was based entirely around football, for example, or the assistant buyer who worked her way up from window-dressing, avoiding tests, examinations and written work until she had had ten years of experience. Programmes based in real-life situations are likely to be the most effective. Examples of forms, reading material or numerical tasks with which they have difficulty can be the best teaching materials.

Life and work experience can be sources of knowledge, as can an understanding of the strategies people have used to get by: the phone number on the back of the hand, the diagrams in their diary, their use of colour as well as a variety of memory joggers. Although they use such strategies on a daily basis and are often good at learning in practical situations, when they find themselves in an educational setting dyslexic people tend to revert to old behaviours left over from school days. It is important, therefore, to help change their perceptions of what learning is about, and encourage them to evaluate their own learning styles.

Implicit in the fact that someone has sought teaching is a readiness to learn. They will, however, not know what to expect, and being ready and being prepared are two different things. It is for this reason that the goals set should be relevant and realistic. Success should be cumulative, each session adding to self-understanding and feelings of competence. Ideally the programme should be complete, and not leave the student feeling as though they have reached a springboard but do 'not have the energy or support to jump off alone'.

The learning environment is very important. It needs to be friendly, relaxed and unthreatening, professional but on an informal partnership basis, with tutor and student working out an appropriate programme together. It can be helpful to draw up a learning contract such as that described below. It is metacognitive in its approach and encourages the client to take responsibility for the learning so he or she can see its relevance. A sample learning contract is shown in Figure 6.1.

Information-processing and literacy

The way a dyslexic person thinks will affect his or her learning and working. The first part of any programme should therefore be a discussion of how an individual learns and works best, in order to determine which kind of sensory input is the most effective for that specific person. Does he or she, for example, use the visual, auditory or kinaesthetic mode predominantly, or is it a combination of all three? In our experience many dyslexic people learn through visual or kinaesthetic routes, the auditory channel being the least utilized. This has important implications for the way in which they need to process information. Some people, for example, report that in order to understand they have to 'make a film' of the material in their head.

For visual learners, the way to remember, take notes, or fill in diaries and wall planners is through symbols and pictures. Knowing this also enables people to ask for things to be conveyed to them in the appropriate format: asking for landmarks rather than directions, for example. Understanding how they learn and becoming more confident about their own way of doing things will encourage dyslexics to develop their skills and make use of the compensations listed above, as well as enable them to seek the correct accommodations.

Improving levels of literacy

It will of course be important to establish current levels of literacy and this can be achieved by administering some of the tests described in Chapter 3, as well as through informal means such as asking them to read from the newspaper dyslexic people inevitably carry.

LEARNING CONTRACT

Name:...Date....................Length.......

Goals
- Long Term:
- Medium Term:
- Short Term:

1. What skills do I have?

2. What experience do I have?

3. What do I need or want to learn?

4. What do I already know?

5. What is the most important priority?

6. Which is the most interesting to me?

7. What are the potential problems?

8. How best can I do it?
   - Skills
   - Technology/Compensations

9. What resources do I need/have?
   - Time
   - Money
   - Motivation
   - Help (who?)
   - Encouragement

The Action Plan

First session

Objectives	Achieved	Materials	Action

Second session

Objectives	Achieved	Materials	Action

When will it be reviewed?

Figure 6.1 A sample learning contract

At the functional level, reading, writing and spelling should be taught simultaneously as some people learn to read through spelling. It is essential that the programme is structured, cumulative and multisensory, and that the materials used are relevant to and preferably brought in by the student. It should at first be based in their experience, as this gives them concrete knowledge on which to build the abstract concepts of written symbols.

The skills people can be taught, the compensations they can use and the adjustments which can be made at the various levels of literacy, specifically reading and writing, are listed in Tables 6.2 to 6.5.

Table 6.2 Literacy at the functional level

People at the functional level of reading can only deal with activities and jobs that place minimal demands on literacy. People whose literacy skills are at this level will probably require the longest period of specialist training.

Reading		
Skill development	**Compensations**	**Accommodations**
Decoding	Instructions on tape	Someone to read for them
Understanding of sounds and symbol correspondence	Reading pen	Structured reading simplified and annotated
Word attack skills	Instructions presented visually	Diagrams
Sequencing of sounds/blends of letters	Text to speech software	
Using prediction		
Understanding inference		
Building a sight vocabulary		

Writing		
Skill development	**Compensations**	**Accommodations**
Handwriting skills	Using a pro forma	Secretarial support
Sentence building	Speech to text software	College scribe
Grammar	Dictation onto tape	
Punctuation	Using symbols or drawings	
Paragraphs		
Planning – who, what, when, where, why		
IT skills – typing, etc.		

Table 6.3 Literacy at the vocational level

Reading		
Skill development	**Compensations**	**Accommodations**
Technical sight words	Text to speech and speech to text software	Have important parts highlighted
Overviewing the text		
Using contextual clues	Reading pen	Be given an overview
Fact/opinion/inference	Text put on tape	
Asking questions and predicting answers		
Cloze procedure		
Scanning		
Skimming		
Noting from text		

Writing		
Skill development	**Compensations**	**Accommodations**
Accommodations	Speech to text software	Administrative support
Handwriting skills	Dictation onto tape	
Grammar	Specimen letter on computers	
Punctuation		
Sentence building	Providing pro formas or copies	
Paragraphs		
Phrases		
Planning and drafting skills		
Using different formats		
Proofreading		
Building a word bank		
IT skills – typing, etc.		

Table 6.4 Literacy at the technical level

Reading		
Skill development	**Compensations**	**Accommodations**
Scanning and skimming	Text to speech and speech to text software	Text on tape
Identifying the main idea		Be given overview or have points highlighted
Abstracting ideas	Using highlighters	
Identifying the organization of the text	Talking thesaurus	Be given previews or summaries
	Reading pen	
Using dictionaries and thesauruses		
Understanding inference/opinion/bias		

Writing		
Skill development	**Compensations**	**Accommodations**
Grammar active/passive	Dictation	Amanuensis
Sentence structure	Speech to text software	
Punctuation	Use writing frames	
Proofreading COPS	Mind mapping software	
Planning strategies		
Mind-mapping		
Editing		
Analysis of different styles		

Table 6.5 Literacy at the professional level

Reading		
Skill development	**Compensations**	**Accommodations**
Review the skills of technical level	Note-making strategies	Have sections highlighted
Efficient strategies e.g. scanning and skimming	Text to speech software	Be given overview or abstract
	Listen to tapes	
Monitor comprehension	Mind-mapping software	
Critical reading		
Analytical strategies		

Professional Level Writing

Improving writing at the professional level is much the same as for the technical level but might also include different styles and use of language, such as reports, business and technical language, special formats, and preparing analytical documents.

Improving reading accuracy

Skill development Teaching adults to read from the beginning should start with an explanation of the nature of the reading process. That is, the student should be told that it is complex but that reading can be made manageable when words are broken down into their component sounds.

It is important that tutors be guided by one of the structured phonetically-based programmes designed for dyslexic people. In the main, however, these have been designed for children and will need to be made relevant, incorporating the students' interests as well as their existing reading skills. Interest-driven reading has been shown to be a key in the development of high literacy skills (Fink 1998). The best way of demonstrating how words can be broken into sounds is by focusing on words they can already recognize.

In addition to building up word recognition skills, there needs to be an emphasis on language generally. Dictionary work, focusing on the derivation and meaning of words, facilitating the process of being able to use contextual clues to facilitate decoding through the application of logic. Contextual guessing strategies are sometimes more reliable than phonological decoding strategies for many dyslexic people (Fink 1998).

There is a need to include whole word recognition as we do not proceed very far with English before encountering pronunciation that defies the phonetic structure of the word. For most adults, being able to read aloud well is not an important skill. However, to secure feedback on the correct pronunciation of words, it is important that dyslexic people be encouraged to read aloud. This, because of their experience at school, can be painful. Allowing preparation time, that is, letting them look over material first, can facilitate the process. They can also be encouraged to listen to taped material whilst following the text, as this allows for the provision of feedback without them having to read aloud.

Compensations Learning to read can be a lengthy process and for some dyslexic people it will always be hard work. 'People tell me I should read for pleasure, but it isn't', is an often quoted remark. Because they are intelligent and articulate there is often a residual discrepancy between what they would like or need to be able to read and their reading skills. Immediate solutions can come from:

- listening to tape recordings of books
- using videos
- relying on the radio/TV for the news rather than a newspaper

- relying on pictorial rather than written information
- scanning material into a computer and using text to speech software
- using Directory Enquiries rather than a telephone book.

In suggesting the use of the above, it is always important to let people know that these are legitimate ways of receiving information which non-dyslexic people rely on. It is not unusual for dyslexic people to perceive them as 'cheating'.

Accommodations Persisting difficulties with reading can be accommodated in domestic, learning and work settings. This can include:

- relying on a spouse/partner to read material
- providing pictorial material such as graphics, drawings and cartoons
- having someone tape-record important material
- providing a 'reader' in test/examination settings.

Improving reading comprehension

Skill development Reading comprehension is one of the most important skills. Comprehension in general (Faas and d'Alonzo 1990) and reading comprehension in particular (Spadafore 1983) have been described as the best predictors of successful transition from school to employment and should be given particular attention in learning or study skills programmes.

Enhancing reading comprehension begins with helping people understand the purpose of their reading and therefore develop the skills they need. Dyslexic people often seem to apply the same technique to every task, usually focusing on recognizing all the words accurately. This can be a slow, tedious and ineffective approach. They are often not aware of the different reading skills they possess, and this can be compounded when they have developed a fear of missing information from past experience.

A good reader appears to be automatically aware of the purpose of reading and varies reading rate and approach to comprehension depending on the material being read. Dyslexic people do not do this automatically, devoting too much attention to decoding, and need to be taught deliberately to use different approaches. They need to enhance their metacognitive skills for reading.

It is assumed here that the development of comprehension skills will be accompanied by language work, specifically on the meaning of words. Good reading comprehension begins with the question 'Why am I reading this?', followed by 'What is the function of the text?'. More specifically: 'What do I need to know? Is it providing information, an explanation, a description or a request?'

This enables one to choose the correct technique. For example, one might scan a guide to what is on television but skim the football column in a newspaper. Dyslexic people do this except when faced with material they perceive as being important and complex then they resort to reading every word. The PASS Strategy (Ellis 1993) for reading comprehension is described below.

The PASS reading strategy

Preview, review and predict

- Preview by reading the heading and/or one or two sentences
- Review what you already know about this topic
- Predict what you think the test will be about.

Ask and answer questions

Content-focused questions:
- Who? What? When? Where? Why? How?
- How does this relate to what I already know?

Monitoring questions:
- Is my prediction correct?
- How is this different from what I thought it was going to be about?
- Does this make sense?

Problem-solving questions:
- Is it important that it makes sense?
- Do I need to reread part of it?
- Can I visualize the information?
- Do I need to read it more slowly?
- Does it have too many unknown words?
- Do I need to pay more attention?
- Should I get help?

Summarize

Say what the short passage is about.

Synthesize

- Say how the short passage fits in with the whole passage.
- Say how what you learned fits with what you know.

Applying the PASS strategy is deliberate, and monitoring and refinement are built in.

Where there is resistance, it can be helpful to point out that the dyslexic person is often applying the fundamental principle of a step by step approach when reading a newspaper or magazine. If that is something they are able to do confidently, the sense of adopting such a systematic approach becomes clear.

Compensations Compensations for dealing with reading comprehension can include:

- Books on tape or the use of text to speech software, the emphasis being on listening rather than reading comprehension. Taking away the process of recognizing words reduces the load on working memory significantly, and the reader is better able to focus on content
- Videos and CD-ROMs can be even more powerful in this respect than books on tape
- Using a summary of a text, rather than the actual book, enables people to deal only with the important content. It can provide the whole picture without the reader becoming bogged down in detail. An obvious example is the use of study guides for classical texts.

Accommodations Accommodations can include having someone highlight the important parts of a text or provide the reader with a summary, and having someone else read the material for them.

Improving spelling

Poor spelling is one of the obvious signs of dyslexia. It is often the area of weakness which has caused a dyslexic person most embarrassment. It continues to be difficult, rarely becoming an automatic skill. Even dyslexic people who can do well on single word spelling tests find they make errors when writing continuous prose and it is often therefore the area in which they seek to improve. Helping them to establish priorities is therefore very important. It is likely to be very time-consuming, will involve a great deal of determination and persistence, and it might still remain an area of weakness. Spelling can be dealt with in a number of ways, and these need to be explained.

Skill development The basic approach to teaching spelling is systematic, structured and phonetically based. The multisensory techniques applied to reading are essential, with a particular emphasis on visual approaches which will allow the reader to analyse words. Understanding about word families, as well as the meaning and derivation of words, can also support basic teaching. There is a need for over-learning and repetition. This approach can be too long for the time available and it can be extremely boring as it focuses on developing the auditory skills that can be an area of significant weakness in dyslexic people. A multifaceted programme is often better and includes the development of strategies for common words using the Look – Say – Cover – Write – Check system, or mnemonics and visual imagery, as well as specific spelling dictionaries for the individual and the words needed for daily living. The other skill that needs to be developed is how to use a Spellchecker effectively. This involves the visual analysis of words, being able to hear the number of syllables in a word, understanding the importance of vowels and knowing what a suffix is. If the reading skills are good, then spellings can be found through using the Thesaurus function.

A spelling programme should include:

- an understanding of the process of spelling – and how the individual approaches it
- an understanding of sound/symbol correspondence and sequencing
- an understanding of phonological awareness
- an introduction to syllables and suffixing
- some basic spelling rules
- a variety of spelling strategies, e.g. visual analysis, mnemonics
- common words vocabulary
- technical spelling needed for work – building up a word bank
- proofreading techniques
- a great deal of overlearning.

Compensations Compensations can include the following:

- keeping a list of key words to hand
- creating a personal dictionary
- using memory devices, such as mnemonics and visual imagery, to facilitate recall. It is, however, important that these provide a rationale, rather than just give the dyslexic person something else to remember
- use of technology such as portable spellcheckers or the spellcheck package of a word processor
- using a voice-activated word processor.

Accommodations These include:

- the provision of technological aids
- having someone proofread work for the dyslexic
- secretarial support, especially someone who can take dictation and audio-type.

Whether someone can take advantage of the compensations and accommodations described above will depend on their competence in spelling.
Conventional word processors and electronic spellcheck devices will only be
of use if someone has basic spelling skills. Bizarre attempts will not be
identified correctly. Voice-activated word processing should be more
effective, but even then this – as well as conventional word processors –
cannot deal easily with homophones.

Dyslexic people need to feel comfortable about the use of the compensations and accommodations described above. Again, the notion of 'cheating'
comes up and needs to be addressed. Often, it can be pointed out that they
need to devote more time to other skills rather than engage in a time-
consuming and perhaps frustrating spelling improvement programme.

Improving writing

Levine (1990) has described writing as an 'awesome juggling act'. That is,
when writing, one has to remember many things at the same time, including
letter formation, grammar, punctuation, spelling, vocabulary and ideas. Putting
ideas on paper is perhaps the activity that places the greatest demand on the
working memory system.

Skill development In our experience most, if not all, adult dyslexics have
sufficient competence in letter formation as to be able to write, or at least
copy, their own name and address and write simple phrases. Their ability to
express more complex ideas is often limited by their spelling skills, as well as
a lack of confidence in their ability to put ideas on paper. Very often, this will
have to do with unrealistic expectations of what writing involves. At a basic
level, writing is essentially communication. It is the expression in symbols of
what they can say. It is important that dyslexic people know that writing is
just that. Communication is enhanced by clear and simple writing and this
should be the first goal.

> I have adopted simple good practices when it comes to writing e.g.
> make sentences no longer than a line. Writing things down exactly
> as I would say them has also been very useful. I have started to read
> a lot, in order to familiarize myself with English vocabulary and
> developed simple techniques to remember how to spell/pronounce
> words. Word processors with their in-built- spell-checkers are a great
> help.

The awesome juggling act becomes less threatening when people are able to focus on matching their own inner thoughts with what appears on the paper. Descriptive rather than interpretative writing separates out thinking from putting ideas on paper. Teaching writing should begin with simple dictated sentences, the most effective being those which relate to their own experience. Keeping the work simple also enables them to deal with the beginnings of punctuation. The more this can be related to speech, the better. When conveyed as pauses in conversation, full stops and commas make sense.

Adults are able to match their own verbal communication with their writing by copying or typing ideas they have dictated to someone else. This is a particularly good confidence-building activity. The next stage is for them to construct their own sentences and produce longer pieces in the form of simple letters or a diary.

A step by step approach to writing is always important and should begin with planning. Even a simple letter will involve several points which need to be covered, and listing these first means that they do not have to be held in memory whilst other material is being written.

> When I went to the centre, we concentrated on sequencing on putting things in order, this helped because people have always commented on how my ideas were out of synch. I've learnt by using my positive skills to overcome some of the problems that I've had. At the centre we concentrated on breaking things down into smaller manageable tasks and then sequencing things under headings. Using a word processor or computer helped as well because I could restructure things and change things at the touch of a button, also by using a computer my handwriting wasn't a problem any more. When I know a system or rules to work by it helps, for instance grammar rules because then I can see how I can construct things in a certain way or order.

Compensations Compensation when there are writing difficulties mainly involves the use of technology. Using a word processor reduces the load on working memory significantly. That is, there are few concerns about legibility, neatness, letter formation and spelling. Voice-activated word processing should allow a direct match between verbal and writing skills.

> A tape recorder and word processor are both useful for clarifying
> ideas by listening to oneself talking or seeing ideas printed out on
> the page. Computers are also invaluable spell checkers. They can
> help speed up output considerably. Unfortunately it takes time to
> learn packages and you pray that your computer doesn't break
> down.

Dyslexic people with poor writing skills can also learn to dictate using a tape
recorder. Even when using technology, however, planning will always be
important.

Accommodations Accommodations include relying on a spouse/partner or
employee to deal with writing tasks. A secretary with audio-typing skills
would allow someone to deal with writing by dictation.

Giving dictation is the preferred way of many professional people who
are not dyslexic and who in fact have highly developed literacy skills. It is,
however, a quick and efficient way of dealing with correspondence.

Improving quantitative literacy

Dealing with numeracy or quantitative tasks is a feature of everyday life – at
work, in education and at home:

> Most individuals are able to generalize the maths they learned in school to the
> wide variety of real-life situations that require math competence. However, for a
> significant number of people with learning related problems, this transfer to
> everyday living remains elusive.
>
> (Patton et al. 1997: 179)

The problems experienced in numeracy by dyslexic people are threefold.
First of all, there are those who have a very poor background in the subject
and will need to go over basic concepts. Secondly, there are people who
understand the concepts but, as a result of their poor memory skills, have
trouble dealing with symbols, remembering sequences in operations as well
as formulae, and dealing with calculations. A third problem which can
compound the foregoing is lack of confidence in their ability to deal with
maths. We do have to deal with arithmetic in everyday situations and this
causes many dyslexic people a great deal of anxiety. Some examples of the
comments they make are:

> Say the word maths and I get cold sweats, hot sweats and twitching.
>
> Shopping used to be agony because of writing cheques. Going into a bank would make me feel sick. I thanked God when shops started printing cheques.
>
> I hate people asking me to work something out in my head. I get flustered and I can't do it. I feel like an idiot.
>
> Checking totals is a nightmare, especially from paper to screen.
>
> I work things out differently and people think I'm stupid.

First and foremost, therefore, assisting dyslexic people to improve their maths needs to start by building up their confidence in their ability. Asking them how they deal with it and approving of their 'alternative' strategy can enhance their confidence.

Skill development Dyslexic people whose background in maths is obviously lacking need to be taught the basic concepts. Much of the teaching of maths they have encountered will have been at an abstract level. They need to begin with the concrete, using very practical examples. For many adults the most important aspect of numeracy is in dealing with money, and this can often be used as a basis for teaching mathematical concepts as well as arithmetic. It is important to establish that they understand the language of maths.

Dyslexic people whose difficulties with maths are procedural – that is, related to dealing with symbols, sequences and calculations – need to be taught strategies that circumvent such problems. Strategies can include the use of concrete aids, including fingers, to help check calculations. Subvocalization (muttering to oneself) can be helpful in preventing the misinterpretation of symbols. Dyslexic people should be encouraged to look at the symbol first and say it aloud. Memory devices such as mnemonics and visual imagery can be helpful for recalling the sequences of operations, as well as in dealing with concepts generally. One woman, for example, learned to imagine boxes in her mind's eye. Their size was determined by a number of items. One box might equal 1 000 for example. If she had to deal with 2 000 she would imagine two boxes.

Having identified the particular problems experienced it is important that strategies are 'task-specific'. Someone who has trouble dealing with sequences of numbers can be taught to identify patterns, using a grouping technique or involving rhyme and rhythm.

Maintaining the place when dealing with a series of numbers can also be a problem. This can be resolved by encouraging people to use a guide, such as a ruler or pencil. One person who had to deal with quite complex accounts could do the maths, but often transposed numbers incorrectly. It brought her into conflict with the Customs and Excise Department over her VAT returns.

It is important to reiterate that the underlying problem with maths is often a lack of confidence. In particular, people will have been in situations where they have expected to resolve a mathematical problem immediately. This is unrealistic and they need to give themselves thinking time, as well as be comfortable about their own way of dealing with the task.

Compensations The most obvious compensation in maths is the efficient use of an electronic calculator. Those that contain a voice-chip so that auditory feedback is provided can be particularly useful.

Other compensations can be compiling a 'ready reckoner', which contains accessible information about weights, measures and conversions. One nurse used this strategy to good effect to help her deal with dispensing medicines. A carpenter had written down his own conversion chart for dealing with measurements.

For people who find writing a cheque difficult they can have in the front cover of a cheque-book a list of numbers with the equivalent word.

The most important factors for me were realizing I had a problem; then telling someone; then seeking advice and specialist help. Seeking advice and specialist help were, ultimately the most advantageous. As a rule I know my own mind and wherever possible I rely on me. With dyslexia I couldn't do this. I found that help had to come from someone who knew what my mind was up to and had empathy for a person in my situation. I am under no illusions, there is no way I could have dealt with this on my own. Once I found people to help me and I found out the knowledge I needed to change and alter my behaviour, I could reduce the affects of dyslexia. Fortunately, it is in my nature to be, in certain situations, obdurate: I was stubborn enough to perceive and effect the necessary changes. Finally, just knowing what is happening and why certain tasks are and always will be harder than they otherwise would be takes a lot of the stress and difficulty out of them.

Accommodations These can include delegation, reducing demands in this regard and relying on an accountant. Supervisors in employment can prepare some of the aids described in the above section on 'Compensations':

Developing basic literacy and numeracy skills should enable a dyslexic to move on, but to be able to cope with more advanced training they need to develop higher learning skills. The appropriate interventions are described in Chapter 7.

Case study D

Reasons for referral

D was referred by his Disability Employment Adviser for a six-month programme of one hour per week to develop his literacy skills, having recently been assessed as dyslexic, to increase his confidence and self-esteem, and to enable him to get and maintain a job. He had been unemployed for several years. His last job experience had been very bad, as he had been subjected to bullying and teasing as a result of his poor literacy skills. He 'left before he was pushed'.

Background

D had experienced family problems. He had found it very difficult to get a job due to the demands on him at home.

Education history

D had always had trouble with reading and writing. He left school with no qualifications. He gained an HND in Catering and worked as a sous-chef in various places. He was finally promoted to main chef, which meant he had to place orders. His spelling let him down, the management lost confidence in him and he lost confidence in himself. He had an assessment and after finding out he was dyslexic, he was keen 'to start again'.

Assessment

Average ability. Very weak memory skills, particularly auditory.
Reading – technical level, instructional stage.
Spelling – well below average level.
Handwriting – weak.
Computer skills – none.

Strengths

Determination. Visual skills. Loved to tell stories to his daughter. Cooking – he is an exceptionally good cook.

Areas of difficulty

Lack of confidence and self-esteem.
Good memory for faces but not names.
Panicked when overloaded.

Goals

To get and keep a job as a chef.
To be able to write a letter.

Programme

Personal development

- To understand dyslexia and how it affected him
- To increase awareness of his skills and abilities to boost his self-confidence.

Skill development

Reading	–	Comprehension strategies
Spelling course	–	Vowels/consonants, syllables, suffixing, key rules
Spelling strategies	–	Visual analysis of words, mnemonics
Memory strategies	–	Linking, association, visualization
Writing	–	Letter writing, job applications, CVs, stories for his daughter
Technology	–	Typing course, basic PC skills
Interview skills	–	Through role play and visualization
	–	How to explain dyslexia and how to present himself.

Outcome

D is now employed as head chef in a large company.

Summary

- To function independently on a daily basis dyslexic people need to reach the upper limits of the functional and lower limits of the vocational level in prose, document and quantitative literacy.
- The skills taught to dyslexic people should be relevant to their needs and draw on their own experience.
- In helping dyslexic people develop their skills it is imperative that they be encouraged to understand the process of learning. Opportunities for immediate success are essential.
- As well as develop their literacy skills dyslexic people need to be helped to find alternative solutions through compensation, and know how to seek relevant adjustments.

Chapter 7
Academic and professional learning skills

This chapter addresses the issues faced by dyslexic people when they make the transition to higher and professional education. The skills and compensations they need to develop and the accommodations that can be made for them are described.

Introduction

To function effectively in further, higher and professional education, people need to be able to do the following:

- organize themselves personally
- cope with independent learning and working
- manage their time effectively
- read and comprehend complex material accurately and fluently
- find relevant information from a variety of sources
- listen, understand and take notes quickly and legibly
- express ideas verbally and in writing
- type quickly
- demonstrate their knowledge and understanding in exams and assessment settings.

Moving on to higher education represents a major transition for dyslexic people:

My first semester was hell, a nightmare, my worst nightmare. It went wrong from week two. The first week was OK, but the second week we were dropped in the deep end, work was piled onto us. I wouldn't have made it but for the support of one friend at home who pulled me through, she said I could do it.

I lived at home, not on campus, so had to travel to London. The journey only takes forty minutes but as the railways are so bad I often had to change trains or they were late. I tried to leave early so that I would have fifteen minutes to recover, but was always late. Then the lecturers would change the lecture rooms so by the time I got there, I couldn't think straight. I was exhausted and it all flew past me.

I had no friends to ask what was going on, where to find things like the library or a photocopier, and I couldn't remember.

I had difficulty organising my time – it was all down to me, and I had so much freedom it was difficult to control. I had so much to organize and remember – different days meant different buildings. I would check and double check. I had to remember to take different files so I colour coded them for different days.

It was all new – places, people, more to do. It was not just the work, it was everything, but I was also having to work so hard just to survive. Then the lecturer said that if I didn't improve my scores I would be out. He said he didn't think I would make it. I knew what the problems were but could do anything, there seemed to be too many to solve in one go.

I was constantly being asked to fill in forms, which just reminded me that I had a problem.

Many of the tutors don't know what dyslexia is.

It is a bit easier now, but I wish the lecturer hadn't said that I wouldn't make it.

This student eventually gained an upper second class degree despite her lecturer's prediction.

The keys to success in higher and professional education

The tasks listed above are all ones that dyslexic people find challenging. Some of the skills, compensations and accommodations that can enable them to become more effective are described below. It is at this level that executive functioning is particularly important, and developing metacognitive skills is therefore a recurrent theme. In terms of the development of skills, the general goal is to enable dyslexic people to become good information processors. Fundamental to this is the notion that the development of strategies is deliberate and requires ongoing experimentation, monitoring, reflection and refinement.

The importance of metacognition

Success at college and in professional education relies very heavily on independent learning skills. It demands confidence and the ability to deal with a great many things at one time. Understanding that learning at this level requires more independence and that the tutors are often there to present information rather than to 'teach' is important. It is essential for dyslexic people to understand the nature of their skills and abilities and of their areas of weakness. They need to know what skills they have, what skills they need to develop, and what compensations and accommodations are available to them.

Dyslexic people already know learning can be difficult for them if information is presented in conventional ways. They might also know it takes them longer to complete work. They have to learn therefore to be much more efficient in their study habits. They have to recognize that many people will not understand the nature of their difficulty. There is evidence to suggest that the success of a student can be a reflection of departmental attitudes towards dyslexia and the extent to which they collaborate with the student and student support services (Scott and Gregg 2000). Dyslexic people do need, therefore, to be able to explain how dyslexia affects them and be specific about their requirements.

It is rarely lack of ability that causes a dyslexic person to struggle at university: it is more often due to a lack of understanding task demands. Having difficulties with organization, getting on with and working with their tutors as well as their peers, and other external matters are factors which may lead to their downfall rather than just their problems with literacy. Misunderstandings between student and tutor can often increase or exaggerate a dyslexic person's difficulties. Students who know that to orientate themselves to university life or a course of professional training will take a long time, and who know what they need to do to make the process manageable, are usually successful. This is particularly important for those who have to balance the demands of a job and further study.

Self-review

Part of improving one's performance is the ability to critically self-review both positives and negatives. Identifying and recognizing strengths and areas for further development is the key. Dyslexic students, because of their past experience, tend to only review negatively. In addressing the issue of 'self-review' of lectures attended, Ellis (1993) suggests the use of the mnemonic CROWN:

C – communicate what you have learnt, the general and the specific things that have been learnt, how different they are and what is new about them

R – reactions. Surprises, corrections, interests, images, conflicts

O – offering one sentence to sum up what a whole lecture was about

W – where are some different places you can use this information or transfer it to?

N – notes. How well did it go today, the best part, the hardest part, and was a personal goal achieved?

As with the Performance Improvement Plan, this is a cognitive strategy for monitoring goal attainments, summarizing, prioritizing, noting and self-enforcement. On a more long-term basis for many dyslexic students, it is suggested that they keep a record of their achievements in which they review or assess their own skills. Some students do it informally in a record or a diary, others are more formal about it and keep a file. Self-review should increase self-confidence as strengths are understood, short-term goals are achieved, and progress is made over a period of time. At university and on professional training courses the goalposts are constantly changing and therefore performance is not always seen to be improving when in fact it is. Self-review also enables the person to set realistic targets for future development.

Students should be encouraged to see feedback as being valid and helpful. They also need to know that they are entitled to reject criticism if it is not useful. How other people see us and our performance from an objective point of view is important, but dyslexic students must learn to accept comments for what they are, consider them and set new goals.

Learning and working styles

The need to learn independently means that students may have to engage in a variety of activities at any one time. They must control the order and pace of their learning. There are a variety of information-processing strategies and the emphasis needs to be on the development of those an individual finds most useful. Understanding whether one processes information best through visual, auditory or kinaesthetic sensory input should influence the strategy adopted when learning. Dyslexic people can deal with images more readily than words, for example, and knowing this should affect the strategy they use for note-taking.

Honey and Mumford (1986) have described four different types of learner. These are:

Activists Activists learn best when working in groups with other people, such as being involved in workshop activities, when they are working to tight deadlines and discussing ideas. Interaction is the key.

Reflectors Reflectors learn best when attending lectures, undertaking project or research work. Working on their own, they are thinking back and reflecting on what has happened.

Theorists Theorists are most effective when reading and evaluating ideas, questioning theories and discussing theories with other people.

Pragmatists Pragmatists prefer to do things, such as being involved in practical problem-solving. They learn best from their work experience or taking part in workshops.

Whilst people rarely fit one category, it is often a useful exercise to outline the differences in approaches to learning as it increases the awareness of the learning process and what it means for them.

Thinking about the way they learn best, and knowing about the various approaches to learning, enables people to develop more flexibility, be more creative, and therefore more effective. It is also important that individuals know when and where they work best. People prefer to work at different times and for different lengths of time. Some people like to be in the environment of a library, where it is quiet and there are no interruptions. Some people like to be in their own surroundings, and others can work anywhere. Everyone needs to know when, where and how they work best but it is essential for dyslexic people: struggling through a difficult text when tired or at a bad time of day can be ineffective.

Time management

For a dyslexic student, working and learning are harder and take longer than for other students, and being able to organize time is essential. Some people like a very rigid plan and are able to stick to it. Others prefer a more flexible overall weekly goal, rather than daily ones. Dyslexic people are not good at estimating how long tasks take and have a poor concept of time generally. Learning support tutors have an important role to play in helping students become aware of where time goes, and how easy it is for it to disappear.

Some universities and colleges allow students greater control in planning their own course through the years of study. When drawing up a schedule of work, dyslexic people need to be especially careful that they don't overload themselves with too many demanding courses. Departments sometimes encourage students to undertake complementary courses that require an investment of time disproportionate to the overall programme. Dyslexic students need to be very selective when this is the case.

University and college life can also be stressful, so relaxation and having fun are important. It is essential for dyslexic people to be able to relax and unwind. However, for some people, even this is a struggle. One student found social situations such as going to the pub so tiring that she couldn't concentrate in lectures. She had to learn to limit herself to one night a week of social activity so she could face the demands of her university day for her first year. As she settled in she expanded her social life:

> Being at University is like being at the bottom of a waterfall.

Skill development This involves being able to assess how long a task takes and knowing when is a good time to work. Realistic goal-setting and prioritizing are other skills which need to be developed. Making timetables and setting timed tasks can help develop time estimation.

Compensations These can be an alarm clock, stop watch, electronic aid or mobile phone, as well as wall charts, wall planners, year planners, day planners, diaries, timetables, Filofaxes and lists.

Accommodations Having friends give reminders and tutors seeing drafts a week before the deadline.

Organization of work

As organization does not come naturally to dyslexic people they need to work hard at it. Knowing this enables them to become deliberate about it and develop their own strategies. Some people like to be very organized and have a good filing system which is kept up to date. Others have a big box. Organizing notes, can be the key to keeping the information under control. The 3Ms described earlier can be useful:

Manageable Breaking the course into sections, course outlines, a reading reference file, lists of lectures, indexes in files and overviews are all essential to making information manageable. Developments in technology mean that knowing where to find information that has been previously covered is as important as being able to remember it, making reading records act as an aide-mémoire as well as facilitating later reference.

Multisensory The use of coloured files, box files, different coloured files and various papers for courses makes organization multisensory. The use of electronic aids is also important.

Memory Aids Filing is a way of revision, but often this means a student has to find time and be disciplined enough to file on a regular basis. Again lists, files, and so on, can act as memory aids as well as make organization multi-sensory.

Reading

Studying at an advanced level requires someone to be able to recognize sophisticated words quickly, as well as assimilate and retain material. Dyslexic people often over-read, focusing on word recognition rather than comprehension. They do not automatically develop systematic approaches to reading comprehension, but these can be taught. Sometimes they are using a variety of strategies but are not aware of it and do not use them appropriately. For example, many dyslexic people do scan and skim when reading a newspaper but do not apply this to their studies. It is important that they know the difference between reading to learn and learning to read.

Skill development Before teaching any systematic reading strategy, it is important to ask students questions about their reading. These include:

- What is your reading like?
- What are the problems you associate with your reading?
- Is your main difficulty decoding the long words, reading aloud or comprehension?

- How do you read – aloud, silently, quickly, slowly or every word?
- Do you miss lines or lose your place?
- Where do you start your reading – at the beginning, and read on?
- Do you read the same way if you are reading different types of material?
- Are you aware of punctuation and the function of paragraphs?
- Are you able to pick out the main idea?

Many dyslexic people tend to read in the same fashion, whatever the text. They are often not aware that there is much more to reading than decoding and remembering what is read. They are not aware of the fact that using a variety of approaches to reading makes it more efficient. The reading process should be targeted, flexible, active and monitored:

targeted – in that the reader knows what information they are looking for
flexible – in that they may change and use a variety of reading strategies during the course of one period of reading
active – in that the reader makes a response to the text. Reading can be very passive when the emphasis is on decoding: there is not time to interact with the text, and therefore it is not easily remembered
monitored – in that if the text is very difficult to read then another strategy should be adopted, or, indeed, the need to read the material at all should be questioned.

Possibly the best known of the reading strategies is SQ3R – Survey, Question, Read, Recite, Recall. Some dyslexic people do not find this effective if it is not sufficiently structured. Other examples are the PASS Strategy described in Chapter 6, and PARTS (Ellis 1993), a systematic reading strategy. The latter is as follows:

Perform goal-setting:
- Clarify why you are analysing the chapter parts
- Identify the goal related to this reason
- Make a positive self-statement.

Analyse little parts (title, headings, etc.):
- Explain the information indicated by the part
- Predict what the section under the part is about
- Tie the parts together.

Review big parts (introduction and summary):
- Search for signal words that indicate main ideas
- Decide what the author thinks is important

- Relate new information to what you already know
- Paraphrase the main message.

Think of questions you hope will be answered:
- Check questions provided by the chapter
- Identify your own questions.

State relationships:
- How does the chapter relate to the unit being studied?
- How does the chapter relate to what you already know?

All these strategies require the student to develop the skills of scanning, skimming and careful analysis. By being more deliberate in their use of these reading can be made more efficient.

Reading comprehension skills can be further developed through the analysis of a text. This includes the organization of the passage, whether it is argumentative or comparative, descriptive, evaluative or discursive. Being able to distinguish between opinion and bias is also important. Knowing the author's intentions and method of organizing ideas can greatly help comprehension of a passage. Continued problems with comprehension should be analysed further. One can ask, for example, 'Is it that there are too many unfamiliar words or that the author is ambiguous in what he is saying?'. It is important for the student to understand that meaning is not always explicit in the text and that each reader brings his or her own meaning to what is being read, based on expectations regarding the text and previous knowledge.

Understanding the patterns of organization do affect the processing of the information and this can influence the way notes are made from the text. Chronological information can, for example, be noted in flow chart form; comparative material can be organized in tabular form. Descriptive information can be arranged as a mind map. Understanding the task demands means that the appropriate strategy can be chosen.

Compensations These can include substituting listening comprehension for reading comprehension by the use of a recording, highlighting important parts of the text, as well as reading summaries.

Accommodations Getting someone else to read to the student directly or onto a tape.

Comprehending diagrammatic and tabular formats

Reading comprehension is not just a matter of dealing with text. Students have to interpret tables and diagrams.

Skill development In terms of the development of skills, Ellis (1993) suggests a systematic approach known as SNIPS:

Start with questions:
- Question to clarify your goals. Why are you analysing the visual aid?
- Question to find out what kind of information to look for.

Picture	What is it a picture of?
Graph/Chart	What is being *compared*? How?
Map	What *key areas* are important to see? Why are they key areas?
Time line	Show the *history* of what? From when to when?

Note what you can learn from the hints:

Look for hints that signal answers to your questions (*e.g. title, captions, lines, numbers, colours*)
Activate your knowledge.

Identify what is important:

Identify the *main message* of the graphic
Identify two *facts* from the graphic.

Plug it into the chapter:

How does the visual relate to what the chapter or unit is about?

See if you can explain the visual to someone:

Find someone to whom you can explain the visual (*explain it to yourself if nobody else is available*)
Tell *what* you think the visual is about and *how* you think it relates to what the chapter is about
Identify what you think are the best hints on the visual and tell *why* they are good hints.

Compensations These can include substituting listening comprehension for reading comprehension by the use of a recording, highlighting important parts of the text, as well as reading summaries.

Accommodations These can include getting someone else to read to the student directly or onto a tape.

Essay writing

A problem with essay writing is one of the most common reasons students and people undergoing professional training advance for seeking help. Putting ideas on paper is the task that most dyslexic people find difficult as there is a high cognitive demand, involving not just writing skills but also organization. Difficulties are often exacerbated by a lack of confidence in their ability to write. Essay writing involves both primary and secondary issues.

Skill development The skills required for essay writing include the following: gathering information on a specific subject; being able to interpret and add original ideas; identifying the key points; developing a line of argument; structuring and organizing thoughts and information in a logical fashion; citing references accurately; being able to write it all down. Essay writing involves the student displaying knowledge and comprehension of a subject, application of the information, analysis of information, the synthesis of information into a new and original form, and the evaluation of information:

- *Knowledge* involves understanding lists of facts and terminology, methods, trends and conventions; also principles and theories and descriptions
- *Comprehension* involves showing that these things can be communicated in other terms or in another form; the ideas are not remembered in the way they have been read but in the way the student has made sense of them
- *Application* involves the student being able to apply the theories into real-life situations
- *Analysis* involves breaking the information into parts and explaining what relationship exists between the whole, being able to identify cause and effect and make inferences, etc.
- *Synthesis* involves using the acquired knowledge in a new, creative, original way
- *Evaluation* is making judgements on ideas, methods and information, and being able to justify the reasons for these judgements.

Understanding these six aspects of essay writing provides dyslexic students with a better idea of what they are trying to achieve. It explains the nature of the task and provides a structure in which to express their ideas, and therefore they can be specific in their approach to processing the information.

It is essential for the student to know what the question is about and why it is being asked: many dyslexic people can miss the point. Process words are extremely important in question analysis: they give an indication of how the essay should be structured. Words such as 'describe', 'analyse', 'evaluate' and 'outline' are each asking for a different way of presenting information. Understanding this can make it easier for the student to structure the essay correctly. One student was disappointed when for one assignment the question set was 'In your opinion, what are the reasons for the lack of women in top management jobs?'. She wrote a very powerful, cogent description of how she felt about the lack of women in top management jobs; however, she failed to give the other point of view because she had taken 'In your opinion . . .' literally. She only got a Third for that essay. It was not the grade she hoped for or expected.

Having analysed the question, then information can be gathered. To improve on their results many dyslexic people need to analyse how they write essays and where exactly they lose marks. Some students do not explain clearly, others do not give sufficient justification for their statements, often because they think it is too obvious, or because they lack confidence in their ideas. Some dyslexic students have developed very contracted writing styles and prefer bullet points; others ramble on. Being able to critically analyse one's own work, however painful, can be productive.

Planning is essential, as a step by step approach reduces the load on memory. Students should be encouraged to develop the technique that suits them, but should find visual strategies the most effective.

Compensations Many dyslexic people are much better verbally than they are at putting ideas on paper. Dictating to tape and writing from the recording can be a useful approach. Developing dictation skills generally, particularly if they can use the services of an audio-typist, enables them to achieve the best match between verbal ability and written work. The use of a word processor means that the cognitive load is reduced because they do not have to concern themselves with legibility, neatness and spelling. They can also reorganize material easily. As technology develops, voice-activated word processing is increasingly being seen as the solution for dyslexic people. They can also use planning software.

Accommodations Accommodations include making sure that technical as well as secretarial support is available. It also involves supervisors and tutors facilitating the process of students being able to structure and organize their ideas. They need much feedback concerning what is expected of them. They need constructive feedback on how they can improve, as well as plenty of time in which to re-draft. There is a danger in allowing dyslexic students extra time to complete assignments, as they can often wind up with a backlog of assignments. Nevertheless, some flexibility over deadlines is essential for proofreading and checking.

Proofreading

Proofreading one's own work is difficult. Often one becomes too close to the material to see the errors: it is easy to anticipate what one thinks is on the page, rather than what has actually been written. As a result of their difficulties with the printed word, proofreading for dyslexic people can be doubly difficult.

Skill development Structured approaches to proofreading can include COPS: checking **C**apitalization of letters, examining the **O**verall appearance, **P**unctuation and **S**pelling (Schumaker et al. 1981). This may seem long-winded, but it is better to break the task of proofreading into small steps rather than trying to do too much at once. Other aids can include:

* keeping a list of errors one consistently makes
* leaving proofreading for at least 24 hours so that it is looked at afresh: this can allow the identification of errors which may otherwise be missed
* reading from right to left can assist, as this prevents anticipation. It enables people to examine each individual word, and excludes the context.

Compensations Compensations for proofreading and checking mainly include the use of technology, such as spellcheckers and grammar checkers. These need to be used carefully as conventional spellcheckers will miss words which are correctly spelled but inappropriately placed, and do not correct homophones. Text to speech software can allow proofreading by listening and many dyslexic people find this very effective.

Accommodations The most obvious accommodation is to have someone else go over the work. Dyslexic people will often do this with trepidation as they fear criticism. It is important so they do need to have someone they trust. They do not need someone who will be 'fussy' as this can be demoralizing.

Grammar and punctuation

Sentence structure and punctuation are often areas of difficulty for the dyslexic person.

Skill development It is not always feasible to embark on a programme to improve grammar but some basic principles often improve the structure and expression of ideas. A basic course in punctuation can significantly improve the quality. Understanding the reason for punctuation – that it adds expression and clarity to a sentence – can usually in itself make a difference to the writing. In particular, many dyslexic people's sentences are either too long or indeed too short. The sentences that are too long are often phrases that are strung together, and either the subject may have been lost or the verb omitted. It is usually better to keep it short and simple, when it is therefore easier to identify that the subject and the verb are present and in agreement. The basic punctuation of commas, semi-colons and colons often greatly enhances the student's writing.

Compensations As has been stated previously, dictation is very helpful, so that there is a match between verbal and written ability. Many dyslexic people cannot see their own grammatical mistakes when proofreading but can hear them when they read aloud or when they make use of Text to Speech packages.

Accommodations Providing a proofreader or secretarial support is the most effective solution.

Spelling

The extent to which spelling remains a problem for dyslexic people is very varied. There are people who have a major spelling difficulty but who do not see it as a problem and therefore write freely, finding other ways of dealing with it. Other people are extremely sensitive about their spelling whatever their level and are easily thrown off track when they make a mistake or indeed if someone points a mistake out to them. It inhibits their thinking. In all cases, the improvement of spelling demands a considerable amount of time and often this is an unachievable goal during their course, so other solutions should be sought.

Skill development The aim of any spelling instruction at this level should be to ensure that the student has enough knowledge to be able to use a spellchecker effectively. Much of the instruction should, therefore, focus on identifying the number of syllables in a word, learning the blends, understanding the suffixing rules, and knowing that there are a variety of vowel combinations.

Other skills involved in spelling include listening for sounds in words and putting them in the right sequence. Once the dyslexic person becomes aware of this they are more likely to approach it systematically. A step by step approach – e.g. listening to the syllables and then to the individual sounds, knowing which sounds or which areas of a word they cannot hear clearly or isolate – enables them to write most of the words they can hear and focuses them on the difficult bits. They can then use their visual skills to check or recall the missing bit. Using other memory strategies, such as visual imagery or mnemonics, will also significantly help the spelling of individual words. Many students report that once they have understood the process, and have let go of the stigma attached to poor spelling, they find their spelling improves.

There are two approaches:

- A short course on spelling strategies, looking at personal spelling errors and developing their own lists focusing on common words and specific technical spellings, using the variety of strategies mentioned above, and utilizing their own thinking and memory skills to help
- A longer spelling course, looking at the key elements of spelling, including a brief history of English orthography. This gives the explanation for why the English spelling system is so complicated; understanding that some words are derived from Greek, Latin or Anglo-Saxon gives a structure that many dyslexic people find useful. Looking at letter patterns, prefixes, suffixes and root words, word derivations and word families can all be targeted effectively to help the dyslexic student analyse the word. It can often help both reading and spelling to improve.

Compensations These include using a hand-held spellchecker or one on a computer. Spellcheckers often eradicate the majority of difficulties but certain errors, such as the misuse of homophones and use of the wrong words, will not be picked up. Dictionaries can be used in conjunction with electronic aids

Accommodations The most effective methods are asking a friend or colleague or having someone to proofread the words.

Listening comprehension

In order to follow training courses, benefit from lectures and presentations, and participate in tutorials, dyslexic people need to develop good listening comprehension skills.

Skill development Previewing is an essential part of good listening comprehension, actively thinking about a lecture before attending. For example, if one were going to a lecture on existentialist philosophy, looking up a dictionary definition beforehand helps. The basic guides available for many complex topics can provide good preparation through giving a structure for the topic and enabling students to establish what is relevant. Reading handouts issued before a training course is also very important.

Another way of enhancing listening comprehension is to ask questions and seek clarification. There are appropriate and inappropriate times for the asking of questions. Lecturers and fellow students can be irritated by constant interruptions.

Listening can also be enhanced by listening for verbal clues – 'firstly', 'a final point', 'on the other hand'.

Systematic approaches to listening comprehension include PQLR. That is:

P Preview and tune in to the lecture
Q Generate questions about the topic for the end of the session
L Listening for the speaker's position
R Mentally review the material so that the important points are remembered.

Compensations In formal learning situations, the most obvious compensation is to take a tape recorder to sessions, which allows one to listen and control information more readily. Particularly useful is a tape recorder with a variable rate and/or a counting device, so that important or not fully understood parts can be specifically identified.

Accommodations These can include providing an overview of lectures or training sessions so that the participants can preview the information. An interactive format can be an effective method of presentation. Students should be encouraged to participate through questions and discussions. Dyslexic people can often deal with visual material effectively, while others prefer a variety of formats, and so the use of diagrams and illustrations can be helpful. Allowing the recording of sessions enables a dyslexic person to listen and focus on understanding the content.

Note-taking

Listening comprehension and taking notes in a learning situation are closely related. Too many people 'take notes at the expense of noting'. It is more important to be able to listen and understand than to be able to write comprehensive notes, particularly as many dyslexic people report that they cannot read what they have written. Note-taking is a very complex skill for dyslexic people because it places a heavy load on working memory. It is affected by a significant number of factors including listening comprehension, processing information, and organizing and recording notes in a legible and fluent fashion. Other variables include how much the student already knows about the subject, how familiar they are with it, their personal confidence in their ability to take notes, and their spelling skills. In addition, note-taking is often related to the way material is presented. If a lecturer presents material in a clear concise fashion, with a lot of cues to the structure of the material, e.g. 'first', 'second', and so on, or provides an OHP which outlines what is being covered, this makes the note-taking task much easier. It is a task that causes dyslexic people to panic as they feel that if they don't take notes, they will not be able to remember what is being said. Some students feel that if they can't take notes adequately, there is no point in going to the lecture.

> At a practical level encompassing visual features into performance-enhancing strategies has improved my effectiveness at taking notes down in meetings and at college lectures. So for example when not taking, I now make greater use – where possible – of diagrams and symbols to supplement key points that I have jotted down. In the past I either avoided not taking altogether or I would attempt to write everything down and give up part of the way through.

Skill development The best approach to taking notes is a minimalist one but it does have to be effective. Here a metacognitive approach aids the efficiency of note-taking. It is a question of matching the individual skills to the topic with the right strategy. Some people find using visual strategies such as drawing pictures, mind-maps or diagrams extremely helpful. Others prefer to write down headings, bullet points and key words. One skill that should be developed is the use of abbreviations, including one's own specific shorthand for technical words. Some people find it is beneficial to divide the page into four quarters, each representing fifteen minutes of an hour-long lecture. This is particularly useful when using a tape machine and can avoid the individual having to listen to a whole hour's tape if they only missed one quarter of it.

Before developing an appropriate technique, people need to identify the purpose of taking notes as it may affect the strategy chosen. They need to identify the themes and ideas being presented. This can be done by listening for signal words, such as 'an important theme', 'a key feature', or statements such as 'and now we will move on to ...'.

Visual aids such as OHPs will often provide a guide to the key words and headings. However, dyslexic people find it difficult to copy down the content of the overhead quickly: this is where the use of abbreviations, particularly for recurring technical words, can be helpful.

Compensations The compensation mainly involves the use of a tape recorder as a back-up to a minimalist strategy. When using a tape recorder, it is important to have one which has a counting device. This enables students to index mark when important points have been made, so that when replaying the tape, they can focus on these. When students have good keyboard skills, taking a laptop or notebook computer to lectures and training sessions can be very helpful. Touch-typing allows one to be able to focus on visual clues, as well as on the overheads, without having to keep looking back and forwards. The notes they have taken will also be legible and can be extended at a later date.

Accommodations Accommodations can include lecturers and trainers providing handouts which summarize the main points of the lecture, and providing reading lists. Students can also rely on other people's notes. Where difficulties are severe, employing the services of a note-taker can be engaged, preferably someone who is familiar with the topic as the notes will be clearer.

Note-making

Note-making when studying is a different task from taking notes in lectures. The student has considerably more control over the information when making notes from texts, videos, handouts, or when making notes of their own ideas for an essay. The purpose of the note-making is important, and the strategy used should be deliberately chosen, matching skills to the task.

Making notes aids concentration and understanding of the subject. They enable the reorganization and linking of ideas, enabling students to rewrite material in their own words, and remember it better.

Skill development A key skill to develop in note-making is being able to identify the key points. This can be facilitated by planning essays and assignments first. Using key words, however, is a skill that many dyslexic people find difficult and this often requires practice. Whenever any notes are taken, it is essential to write down the source of the notes, the date of the lecture or seminar, or the book title reference page. A personal comment on the interest, understanding and importance of the text or lecture also helps recall. Notes should be as personal as possible. As long as they are effective for students, in that they can decipher them, the way in which they are taken is not an issue: it is important, however, to remember that they might be needed in the future. Reviewing notes shortly after they are made can ensure they are sufficient, as well as provide a starting point for revision.

Compensations These can include talking into a Speech to Text software package; using a Dictaphone, and having the notes typed up; and using a note-making pen scanner that enables one to scan quotes from the text and transfer them straight to a computer. Photocopying important texts and highlighting the key words can also be helpful.

Accommodations As mentioned in the previous section the accommodations are using other people's notes, being given highlighted texts or abstracts and copies of overheads or handouts.

Revision and memory skills

Applying and using new knowledge involves being able to remember what has been learned, and central to this process is being able to revise properly. This is particularly important to dyslexic people as the automatic retrieval of information does not come easily to them. Revision should be an ongoing and active process. It can begin with adding new information to notes taken during the course of a lecture. Ideally, revision should start at the beginning of a course of work and training. Reviewing material on a regular basis makes it easier to recall. The purpose of revision is usually to reorganize the information that has been given so that it can be recalled clearly and appropriately under timed conditions. Examinations are aimed at assessing ability and knowledge, but they also assess the ability of the individual to organize information on paper quickly. Revision must therefore involve storing information and training to retrieve it quickly.

Skill development Metacognitive awareness increases the efficiency of revision, and it can be made manageable, memorable and multisensory, following the 3M model described earlier.

Make it Manageable Revision should be targeted and systematic. It is made manageable by knowing what has to be done; course outlines are very helpful. The next step is to rate how well the information on a specific subject is known, and what its relative importance is for the examination. Planning a timetable and breaking it into manageable parts is essential. It is a more effective use of time if specific topics are targeted each day. The revision plan must, however, be flexible.

Revision should build on what is already known. A five-minute brainstorming period at the start of a revision session activates knowledge and gives a clear indication of gaps, showing therefore what needs to be revised. Likewise, at the end of a session, a quick mind-map or notes outline can be a good self-test of what has been revised and learned. Furthermore, it is a way of practising the retrieval of information at speed, an important part of the examination process. Reducing the verbal material makes managing the information easier, summarizing in keywords, pictures or symbols so that minimal cues will access material from long-term memory.

> I wanted to send some examples of my revision notes. I found it useful to see other students' work when I cam and I hope you may find it useful to show others. As you can see from the cards, I was having difficulty learning the subtle differences between similar conditions and had to try to find a way of making the differences memorably obvious. Friends were horrified that I cut up my expensive textbooks but if I never took them off the shelf to read and could never understand the text, they were not a lot of use to me even if they were shiny and expensive.

Make it Multisensory Making revision multisensory can include discussing information with a friend, using a tape recorder, listening to music, drawings, visualizing and highlighting or note-making using different colour pens.

Make Use of Memory Aids Memory aids include mind-maps, cards, flow charts and pictures. Displaying these on walls and whiteboards in various places means that information is frequently reviewed. A combination of memory aids is the most effective. One student, when trying to learn all the names of the plants that she had covered in her horticultural course, wrote the names and drew the pictures of all the hothouse plants and put them in her kitchen; the water plants were on the walls of her bathroom, and all the cool plants were on the walls of the sitting room. In the examination she could visualize herself in each room, locate the picture on the wall and therefore remember the name of the plant and the spelling. This type of revision strategy is very active, multisensory, extremely creative and can be recommended. Another student had wallpaper strips round her wall providing a time line chart for her history studies. Other students have mind-maps on their walls, or colour-coded flash cards with symbols to identify the day the lecture was given. Having a visible timetable on the wall, and ticking off the days and the information covered, can also be a good memory and confidence booster.

Compensations Compensations can include studying a minimum number of subjects in depth: rather than trying to acquire a widespread knowledge when preparing for examinations, focusing on a few topics can make it easier to recall specific material.

Compensation can also come from putting material on tape and listening to it whilst engaged in other activities. Talking can be a very powerful way of learning, and so revising with a fellow student or students can facilitate understanding and therefore recall.

Accommodations Accommodations involve having regard for the fact that dyslexic people can easily become overloaded and have difficulty with the automatic retrieval of information in an examination setting. Modular courses, where examinations cover a small number of topics and are frequent, can suit a dyslexic. Multiple-choice tests place fewer demands on automatic recall, although these do present other difficulties. The timetabling of examinations can also reduce the demands on the dyslexic person. There should be no more than one each day, and there should also be a good time spacing between examinations.

Examinations

Examination techniques should also be part of a revision package and, for the dyslexic student, as much practice as possible is essential. At university and on professional training programmes, the culmination of a course is often a set of examinations for which they have had no previous practice. All students have to deal with an element of the unknown; younger students will have had the discipline of facing GCSEs or A-levels and will have had practice in examinations but not at a more advanced level. Mature students will not have had this experience and examinations can be daunting.

> Now that I understand why I find it difficult to face the ritual of examinations, I have taken practical steps towards making examinations less demanding. For example, I have arranged with my college to use a word processor rather than handwriting examination papers; I now also take additional time to sit each paper. But more importantly than this, because I am gradually developing an understanding of dyslexia and the problems it causes me, I appreciate my own effort all the more when I achieve a respectable result in an examination.

Skill development A dyslexic person can find that examinations tap all their weaknesses, in that they require the automatic retrieval and organization of information at speed. It is important for the dyslexic person to know that examinations require different skills than those needed for completing an assignment. They rely heavily on the recall of what they know and the effective use of information. In answering a question successfully, it may be sufficient for them to recall only four or five important facts, so long as they can demonstrate why these facts are the central issues and show that they know how to apply them.

Time management is one of the keys to success in examinations and many students run out of time even though they have been allowed extra. Successful students have found that extra time is best spent at the beginning, reading the questions carefully and planning answers, rather than at the end, doing too much proofreading. It is advisable for students to have a watch on their table so that they can monitor the time passing. Some students find it extremely helpful to try to allocate marks within their questions. Being able to do this comes from practice using past papers. It is very important that the dyslexic student knows the format of each exam, the kinds of questions and the equipment they need and has as much practice with planning answers as possible.

Preparing an action plan for how the time is going to be divided up can help, as can deciding on an order in which to answer the questions. Highlighting the key part of the question and the process words can be essential in making sure it is answered appropriately. Answers should be planned to help the person stay on track and remember the point of the question. It can be encouraging to tick off the questions as they are completed.

Becoming familiar with the place where the examination is to be held, double-checking the timing of the session, and finding out how long it takes to get there can reduce stress. It is imperative that all the accommodations for the examination are in place well beforehand.

> Thinking more constructively about my skills and abilities has helped me to understand why I struggled in my formal school examinations and why I find sitting examinations for my current degree studies so demanding. Under the intense pressure of examination conditions my ability to recall information – which dyslexia impairs anyway – becomes disengaged to an even greater extent; this and my slow rate of writing lead to my becoming frustrated with the entire process.

Compensations These involve developing alternative skills such as competence in word processing, and taking examinations verbally.

Accommodations Accommodations in examinations involve making special arrangements for dyslexic candidates. These can include:

- Allowing extra time to take into account a number of factors such as the reduction of stress, slow rates of reading and writing, difficulties with comprehension, the need for planning and proofreading.
- Allowing the use of a word processor – where this has become the main way in which a student communicates in writing, and there is a discrepancy between their verbal ability and their written expression, allowing the use of a word processor would seem appropriate.
- Where students have significant problems with reading, examinations could be presented on tape, or the student could be provided with a reader.
- When a student has handwriting difficulties but does not have sufficient competence with technology to use it, they could be allowed to write out their examination paper and then dictate it on to tape for transcription.
- A combination of written and verbal examinations would allow dyslexic candidates who have difficulties with written expression to demonstrate their knowledge and competence.

- Duplicate copies of examination papers, which enable students to see both sides of the paper at once, can be very helpful.
- Examination papers can be produced in large print, and, sometimes, in different colours where there is a sensitivity to colour and background.

Concerning the first item above, that of extra time, the Higher Education Funding Council working party's survey on Dyslexia Provision in Higher Education revealed that 99 per cent of institutions allowed extra time for dyslexic students in written examinations. This does not, however, mean that the matter is without controversy. There are two particular issues:

- Academics and non-dyslexic students have complained that dyslexic students are being advantaged by being allowed extra time.
- There is disagreement on the issue of how much extra time should be allowed.

With regard to the first issue, systematic studies (Kay Runyon 1991; Alster 1997) have demonstrated on both reading comprehension tasks and algebra tests that extra time appeared to minimize the impact of being dyslexic rather than advantage students. That is, it made a considerable difference for students with learning difficulties, but little difference to those without. Extra time is therefore thought to 'level the playing field'.

The issue of how much extra time a dyslexic candidate should be granted is more difficult. Some institutions make a blanket provision of 10–15 minutes per hour, whilst others vary it according to the extent of the student's difficulties. The HEFC's report criticizes blanket arrangements as they are contrary to the fundamental requirement that in all cases of disability, arrangements should be on an individual basis, dependent upon needs. To overcome this, the working party recommended that students whose dyslexia is mild should be provided with a minimum of 10 minutes per hour; students whose difficulties are moderate should be allowed a minimum of 15 minutes per hour; and in cases where the effects of the dyslexia are severe, a minimum of 15 minutes per hour should be allowed. In a footnote, however, the HEFC comment that, in most cases, students whose dyslexia is severe will require an individual evaluation of their examination require-ments, which may result in a greater allowance of additional time.

The problem with this is that deciding criteria for the degree of dyslexia is very difficult. Further, there is no systematic way of determining whether 10 minutes is better than 15 minutes. Both Kay Runyon and Alster found considerable variation amongst the students in their studies with regard to the amount of time they needed to complete tasks. The former found the amount of extra time needed ranged from 4 to 29 minutes, whilst the latter discovered that the amount of time needed varied between none and 44 minutes. There is an issue of how one determines who needs what, and in addition it could become an administrative nightmare. It is perhaps too soon to be prescribing specific amounts of time; however, it is clear that 'given sufficient time, dyslexic college students can perform at levels comparable to their non-disabled peers . . .' (Mosberg and Johns 1994: 134).

Statistics

Many people entering higher education or undergoing professional training are required to complete courses in statistics. Some dyslexic people find this very difficult, as they have a poor background in maths, and because their weak memory creates problems in areas such as sequencing and recalling concepts. They will be expected to operate at an abstract level and learn new terminology which they have to remember. Recalling the difference between 'quantitative' and 'qualitative' can for example be difficult. Issues of confidence in their mathematical ability arise.

Skill development The teaching of statistics needs to be as concrete as possible, using practical examples. It is important to tap understanding and reasoning, rather than automatic recall. In particular, when learning the language of statistics, terminology such as 'data', 'mean', and so on, need to be explained in a concrete way, and with a rationale.

Dyslexic people can also be taught very specific strategies for recalling the operations involved in statistics. It is a subject that can be made very visual by the use of graphs and tables. Mnemonics can help in remembering sequential patterns as can memory techniques that rely on making connections.

Compensations The most obvious compensation is to use a computer to perform statistical operations. Dyslexic people will, however, need to understand the concepts if they are going to perform the correct operation. Using a computer or calculator is not, therefore, cheating. A 'self-prepared' manual containing basic concepts, definitions and formulae can be a useful aid.

Accommodations The most effective accommodation is relying on a statistician when needing to analyse and interpret data. It is probable that most people for whom statistics is not a daily task need to rely on others or go back to books and manuals, whether or not they are dyslexic. It can be helpful to provide simple guides with very clear instructions regarding the procedures which should be used.

Many dyslexic students can understand statistics at a conceptual level but find it difficult to deal with tests and examinations. If the purpose is to demonstrate understanding so as to ensure that students are able to interpret research material correctly, setting a project or open-book type of examination, in which they can refer back to sources and do not have to rely on memory, would be appropriate.

Presentations

For some dyslexic people, presentations are the best possible way of displaying their knowledge and their abilities, as they are better at talking than writing. Others consider it a nightmare as they have trouble with word finding. Presentations can be given for a variety of reasons, including as a method of assessment. They can be an exercise in developing communication or life skills, or the starting point for discussion of a subject at university. They are also increasingly used in the workplace as a way of reporting to colleagues.

Skill development It is important to know the aim of the presentation, who the audience is, and the duration. If it is longer than 15 minutes it is important to break it up to maintain the audience's attention. The general principles should be to clarify the main aspects of the topic, and not to be too ambitious about what is covered. In some cases the presentation will be very formal and questions will be taken at the end; in others there will be interaction with the audience. Planning, structure and confidence are key elements.

The 3M principles of making tasks manageable, memorable and multisensory are, once again, useful here. How the dyslexic person presents the information is a question of personal style - some people like overheads, some like computer software and others prefer cue cards. Illustrations and diagrams often make the points clearer and serve as a memory aid.

Dyslexic people need to know that there are three elements in the process of verbal communication - the words you use, the way they are said and body language. It can be reassuring for dyslexic people to know that it is not just the words that have impact and that anyone can make a mistake. The way in which the information is delivered must be considered: variation in tone and speed of delivery are important. Many people speak too quickly when they are nervous, and this is when the use of visual aids can help.

The dyslexic needs to feel in control of the presentation and it can be a good idea to have a contingency plan if things start to go wrong. They may also need to explain, without using the words 'dyslexia', that they have trouble with words when they are in a nervous or stressful situation. One person, for example, used it as an advantage as he warned the audience it would help to keep them on their toes and make them listen carefully to what he had to say. It is important that they know that they are allowed to say 'I have lost my place' or 'Now where was I?' and that this occurs when others give presentations.

Compensations Making a video or using a computer package such as PowerPoint reduces the load on memory. This can be easier than trying to keep overheads in order and on the projector at the right time. It enables the presenter to focus on talking.

Accommodations These can include having a helper to operate the equipment or to write on the flipchart, since the burden on the presenter is reduced.

Working in a group

Working in a group can be advantageous for dyslexic students but can also present significant problems. Many dyslexic people prefer to work on their own because they lack confidence when working with others. They prefer to work according to their own routines and in their own way. Many university and training courses, however, now have a 'groupwork' component, partly because it helps develop the ability to work in a team. It is also thought to help build self-confidence. For dyslexic people, it can be difficult because it might reveal their weaknesses, and they can feel that they are letting the group down if they cannot perform at an expected level. It also places demands on their time in that they have to be at meetings on time and complete work to deadlines.

Dyslexic people can be very sensitive and somewhat defensive. This can lead to difficult working relationships. It is important for the dyslexic person to know that working in a group or a team can be difficult for anyone and the problems they may be experiencing might be the same for others but exaggerated. If the team is really not working well, it is essential for them to seek outside help from a tutor, rather than allow the situation to deteriorate too far.

These old demons are still there. Several nights ago at the university someone had written 'your' instead of 'you're'. Another person turned to me and asked me if the original spelling was wrong. My reply was no, probably because 'your' is very similar to 'you're'. Nothing came of this incident, no one, apart from me, probably remembers it, it lasted about two seconds. Yet, the anxiety upon leaving myself open to petty ridicule was there, worse, someone could question my intellectual capabilities. I felt my confidence waver slightly, and although it only lasted a split second it was noticeable to me. That said, I know 'what the score is': why these things happen. Moreover, my ever-growing self confidence means I don't feel any need to 'prove' how clever I am and such events are rare and brief: I soon realize what is happening and take control of my reactions.

Skill development Dyslexic people are likely to encounter misunderstanding, so they need to be able to explain their situation and offer solutions for any potential difficulties to avoid conflict. It is an area in which they can do well as they often generate creative and original ideas, solve difficult problems and present information very effectively. They need to be able to say what they are good at and avoid situations where they may display their weaknesses. They might, for example, suggest that someone else takes the minutes, if they make the presentation. On some courses, documentation needs to be kept on each meeting. Using a pro forma outlining who is present and key areas to be discussed, with a summary of the points covered during the meeting, can be a good idea.

Compensations These can include using a tape recorder and Dictaphone, the former as a way of recording proceedings and the latter for making contributions.

Accommodations These can include having someone take notes of the meeting, and the delegation of specific tasks generally, each person taking on specific roles.

Tutorials

The tutorial is a key part of university life for students. It is a chance to gather information, develop ideas, focus their thinking and gain confidence. Tutorials also enable students to keep on track with their course. For many dyslexic students, tutorials are not as effective as they should be, and yet the success of the dyslexic student is dependent to some extent on the tutorial support that they have been given. Unless they have had personal experience many tutors are unlikely to understand dyslexia. Some students report that their tutor has been very good, enabling them to access the information they need, whilst not doing the work for them. Others have suggested that their tutor has tried to control the situation to the extent that it was not the student's own work that was presented in the end. Some students also report that their tutors try hard but do not understand, and tend to make things more difficult. A dyslexic student's confidence can easily be undermined.

The role of the tutor

It can be difficult for tutors to know exactly how much help should be given. Why, for example, should they direct a dyslexic student to a greater extent than one who has financial worries or other concerns? What are the criteria for support? Should one student be given extra time to complete the work because they are dyslexic and another not, even though the latter has pressing family concerns and can only work late at night? These are difficult issues and the students need to acknowledge this. Organizational policies help outline procedures. The experience the tutor has of dealing with dyslexic students in the past is a significant factor.

It is often successful dyslexic students who are best at developing the understanding of tutors and lecturers. Some tutors have reported that working with dyslexic students has improved their own teaching and professional development. Equally, they have found some of the strategies used by dyslexic students to be helpful for themselves (Scott and Gregg 2000). Certainly, it enables the lecturer to suggest specific study skills that will be relevant to the discipline. As one student said:

> My tutor is great, he has so much knowledge on the subject as it really interests him, but what he can also do is give me the key points. I then go away and think about it, and return to him with new ideas. We have some great discussions and I then find I can write down the outcome easily.

Sheridan (cited in Scott and Gregg 2000) has suggested that if attention to dyslexic students leads to heightened consciousness of the importance of skilful teaching, then the presence of these students on campuses will have made a significant contribution to the improvement of higher education.

Skill development When working with dyslexic students, a tutor needs to increase his or her understanding of dyslexia and recognize that it affects each individual in a different way. Dyslexia is an information-processing difficulty and it is important for the tutor to know that this sometimes creates a problem with verbal as well as written information. Some students leave tutorials feeling as confused or as uninformed as they were when they went in because they have been too frightened to ask for clarification for fear of seeming stupid. The tutor needs to ask specific questions and clarify that the student has interpreted what is being said in the way that it was meant. Dyslexic students need positive feedback on their performance. Mistakes can be important learning tools and constructive criticism enables them to see how to improve. When returning essays, it is helpful if tutors give clear recommendations and suggestions about content and style and, if possible, talk it through with the student. Similarly, reviewing examination scripts can also significantly improve performance: often students don't know or remember what they have done wrong and are likely to repeat errors. Tutors can also help provide key points of information in areas around which the student needs to work. It is also helpful if students are allowed to present a first draft to ensure that they are on track. Tutors do need to remember that the amount of time and effort that may have gone into a first draft can be considerable and that even rewriting can take a dyslexic much longer than expected.

Compensations The tutor could allow tutorials to be taped and provide a summary of the key points at the end of the session, as well as a written list of suggestions of work that could be covered ahead of time.

Accommodations These involve being flexible over deadlines, seeing more drafts and plans of assignments, and being in closer contact with the student.

The role of the student

Students need to develop an understanding of the parameters of the tutorial. It is important for students to be prepared, to know what the tutorial is going to be about, and to know how to ask the right questions. They need to know how to frame what they are asking for. They are more likely to get a positive response if they ask a positive question: for example, 'I thought X's discussion was excellent, I wonder if you could direct me to somebody with another point of view so I can clarify my ideas?' Students need to ask if they can take a tape recorder to sessions so they can concentrate on listening and understanding the content. A summary or a brainstorm, either at the end of the session or shortly afterwards, can help to recall the material.

Compensations These can include prepared notes which summarize the session, and using a tape recorder.

Accommodations These can include finding time to discuss the session further with another student, and the provision of extra tutorials.

The keys to success

The factors influencing the success of students can be summarized as:

- feeling in control of their learning and the information that they have to deal with
- having a range of strategies to enable them to overcome some of the difficulties that they face
- support from both their family and their friends
- a stable environment in which to live and work
- sympathetic tutors and friends on the course with whom they can exchange ideas and borrow notes
- the appropriate choice of course and options
- having an interest in the subject they are studying
- feeling comfortable in their environment
- persistence, determination and hard work
- being able to talk to other dyslexic students, to share experiences and exchange strategies.

The responsibilities of colleges and universities

Support for dyslexic students has improved significantly in recent years but much still needs to be done. The Disability Discrimination Act 1995 requires colleges and universities to provide a disability statement but there is a need for:

- more awareness training for academic and administrative staff. Both groups need to recognize that to access some of the compensations and accommodations at university dyslexic students have to deal with paperwork they can find difficult

- greater awareness and understanding amongst tutors and lecturers that would improve the teaching/learning process. If universities are institutions that foster independent learning, then they should be able to accommodate the dyslexic student's needs
- more practical and departmental support in terms of accessing knowledge, specialist support directed towards developing literacy and learning skills, and counselling support to help the dyslexic person overcome some of the psychological and emotional issues that affect their learning
- more self-help groups, that would help the dyslexic student feel less isolated.

Some mature students undertake access courses prior to attending university: these can be very helpful in developing the skills a student needs to embark on a career in higher education. The difference between the level of support provided during such courses and that available at university level is sometimes considerable. There is a need for a carefully planned transition process, directed at independent learning. This could greatly relieve the stress on the dyslexic student and reduce the demands on the tutors at university.

Study skills course outline

Although dyslexic people need individual support which addresses their specific needs it can be helpful to work within a structure, and courses are sometimes successfully conducted with small groups. A suggested programme for a Study Skills Course is as follows.

Aim

This is a learning skills development course. The aim is to develop your understanding of dyslexia and how it affects you; and to recognize and develop your skills and learn more effectively. It also aims to provide you with a choice of strategies to help you throughout your course and beyond.

The initial interview

- priorities for learning – aims, goals and reasons for doing the course
- discussion of personal learning profile
- strategy and programme planning.

The programme will include some or all of the following, depending on what is needed.

Self-understanding

What is dyslexia?
- definition
- thinking skills and learning styles
- metacognition
- memory strategies.

Skill development

Organization of time and work:
- the importance of organization
- time management
- organization of work.

Reading skills:
How do you read?
- different types of reading, e.g. critical and analytical
- efficient reading strategies, e.g skim and scan.

Writing skills:
- essay writing made manageable
- question analysis
- different structures
- planning

Note-taking:
- the purpose of note-taking
- various different methods.

Spelling, punctuation and grammar:
- making it multisensory.

Revision and examination techniques:
- making revision manageable
- how to handle exams.

Dyslexia in the future:
- challenges and dilemmas.

Other areas that might be covered if required are: writing a dissertation, listening skills, presentation skills and how to deal with an interview.

Case study E

Reason for referral

E came to the Centre for an assessment because he was experiencing significant problems in his work as a policeman. He was continually losing things, his notebook for example; he had difficulty remembering his daily instructions and he was aware that it took him longer to produce written work. An assessment revealed that he was dyslexic. In his initial skill development session, he was relieved to discover that there was a reason and an explanation for his difficulties. He was also extremely motivated to find solutions.

Background information

E had not enjoyed school; in spite of working very hard, he had never achieved grades that his teachers felt he was capable of attaining. He was an only child but his family situation was complicated and E felt that this might be a reason why his teachers at school did not ask why he was not more successful. He left school after gaining modest GCSEs. He did a variety of manual jobs and clerical office work, and as he disliked office work, he joined the police force in his early 20s. He enjoyed being a policeman and, on the whole, was very good at it. However, he was keen to climb the promotion ladder.

Assessments

E's assessments revealed that he was a man of considerable abilities. His IQ was high, his verbal scores falling within the high average range, apart from Digit Span and Arithmetic (mental), which were slightly below average. His non-verbal performance was weaker but still within the average range. His language skills were extremely good, he could express himself articulately and with confidence. E reported that he generally got on very well with people. He liked being part of a team.

E's assessment revealed that his reading, despite being at the Professional level, was slow and his comprehension was weak. He reported that he had to read text two or three times in order to assimilate the information. His writing was slow at 15 words per minute. E expressed his ideas clearly but his sentence structure was weak and his punctuation erratic. His spelling was of a sufficient standard that he could make use of a spellchecker on a word processor. E himself said that he had difficulty remembering things: people's names, instructions and where he had put his possessions. He also said that his reading was far too slow.

Goals

E's goal was to complete a degree course in Police Studies.

Programme plan

E's programme was aimed at developing his understanding, and improving his reading, essay writing and memory strategies. The outline of his programme, over a course of ten sessions, was as follows:

- Dyslexia and how it affected him
- Reading skills – skimming and scanning techniques
- Comprehension strategies
- Memory strategies
- Mind-mapping skills
- Essay writing, including the purpose, gathering information, planning techniques, grammar, especially sentence structure, and proofreading.

Outcome

The knowledge that he was an intelligent man, and the fact that there was a reason for the difficulties he experienced, gave E a great deal of confidence. He began to look at the way he was doing things and finding new ways of overcoming some of the problems. He practised many of the strategies we discussed during his course; for example, he found the mind-mapping session extremely useful. He returned the following week with mind-maps of his time, his essays and notes for his reading. After the reading session in which we discussed scanning and skimming strategies as an aid to comprehension and improving reading speed, he said it had cut down the time it took him to read his newspaper from four hours to one hour.

E has now completed his Police Studies degree and has remained in the force, moving to more specialized duties. He has kept in touch with us and when asked to comment on his experiences he sent us the following poem:

Moving On

At school you were stupid, a bit of a fool.
Hit round the head; admonished, quite cruel.
You could think of the big things, argue and call, but ask you to
write it, no ... not at all.
Your spelling creative; your writing was poor. So they heaped on
the scolding, you would always take more.

They said you were lazy, to buck up and work.
With more concentration, you'd get a perk.
You're friends thought you odd; to mix was a trial.
To talk to your fancy, took a great while.

To avoid humiliation, you'd sought to fail.
You weren't lazy or stupid, you tried and how.
But no matter what effort, the way always barred.
Your classmates progressed, while you stayed behind.

So what was the matter, were they all blind?
You could do better; you knew that for sure.
But who would listen, who would be kind?
You went with your feelings, they told you at last.

Confirmed your suspicions, that you are not daft.
A bit of a problem, inconvenient, but at last.
Yes they can help you, to attain what you seek.
But you surge with great anger, confused with relief.

So how did they miss it, why weren't you briefed?
Self-pity, annoyance a natural response, to wallow and
grumble ... is that what you want?
But what ever has happened cannot be changed. Remember, but
don't be swallowed in pain.
You can sit in a circle, cry and complain. Demand restitution,
seek money ... personal gain?

Or you can accept what has happened, go out ... prove they
were wrong.
The question my friend, is can you be strong?
Put it behind you, look forward, make your own perks.
You can prove to that teacher that you weren't a berk.

Summary

- Higher and professional education present dyslexic people with considerable challenges. Moving on to these levels of education and training represents a significant transition.
- Successful adaptation at this level is heavily reliant on the development of a dyslexic person's metacognitive skills, as these enhance executive functioning.
- The specific skills which should be addressed include reading and listening comprehension techniques, essay writing strategies, note-taking, proofreading and organization.
- At this level technology has a great deal to offer in terms of compensation.
- Institutions, tutors and trainers can make reasonable and sensible adjustments that allow those undertaking courses of higher and professional education to show themselves at their best.

Chapter 8
Career development and guidance

This chapter describes the issues involved in providing career counselling for dyslexic people, as well as their continued career development. A decision-making model of career guidance is outlined.

Introduction

Peel (1992) suggests that the most useful definition of 'career' is the broadest and cites the *Shorter Oxford Dictionary* as defining 'career' as 'a person's course or progress through life'. He intends this to include paid and voluntary employment, both full and part-time, self-employment, domestic roles, and periods out of paid employment. It has been suggested in Chapter 2 that it is transitions across the lifespan which constantly present dyslexic people with new challenges. Assisting with careers development and the provision of suitable career counselling and guidance can be among the most important but the least resourced areas of professional work. Appropriate career guidance at school and ongoing counselling and development are among the professional activities which can assist a dyslexic person to achieve 'goodness of fit'.

Approaches to counselling and development

There are essentially two views of career, the organizational and the individual (McCormick and Ilgen 1985). The former considers careers within the context of organizations, whilst the latter considers the nature of the people involved for explanation of career events. Although there are competing views, a common theme which runs throughout much career development is that, although the process of career development is similar for all students, many issues are unique to the individual, especially those with disabilities (Wehman 1996). The view taken here therefore is that career development and counselling should be individualized to meet the unique needs of dyslexic people.

The individual view draws on the developmental changes that are part of the continual process of maturing and ageing. Maturation is usually broken down into stages, identified by dominant behaviour present at those periods in one's life. Levinson (1978) exemplifies the individual orientation towards careers. According to his theory, all of us mature and develop whilst passing through a sequence of eras, each lasting about 20 years. In particular, there are four significant eras or stages in each of our lives:

- childhood and adolescence: age 0–22
- early adulthood: age 17–45
- middle adulthood: age 40–60
- late adulthood: age 60+.

Within the early adulthood stage, Levinson included three subphases:

- entering the adult world
- age 30 transition
- settling down.

In the first, the individual is faced with some major transitions. They begin by shifting from the role of a child in a family to becoming a 'novice adult', with responsibility for his or her own life. One of the major decisions with long-term implications at this time revolves round the choice of a career. Levinson argues that at this time it is necessary for people to be able to explore alternatives which may be open to them and to try out some of the possible roles to see 'how they fit'. During the moves from one stage to another the transitions become important: these are major changes from what was done in the past.

In addressing the issue of career development and transitions for people with learning difficulties, Wehman (1996) lists several key aspects of career development that need to be considered, including the following:

- Career development is a process that begins at birth and should continue throughout life
- Early career development is essential for making satisfactory choices later
- Significant gaps or periods of neglect in any area of basic human development can affect career development and the transition from one stage of life to another

- Career development is responsive to intervention and programming when the latter involves direct instructions for individual needs.

The first two of these in particular address the importance of adequate career counselling at school and college. There are various theories of career choice but Yost and Corbishley (1987) argue that, although there are contradictions between them, there are central themes which have implications for career counselling. These include the assumption that people make career decisions out of the context of a lifetime of experiences; that people have strong expectations of work and, therefore, the exploration of intra-personal satisfaction they expect or derive from work is important; there is a need for skills specific to job selection, acquisition and retention which need to be assessed or taught; there are personal, social and environmental factors which need to be explored as these can be a barrier to deciding on or pursuing a particular career. On this basis and in the absence of a comprehensive career theory, they take a pragmatic view and argue for a decision-making model which acknowledges the influence of the central themes of the various theories. A decision-making model, they argue, has the advantage of focusing on the established core of career choice – that is, the centrality of decision-making. It also has considerable face validity for clients and allows a good deal of flexibility. Their model, adapted for use with dyslexic people, is outlined below.

Career guidance: a decision-making model

The model proposed by Yost and Corbishley (1987) has eight stages, as follows:

- initial assessment
- self-understanding
- making sense of self-understanding data
- generating alternatives
- obtaining occupational information
- making the choice
- making plans to reach the career choice goal
- implementing plans.

Initial assessment The aim of this is to gather personal and employment information about the client and to arrive, in collaboration with the client, at a feasible career counselling goal that the client is motivated to pursue.

Self-understanding The client explores his or her values, interests, experience and abilities that relate to the present goal. In addition, assessment is made of psychological issues that may affect career counselling.

Making sense of self-understanding data The information gathered in the previous stage is synthesized into a coherent set of statements which indicate the client's desired outcomes for a career choice. These will be used as a reference point in future stages. Personal and environmental barriers to success in pursuing the desired career are summarized.

Generating alternatives Using the information acquired thus far, counsellor and client develop a list of possible career alternatives without making any judgement about the value of the options.

Obtaining occupational information It is important to learn as much about each option as is necessary to make an informed choice. The list of options is narrowed.

Making the choice The client makes a choice among options – any psychological problems which arise should be dealt with at this stage.

Making plans to reach the career choice goal Contingency plans are worked out to handle any setbacks which might arise.

Implementing plans The client takes whatever action is necessary to achieve the selected career goal. This could include further training or education, learning how to present oneself on paper and in person to prospective employers and conducting a job search.

Career guidance and the dyslexic: a model

Dyslexic people should not be excluded from particular occupations: they can develop strategies for dealing with memory tasks as well as with organization. Developing a list of unsuitable occupations similar to that which is prepared for people who are colour-blind would not be helpful.

Initial assessment

The aim of this is to gather personal and employment information about the client. This should include the usual information about aptitudes and abilities.

Careful thought should be given to the question of aptitude and ability testing. Pencil and paper and/or timed tests can be unsuitable as they often provide more information about the clients' dyslexia than they do about their abilities. Reid (1999) has, however, reported some success using the Morrisby Test with dyslexic adolescents, particularly in boosting their confidence in their abilities. Being diagnosed as dyslexic will have involved an assessment process, including a wide-ranging intelligence test such as the WAIS. Ability testing can therefore be redundant.

Holland's Self-Directed Search which is untimed and provides a self-rating with regard to interests, competencies and abilities can be useful here. There is a Form E which takes into account reading levels. Holland's theory of vocational education and planning emphasizes the match between character-istics of the person and those of the environment. It is based on the assumption that we gravitate towards academic subjects and occupations we think we will find attractive, and think we will succeed in (Holland 1973, 1985). The Self-Directed Search was developed to assist individuals and counsellors to assess characteristics and provide information for improving career decisions.

Holland's theory assumes that most people can be classified into six general types which reflect their orientation towards careers and these are shown in Table 8.1. It should be remembered that, as with any labelling system, there is considerable variance. The types or categories only give a general impression, the exact mix varying from person to person. The specific descriptions within a category are not precise either, they are just meant to provide a general impression of the types of traits that make up the category. Holland's theory also assumes that some types of job environment match these person types. Given these two conditions, people and jobs, the final assumption is that people search their environment for jobs that allow them to use their skills and abilities, to express their attitudes and values and to perform work roles that agree with their general orientation towards work and people at work.

Completion of the Self-Directed Search using Form E leads to a two-letter code being provided. This combines the types and can be checked against a list of suitable occupations.

Dyslexic people use the Self-Directed Search sensibly and answer it honestly. There are of course risks, mainly based on assumptions people might make about themselves. These include:

- The publicity given to gifted dyslexics, particularly those with very strong visual creative abilities, can result in dyslexic people agreeing with all items relating to abilities and career choices in those areas when this is

unrealistic. That is, there is a risk that they might adopt a 'should' rather than 'can' approach
- Many dyslexic people underestimate their ability and can therefore be reluctant to check items for which they would assume they would need more ability and competence than they have
- The damage done to the self-esteem of some dyslexic people means that they will be 'trying to prove something' and only check items which lead them to making choices which are entirely unrealistic.

The use of the Self-Directed Search for people with learning difficulties has been systematically researched. Having considered this, Taymans (1991) makes the following six recommendations:

- One to one administration of the test is recommended. This has the advantage of enabling the test taker to ask questions about reading and understanding words which might be unfamiliar
- It is helpful to develop demonstration and practice items so that it can be ensured that the format and types of questions to be answered are understood
- A list of alternate words or phrases to help explain unclear items can be developed
- The administrator of the test should keep a record of any specific problems the test taker seemed to encounter
- Scoring should be undertaken by the administrator of the test with the client participating to verify agreement of scores and personal interests
- There is a computerized version of the Self-Directed Search which might be preferable for some people.

Helping dyslexic people to identify their abilities and understand their inefficiencies seems to be an important part of vocational guidance work when dealing with those leaving school and for the career counsellor working with those who have reached a critical point in their working life. Buchanan and Wolf (1986) found evidence of the lack of ability to assess their own strengths and weaknesses amongst students with learning disabilities.

Self-understanding

The client explores his or her values, interests, experience and abilities that relate to the present goal. In addition, assessment is made of psychological issues that may affect career counselling. One important issue is personality and this is sometimes evaluated, both within organizations and by career

Table 8.1 Holland's classification of person and environment characteristics. (Adapted from: McCormick and Ilgen 1985)

Type	Person characteristics	Environment characteristics
Realistic	Aggressive Mechanically orientated Practical minded Physically strong Conventionally masculine Acts out problems Avoids interpersonal tasks Prefers concrete to abstract tasks.	Requires explicit, concrete, physical tasks Outdoors Needs immediate behaviour Needs immediate reinforcement Makes low interpersonal demands.
Investigative	Thinks through problems Scientifically inclined Inventive Precise Achieving Shy radical.	Requires thought and creativity Task-idea orientated Makes minimum social demands Requires laboratory equipment but not high physical demands.
Artistic	Original Asocial Dislikes structure More conventionally feminine Emotional.	Interprets and modifies human behaviour Has ambiguous standards of excellence Requires intense involvement for long periods of time Works in isolation.
Social	Responsible Humanistic Accepting of conventionally feminine impulses Interpersonally skilled Avoids intellectual problem-solving.	Interprets as well as modifies human behaviour Requires high communications Helps others Emphasizes prestige Delays reinforcement.
Enterprising	Verbally skilled Power and status oriented.	Needs verbal responses Fulfils supervisory roles Needs persuasion Needs management behaviours.
Conventional	Prefers structure High self-control Strong identification with power and status.	Systematic, routine Concrete Makes minimal physical demands Indoors Makes low interpersonal demands.

counsellors, using the Myers-Briggs Type Indicator (Myers and McCauley, 1985). Again, this is based on type theory, Myers proposing 16 psychological types, each described in terms of four preferences. The concept of preference is important to the theory and in administering and interpreting the MBTI. Preference means 'feeling most comfortable and natural with'. The MBTI is designed to measure preferences rather than abilities, skills or how well developed the preferences are. It is essentially a categorizing measure, the scores achieved indicating the degree of confidence in the chosen preference, not the degree of development.

The type theory suggests four pairs of preferences: Extraversion (E) and Introversion (I); Sensing (S) and Intuition (N); Thinking (T) and Feeling (F); and Judging (J) and Perceiving (P). 'E', 'I', 'J' and 'P' are called attitudes; 'S', 'N', 'T' and 'F' are called functions. A person's type is described in four letters, one from each pair of preferences.

Myers's theory assumes there is a 'true type' and people develop this 'normally' over a period of time. 'False type' development can result when there has been interference with normal development of true preferences. An example of someone who has developed a false type would be a person whose ideal self-concept includes a preference for thinking but neglects their true preference for feeling. According to type theory, such a person would be 'acting out of character'. The general motives associated with each dominant function are shown in Table 8.2.

Table 8.2 The association of general motives with dominant personality functions proposed by Myers (Myers and McCauley 1985)

Introverted Sensing (IS)	To work quietly and systematically on something practical or tangible
Extraverted Sensing (ES)	To work with machines or objects in an easy-going, sociable setting
Introverted Intuition (IN)	To develop new theories and ideas
Extraverted Intuition (EN)	To change the environment/situation
Introverted Thinking (IT)	To analyse and understand ideas
Extraverted Thinking (ET)	To organize and criticize the environment/situation
Introverted Feeling (IF)	To work quietly and individually on something which is highly valued
Extraverted Feeling (EF)	To help others

In terms of personality assessment, however, it might not be necessary to administer tests. As mentioned in Chapter 2, persistence and determination have been shown to be important factors in determining the success of dyslexic people. This will have been manifested during their academic and work careers. It can also be important to assess the extent to which their experiences at school and perhaps at work have affected confidence and self-esteem.

Assessing the extent to which dyslexia is still affecting literacy, memory and executive functioning is especially important. Persisting problems with literacy do, of course, make a difference. Even residual difficulties such as slow reading and writing would make some occupations onerous. Abilities such as verbal fluency would also be relevant as strengths in this area might compensate for weaker written language skills.

In helping dyslexic students to explore their values, interests, experience, and abilities that relate to their goals, considering the extent to which they understand their condition and how it affects them would seem to be particularly important. Denial of their weaknesses or failure to recognize possible problems could prevent them from achieving their goals.

Dyslexic students occasionally deny that they have problems with literacy and learning. Sometimes they perceive it as a school problem, and once they are leaving an academic environment they think it will no longer be a problem. Further, they have a realistic concern that people will focus on their weaknesses rather than what they can do. The importance of self-understanding has been a recurrent theme throughout this book. Many dyslexic people have been given a label but have never had a reason as to why they find certain tasks difficult. The following conversation is not uncommon:

Question:	What does being dyslexic mean?
Answer:	That you have trouble with spelling
Question:	Why do you have trouble with spelling?
Answer:	Because I am dyslexic?

People need to understand why tasks are difficult if they are to make sensible career choices, as well as plan for transitions.

Making sense of self-understanding data

The information gathered is summarized into statements or goals which can be used as a reference point. For dyslexic people, it would seem to be particularly important to summarize the obstacles their dyslexia might present in pursuing their desired career, and the skills, compensations and accommodations they might need.

Further, it is important to make them aware of the possibility of their dyslexia adding to normal occupational stress and fatigue. For example, the teenager who wanted to become an air traffic controller need not have been dissuaded from pursuing this occupation despite the fact that she still had trouble with sequential tasks and with labelling, including right and left, correctly. She could have used strategies to overcome such difficulties; however, it was pointed out that she would be putting more pressure on herself in an already stressful occupation.

It is also important that dyslexic people do not fall for stereotypes such as the assumption that, as dyslexics, they will have good spatial abilities and should therefore enter into artistic endeavours or work with computers. In a study of high school students, Hearne et al. (1988) found that learning disabled students were no worse or better than their non-disabled peers in terms of an aptitude for working with computers.

Generating alternatives

Using the information acquired thus far, counsellor and client develop a list of possible career alternatives without making any judgement about the value of the options. This should not differ greatly from working with non-dyslexics, but the options should be realistically based on the information provided from the previous stages.

Obtaining occupational information

This involves learning as much about each option as is possible and narrowing the list of options. Here again, it is important to consider the limits that dyslexia might place on the client. The question 'What aspects of the job might make it unsuitable for me?' is particularly important. Another issue at this stage might be the route to qualification for an occupation. Would, for example, an NVQ or a National Diploma, followed by an Advanced Diploma, be an easier and more relevant pathway to a career rather than GCE A-levels. The extent to which allowances will be made for a client's dyslexia on a particular course of study or training is an important issue, as is the nature of course assessment and evaluation.

Vocational guidance counsellors working with dyslexic people might find themselves needing to encourage their clients to pursue courses of training for occupations they had ruled out because of their difficulties. Plata and Bone (1989) studied the way in which disabled adolescents viewed the importance of particular occupations. They found that students in their sample perceived skilled, semi-skilled and unskilled occupations as being more important than managerial and professional occupations, despite the fact that some were of well above average intelligence. It might therefore be that the school experiences of some lead them to underestimate their capabilities and potential.

Making a choice

The client makes a choice amongst options based on all the above information and this is no different from the situation faced by non-dyslexic people.

Making plans

The purpose at this stage is to make plans to reach the career choice goal. Where the choice might be affected by the outcome of school or examination results contingency plans should be worked out. Alternative routes to the same career paths should be considered.

Implementing plans

The client takes whatever action is necessary to achieve the selected career goal. This can involve:

- pursuing further or higher education or a course of vocational training
- developing the literacy and learning skills required for a course of training or a particular job
- developing memory and organizational skills
- developing the use of compensations, including technology
- preparing a curriculum vitae
- practising filling in application forms (see below)
- considering the issue of disclosing the client's dyslexia (see below).

It is often a requirement that application forms be prepared by hand. Typed applications are better than handwritten ones but if an employer insists that they should be completed in one's own handwriting, it could be an important indicator that it is not going to be easy to achieve 'goodness of fit'. That is, an employer who insists on handwritten applications could be fussy about neatness, and if this does not come naturally, the dyslexic person will not fit in. They could of course insist on typing the application and add a note saying they are dyslexic.

The other reason an employer might require a handwritten application form is so that they can conduct a handwriting analysis. It might seem glib, but the relationship between handwriting analysis and job performance is poor and its use as a selection method says something about the decisions which are being made in the organization.

Dyslexic people need to consider the issue of 'disclosure' carefully. This is a personal matter and there is no easy answer. They must, however, consider it so they can become clear in their own mind as to how they might deal with it when it arises. If it is likely to become obvious immediately, disclosure is perhaps best. It is important that dyslexic people focus on what they can do and what they need. This could include:

> You should know that I am dyslexic which means than I am inclined to be very thorough in the way I read and sometimes take more time.

> I am dyslexic, my reading is fine but I still have some trouble with spelling. Would it be OK to use my laptop computer at work?

> I am dyslexic but have sorted out my reading, writing and spelling, but sometimes can't see mistakes I make. Is there somebody who would be able to proof read my work for me?

That is, they should say that they are dyslexic but tell people how it affects them and what they need to do about it.

Hoffman et al. (1987) found that filling in application forms, as well as knowing where to find a job and how to get training, were major problems. One client sought help because preparing her application was proving difficult, despite the fact that she had a degree in Fine Art and a postgraduate diploma.

At stage 8, implementing plans, it can be useful to prepare a written action plan such as that shown in Table 8.3.

Table 8.3 A typical action plan. (Adapted from Nathan and Hill 1992)

Action Plan

1. My goal is:
2. My action steps are:
3. Number the Action steps in a logical sequence.
4. Write down your plan:
   - Over the next week I will ...
   - Over the next month I will ...
   - Over the next 3 months I will ...
   - Over the next 6 months I will ...
5. Decide when you will review progress.
   - My review date will be ...

Case study F

F Male   Age 27

Occupation: Chef – holding City and Guilds Qualifications. He had worked in the catering industry since leaving school.

Initial assessment

Although F was still interested in catering work and was competent, he was feeling bored and could not see a future for himself whilst continuing to work as a chef.

F was also in the Territorial Army where he had gained Non-Commissioned Officer status. He enjoyed the structure and routine, as well as having a supervisory role.

Self-understanding

F had been diagnosed as being dyslexic. Assessment showed him to be of above average intelligence but to have poor auditory memory.

F's reading skills were at the professional level but he read slowly and had difficulty with comprehension. His writing and spelling skills were limited.

Although in many ways a confident young man, F did have poor self-esteem with regard to his academic ability.

Completion of the Self-Directed Search suggested that he was an 'S.E.' type person, 'S' meaning social and 'E' enterprising. This is consistent with him working in the hotel and catering industry.

Making sense of self-assessment

On the positive side, F had good general ability, as well as good practical skills. He had a knowledge of the catering industry and some experience of supervision through his work in the Army.

On the negative side, F had low self-esteem regarding academic matters, as well as problems with literacy.

Listing alternatives

One of the main alternatives seems to be in hotel/recreation management.

Occupational information

Hotel and catering management courses were available at further and higher education level.

Making a choice

F decided that he would like to pursue a hotel and recreation management course so that he could remain within the catering industry but move up to management level.

Making plans

The timing of the interview was such that F would not be able to begin a course immediately but he did agree to make enquiries about suitable ones. He thought that a further education programme might be preferable to higher education as this was more likely to be coursework assessed.

Implementing plans

F formulated the following action plan.

Action Plan

- My goal is: *To qualify and work in the management side of the Hotel/Recreation industry.*
- My action steps are: *Gain admission to a course. Prepare for the course by developing my writing and spelling, learning to type, as well as learn how to study.*
- Number the Action steps in a logical sequence.

Write down your plan:

- Over the next week I will *Find out about courses*
- Over the next month I will *Start lessons with a tutor*
- Over the next 3 months I will *Learn to type*
- Over the next 6 months I will *Make sure that I have all the skills I need to complete a course.*

My review date will be *in 2 months.*

Career development

Peel (1992) describes career development as the 'life-long process of fostering and cultivating the shape of the individual's working life so as to make the best use of inherent talents, skills, knowledge and interest for that person's and the employer's benefit'. It should be forward-looking and concerned with potential, that is, the potential of individuals and of the situation in which they are or may be in the future. Career development does not necessarily involve promotion as it can also mean making a present job situation more satisfying and enabling someone to be more effective for their employer. In assisting dyslexic people, organizations can access a number of resources including:

- further and higher education, as well as vocational training
- human resource specialists within the organization
- government and private advisory agencies, including schemes designed to support disabilities such as Access to Work
- literature and learning aids
- any professional organization an individual might belong to
- managers and peer groups
- the individual's abilities and personality.

Positive career development can benefit individuals in terms of them fulfilling their potential, as well as the organization itself in terms of the contribution that person will make.

As well as accessing outside resources, organizations can support dyslexic people through coaching, tutoring and mentoring. Coaching largely refers to advice whilst on the job. It is usually an individual activity and focuses on the facilitation of skills that a person needs to function more effectively. Tutoring is usually provided by subject experts: an example would be someone who needs to have a better knowledge of accountancy being tutored on an individual or group basis. Mentoring usually involves a more senior and experienced person helping an employee on a personal, one to one, and probably long-term basis. The assistance they offer is general rather than subject-related. Mentoring can help in a number of ways, including overcoming problems with relationships, difficulties in studying, devising projects, offering new perspectives and insights, motivation and time management. Mentors can come from within or outside an organization.

Summary

- Career counselling is a professional activity which can assist dyslexic people to adapt positively to transitions.
- A decision-making approach to career counselling can enable dyslexic people to make sensible and realistic choices, based on a knowledge of their strengths and weaknesses.
- Preparation of an action plan can assist in the setting and achievement of realistic goals.

- Dyslexic people may need continued support in the development of their careers through coaching, tutoring and mentoring.

Chapter 9
Dyslexia at work

In this chapter the challenges facing both employers and employees are outlined. The skills, compensations and accommodations that address work-related tasks and that can enable dyslexic people to work effectively are described.

Introduction

Being dyslexic is not a barrier to occupational success: there are too many dyslexic people in all occupations to refute this. Some occupations are more dyslexia-friendly than others, however, tapping the dyslexic person's strengths rather than their weaknesses. There are undoubtedly dyslexic people who are in the wrong job, that is, they are in a situation where the demands on tasks they find difficult outweigh those on their competencies and strengths. The difficulties facing a dyslexic person at work can be exacerbated because the challenges they face are not obvious, being concerned with organization, social skills and coping with transitions rather than literacy. Many dyslexic people, having survived the traumas of the school system and leaving with few qualifications, find learning 'on the job' more effective. As they deal with the problems they face, they may learn to avoid situations involving literacy skills and become very well organized in work. They certainly may have more confidence than they had in school, being evaluated on their performance rather than through tests and examinations. This, however, will only be maintained if they have opportunities to continue developing their literacy, learning and technological skills and if, like any employee, they feel valued.

The employer's role

Enabling dyslexic people to feel comfortable and allowing them to use their skills is a matter of establishing the 'goodness of fit' referred to in Chapter 2. It can be improved through encouraging a positive attitude towards dyslexic people. The ideal situation is one in which there is a 'whole-organization approach', that is, where there is a good understanding of dyslexia and a network throughout the organization to support the dyslexic employee, or well-developed 'social ecologies'. Often several individuals in the same organization have to fight for acknowledgement, resources and special training. This is a waste of time, resources and energy for all.

One of the problems facing dyslexic people is that it is a 'hidden disability'. Dyslexic people can be 'different' but supervisors and colleagues don't know why. A whole-organization approach should therefore begin with awareness training, directed towards increasing everyone's understanding. It should include information about the nature of dyslexia, and how it affects people individually and in the workplace. The emphasis should be on solutions rather than problems, and it should be stressed that many of the adjustments made for dyslexic people can improve the working environment for everyone. There is, however, a need for balance: it is easy to exaggerate the difficulties, portraying dyslexia as an insurmountable problem, when it isn't. At the same time, by highlighting simple solutions the difficulties experienced by dyslexic people on a day to day basis can be underestimated:

> I have been informed that after 12 years of schooling and 10 years of work that I have dyslexia. I still don't understand what it is and how it affects my daily life but the attitude of others does stand out when they get told.

Awareness training can be followed up by establishing support groups, identifying named staff who can be contacted for advice, setting up a mentoring system, and arranging specialist input when necessary. In general there should be a coordination of and cooperation with staff responsible for human resources, equal opportunities and in-house differentiation in selection, training and appraisal:

> My employer has organized training and this has been pointing out
> issues and that my current operations are how people with my
> condition may deal with it. If it sounds like I have an illness its
> because that is how I've felt since I have been told. My level of
> confusion has increased and no one seems to be able to help.

In designing an awareness training programme it is important to
acknowledge that, in general, people are comfortable with their 'sameness'.
Walker (1994) has recommended that organizations should value differences
as an approach to affirmative action and equality of opportunity. Rather than
allow differences to create discomfort and conflict, she suggests that they
should be seen as something that can 'fuel creative energy and insight ... [as]
points of tension that spark alternative viewpoints and ideas, and ignite the
kindling process behind creativity and innovation' (1994: 212).

Walker's Valuing Differences Model is based on four principles:

- People work best when they feel valued.
- People feel most valued when they believe that their individual and group
  differences have been taken into account.
- The ability to learn from people regarded as different is the key to
  becoming fully empowered.
- When people feel valued and empowered, they are able to build relationships in which they work together interdependently.

She suggests that valuing difference is a way of helping people think through
their assumptions and beliefs about all kinds of differences, facilitating both
individual personal growth and an organization's productivity. Recognizing
and valuing the 'differences' manifested by dyslexic people will facilitate their
success and contribute to that of the organization. As Armstrong has written:

> Managing diversity is about ensuring that all people maximise their potential and
> their contribution to the organisation. It means valuing diversity, that is, valuing the
> differences between people and the different qualities they bring to their jobs
> which can lead to the development of a more rewarding and productive
> environment.
>
> (Armstrong 1999: 804)

Employers do, however, need to take action through specific initiatives.
Among the ten most successful of these described by Kandola and Fullerton

(1994) which would be relevant to dyslexic people are: buying specialized equipment; employing helpers; and training trainers in equal opportunities. Employers should consider the 'reasonable adjustments' which can be made to allow dyslexic people to show themselves at their best. They need to be aware of their legal responsibilities, specifically meeting the requirements of the Disability Discrimination Act (DDA) 1995 which is described in more detail in Chapter 10. Employers should be able to answer the following questions (adapted from Wehman 1996):

- Do you provide information to job applicants and employees about their rights under the DDA?
- Have you informed supervisory staff of their responsibilities under the DDA?
- Have you ensured your employment practices and procedures do not discriminate against applicants or employees who are dyslexic?
- Do you make adjustments for dyslexic applicants during the selection process and when employed by you?
- Can you identify the main skills involved in jobs, and do interview questions focus on whether an applicant has or can acquire these skills?

Employers do need to consider financial issues but often cost considerations are minimal. The two questions they really need to address are:

Can we alter the job?
- restructure the job
- extend a training period
- provide alternative training
- modify work schedules
- reassign tasks
- provide a mentor or coach.

Can we alter the workplace?
- change the work station
- provide organizational aids
- allow flexible working hours
- provide appropriate technology.

The remainder of this chapter addresses many of the issues raised by these questions.

Challenges facing dyslexic people

The most common challenges facing a dyslexic person at work are in areas such as:

- organization
- overload of work
- time management and work prioritization
- demands on written language abilities
- carrying out instructions
- unsympathetic colleagues
- dealing with distractions of noise, people and place.

These issues can all have a negative influence on the performance of anyone at work, but they are more challenging for dyslexic people, affecting self-confidence. The negative feelings they experienced at school are rekindled. Their managers' confidence in their ability to do the job can also be undermined.

> There are people at work who undermine me but it has been covert and therefore it is difficult to put your finger on it. I was passed over from promotion but have since been moved to a new job and promoted to the same level on a temporary basis so I proved that I can do it. My confidence is very fragile. I don't think I have done much wrong, but I just want to make sure I get the procedures right because I know I can do what the job entails and somebody of my ability should be able to get a great deal further.

The manager's role

Managers have a key role in enabling dyslexic people to work at a level commensurate with their ability. They need to be clear about what is required and consider what can be achieved through the right adjustments. It should always be remembered that dyslexic people:

- process information differently
- often perform less well in written tasks than is expected

- can be defensive in new training situations because of their past experience
- always need positive feedback
- can lack confidence and be reluctant to ask questions
- have skills and abilities they themselves do not recognize.

They are not unique in this, of course, and many people are initially bewildered in a new job or when faced with change. One training manager, after demonstrating what was required to a group of employees, was heard saying, 'This is easy, you would have to be an idiot not to be able to do it; are there any questions you would like to ask?'. He then observed, 'Nobody ever asks questions, I don't understand why'! This incident illustrates how easy it is to convey the wrong message. Effective communication is one of the keys to productive training.

Unlike education, which is linked to the goals of individuals, training is 'role-specific'. It starts with the requirements of a particular organization and, within that, of a given job (Miner 1992).

Success at work depends on several factors, including:

- knowing one's own individual skills and abilities
- knowing what the job demands are
- feeling comfortable in the environment in which one works, that is, having the chance to use one's skills and knowing they are valued
- the 'social ecologies' or the support of other colleagues to help circumvent any problems that they might encounter
- the ability to reflect on and evaluate one's own performance.

Understanding the demands of the job is part of career counselling and initial training. It can be enhanced by employers, managers and supervisors helping people to understand the nature of the job, as well as their skills and abilities.

Task analysis is essential to effective performance at work. To do a job effectively one has to analyse what the demands of the job are. These are often written in a job description, but it is important that the dyslexic person is able to understand and interpret what is expected of them, as well as the skills the job may require. They need to be encouraged to ask questions such as 'What does the job involve?' and 'What is the best way for me to tackle it?'. The application of the Performance Improvement Strategy described in Chapter 5 can improve performance at work through strategy selection and monitoring. Some people make more than one plan when deciding what to do, always having a Plan B. Contingency plans are often a good way of maintaining a feeling of control over a situation.

Understanding task demands and using a strategy employed successfully in a previous job situation but adapted for the current one can lead to efficient performance. Automatic strategy selection and generalization are, however, contingent upon effective executive functioning: to dyslexic people, therefore, each situation can be a completely new one. They fail to transfer and generalize successful learning and working experiences across to new situations. Graduates, for example, do not use the skills they developed for planning essays whilst a student to report-writing tasks. They can also fail to change an inefficient method because they are so busy trying to keep up with current job demands they do not have time or confidence to think about changing something in order to improve it. They will often work in the way they have been told to work by a line manager and be too worried and frightened to adapt and use their own strategies. In this situation it is important to explain to the line manager the reason for the change of routine or system.

Changes at work

Dyslexic people find adapting to change challenging, and one of the problems facing them is that there has been a great deal of change in the workplace in recent years. This is a continuing process, the rate of change being quite overwhelming. There are three areas of potential difficulty.

First, a change in job requirements places obvious demands as the person is likely to have to learn new skills. One woman, for example, was a very good playgroup leader whose job changed, in that she was increasingly required to write reports and keep daily logs. This placed tremendous demands on her literacy skills which were very weak, and she was unable to develop them in the time required by her supervisors. She left her job, which was a great loss to the children of her locality.

Second, changes of personnel can affect a dyslexic person's performance. They may have to display their weaknesses and difficulties to another person who has no understanding or interest. This can destroy their confidence in their work. It is often a change in management personnel which prompts people to seek help and advice: it has been a lowering of self-confidence rather than skill deficits that has undermined performance in work. Changes in support staff can also affect performance: one highly successful man's personal assistant left, and was replaced by someone who was less organized. As a result he needed to spend more time sorting out problems, and his own work suffered. Getting used to new colleagues can also create difficulties in social interactions.

Finally, changes in the environment can affect performance. This is not usually a long-term problem but it can take dyslexic people longer to settle into new surroundings. It is at such times that they should anticipate that it might take them longer to do their job than usual. They can also be distracted by noises around them. Certainly, if they have moved into an open plan office, many dyslexic people find it extremely difficult to concentrate. Here it is external factors which are creating the problem and the solution lies in modifying the environment.

Support in the workplace

Coaching and tutoring

The words 'coaching' and 'tutoring' are used synonymously, despite the fact that they can mean something different. 'Tutoring' usually describes help given to learners by subject experts, in the context of a specific course of study or acquisition of specific skills. In this context it refers to 'off the job' learning. Individual tutoring or tutor groups composed of students following the same course can be particularly helpful, offering as they do opportunities for exchanging views and experience, debate and general support. We have advocated elsewhere individual tuition, and if tutorial groups are to work, they need to be kept small. Ideally, they should not be too demanding in terms of the need to attend, but should be frequent.

'Coaching' can refer to 'on the job' advice or to an activity that bridges 'on the job' and 'off the job' learning. Both coaches and tutors need to have a good understanding of the nature of dyslexia.

Mentoring

Mentoring involves making available an experienced person to help an employee or learner on a personal, long-term, one to one basis, offering general rather than subject specialist help. Mentoring can help with overcoming relationship problems, difficulties in studying, the application of theoretical knowledge, devising projects, and bringing fresh perspectives and insights when facing personal problems associated with study, self-motivation and time management. It can be of value as part of an induction process, especially when an employee is 'different'.

Addressing challenges

Organization

> Dyslexic people ... may have to organize their lives differently from others, but that does not mean that they perform less well. Indeed, in many instances it will be found that the problems that they meet are little different from those met by everyone else – but they are exaggerated and made more obvious.
>
> (Hales 1995:88)

Organization can cover several dimensions including time management, general organization for work, personal organization and organization for learning and training. Some of these issues have already been addressed in earlier chapters and there is inevitably a certain amount of repetition here.

The dyslexic person's weakness in terms of organizational skills is a direct result of their inefficient working memory, particularly its impact on executive functioning. Organization involves sequencing information and behaviour, as well as keeping track of sets of instructions. For example, a receptionist needs to be able to hold in memory a sequence of instructions or facts long enough to organize them on paper, or she will not be able to accurately record telephone messages; a secretary asked to file papers needs to be able to locate the correct file if she is to keep the files organized; a despatch rider needs to be able to hold on to information about directions and routes and be capable of translating such information from maps if he or she is to get to the destination.

Organizing one's work and workload is a commonly reported difficulty. If people have trouble organizing themselves, being promoted to a managerial position could be stressful as they then have to organize others as well. At the same time this can act as a catalyst, leading to people becoming highly organized; some become so meticulous that every event is recorded in a diary and their determination to plan and organize activities results in them becoming very reliable. Paradoxically, it is the fact that they are so well organized that indicates they have a fundamental weakness in organizational skills.

Dyslexic people can be taught organizational skills and it is often one of the areas requiring most attention. Becoming better organized involves:

- understanding the nature of the task
- goal-setting (targets and priorities)

- planning time
- monitoring
- lists and classifications
- filing.

It is not unusual to meet dyslexic people who have in fact become very highly organized, and some of the skills and compensations which they have and which can be developed, as well as the accommodations which can be made, are shown in Table 9.1.

Time management and work prioritization

Skill development Time management and being able to prioritize the work are skills that are becoming increasingly important in the workplace. The skills involved in doing this include developing an awareness of time, being able to estimate how long a task will take, and being able to allocate the appropriate amount of time to it. It also involves being able to determine which are the most urgent or important tasks, and being able to place them in an efficient order. This can be achieved by brainstorming and then ordering the tasks. It can be a good idea to consider potential pitfalls in the plan, and build in contingency time for tasks that take longer than expected or last-minute demands from colleagues or supervisors. Setting targets, making plans and monitoring progress are all important. Reviewing where time has gone is also essential: telephone calls can take up much more time than anticipated, either because the conversation goes on longer than expected, or because it can often take several calls to actually make contact with the right person. Reading emails and listening to voice mail can also take much longer than planned for.

Another common problem with prioritizing is that an employee can be asked to do something by several different people:

> Everyone always thinks their work is the most important – how do I know? My solution is to do the most recent one so I never seem to complete a task.

Many dyslexic people do feel that their workload is too great. Discussing this with their line manager and establishing a system for allocation is important.

Implicit in the model of working memory described in Chapter 1 is a need for dyslexic people to undertake the most demanding tasks when their concentration is at its best, and usually when the office perhaps is at its quietest. Difficult tasks will take less time to do if energy levels are high. It is important to try and achieve a task without interruptions. Planning use of

Table 9.1 Organization issues

Organization of time

Skill development	Compensations	Accommodations
• concept of time • estimation of time for task • planning • previewing skills • contingency planning.	• electronic organizers • watches, alarm clocks • diaries, Filofaxes • wall charts, planners • time management software.	• secretarial support • friends, colleagues or supervisors providing reminders.

Organization of work or dealing with work overload

Skill development	Compensations	Accommodations
• planning • prioritization • task analysis • time management • reviewing skills • goal-setting • use of space • filing.	• urgent/important tray • colour coding • review list • filing system.	• extra time with colleague to plan • work prioritized with markers • checking with colleague.

Personal organization

Skill development	Compensations	Accommodations
• daily chores plan • weekly timetables • personal finance skills.	• to do list.	• family member to consult.

Improving concentration and attention

Skill development	Compensations	Accommodations
• orientation to task.	• earplugs or headset to cut noise • use answerphones or voice mail to control phone calls.	• flexitime to check-ins with colleagues • work when quiet • change position of desk • flexitime to work • a screen to block off.

time on a daily basis requires self-discipline. It also requires flexibility if someone is to feel in control. It can help if specific times in the day, such as lunchtime, are set as markers: at these points, a person can review the day's plans, evaluate their progress, consider how events may have changed priorities, and be prepared to make appropriate changes.

Compensations These mainly involve the use of electronic organizers, watches with timers, Filofaxes, diaries, and time management computer software.

Accommodations These can include the use of secretarial support, line managers providing reminders and helping to plan work or assign specific tasks, and colleagues checking how the plan is going.

Organization of work and the workspace

Skill development Ideally, the dyslexic person needs to develop their own system of organization so that it is appropriate to them. Some prefer to be highly organized with everything filed away neatly and tidily in filing cabinets, other people prefer boxes or piles of things.

The workspace is an important consideration as it can be essential both to looking and to feeling in control. Keeping a tidy desk is something that can be important but difficult for a dyslexic person. Further, 'hot desking', where employees are expected to work at the desk available, has become increasingly popular as a way of maximizing the use of office space. This can make the personalization of desks and the development of personal systems difficult. It is, however, best for dyslexic employees to set up their own systems, and to have their own ways of organizing their desks and, if possible, of establishing their position. What has to be done should be made as manageable as possible, and systems should be reviewed frequently to see if minor adjustments should be made.

Compensations These can involve the use of trays marked 'Important' and 'Urgent' on desks, as well as wall charts and pinboards. Some dyslexic people find colour-coding very helpful. Electronic memo devices can be used to provide reminders.

Accommodations To a large extent these just require supervisors to provide the materials and equipment the dyslexic employee needs. Their contribution to finding sensible solutions, as well as enabling the employee to feel it is all right to 'do it their way' is, however, crucial. One solution to hot desking, where allowing an employee to have her own desk was impossible, was to allow her to move between just three desks rather than the 15 in the office.

Reading at work

People only need the reading skills that they *need*, and reading tasks at work vary. Some occupations do not require much reading at all and many dyslexic people have managed with little or no literacy skills. People often have a technical sight vocabulary in order to deal with the demands of their job. Increasing demands for qualifications and the use of technology are placing much greater emphasis on literacy skills. When people once used the telephone it might now be expected that they use email. People who can produce quite complex reports can be flummoxed by a relatively simple email if the content is unfamiliar. The speed of email has meant that people often have less time to deal with the information before a response is required, and this can increase stress and affect an individual's performance. As White (1992) has written:

> In the past it could be successfully argued that higher levels of basic skills would increase one's vocational chances. This may no longer be true. What is needed now and in the future is not simply more of the same basic academic skills that have been taught for 20 years: adults are expected and will be expected to use these basic skills to solve problems and communicate with others; adults are expected and will be expected to listen to others, be able to negotiate, and work as team members.
>
> (White 1992: 456)

Many jobs now involve a large amount of reading – letters, reports, leaflets, minutes of meetings, and so on. Comprehension and getting information from text are the most important skills in the workplace. Reading skill development has been discussed in Chapters 6 and 7 but it is important to note that people can meet the literacy demands of their jobs by specific strategy development and with certain compensations and accommodations made available to them. The PASS strategy referred to earlier – that is, knowing the purpose of the text and the reason for reading it – can be instrumental in enabling a person to improve their skills.

There are occasions when people at work will be asked to read aloud. This might be just a social activity such as reading out an article from a newspaper or the horoscopes, but can also be work-related – reading a letter or a report. Dyslexic people should be able to decline reading aloud without embarrassment. A simple 'I prefer not to read aloud' will often suffice. Alternatively, 'I am sure you will read aloud better than I can because I don't enjoy doing it' will do.

Reading for information

Skill development Scanning, skimming and careful reading, as well as knowing when to apply them, are the most useful skills to develop for reading at work. It is also helpful to build up a subject or technologically specific vocabulary. In addition, for some critical review, analysis and research skills are important.

Compensations These can include having somebody highlight the key points; reading aloud to tape and listening later; asking for an overview or an outline before reading a report. Equally, asking a colleague how they feel about a report before actually reading it can give a great deal of information about the content and therefore make it easier to understand. Using a scanner and Text to Speech software can allow reading by listening.

Accommodations These can include providing someone to highlight key points or read material to tape. Some dyslexic people do not like reading off a computer screen and therefore emails are easier to deal with if they are printed. It can also help everyone in the office if the presentation of written work is considered, some fonts being easier to read, as well as layout and colour improving readability.

Reading complex material

A systematic approach such as applying a critical reading technique to workplace documents can improve comprehension. This involves:

- reflecting on the purpose and the author's viewpoint
- getting an overview from scanning the material for layout, length, organization, tables
- skimming the headings
- reading the abstract, summary, conclusions or recommendations carefully
- recognizing the style of certain sections or the whole document. Some will be descriptive or informative, others evaluative or discursive; some will be persuasive or promotional, others analytical
- carefully reading the important sections – this could be the whole document, which may require highlighting or note-taking of key words to aid memory and comprehension. It may also mean that it should be done in stages, or by taking breaks and allocating time for reflection on the text

- interacting with the text as it is being read can also help. Is the line of argument or reasoning clear? Does it make assumptions? What can be inferred from the text? What can be deduced? How else could it be interpreted? These are all questions that increase comprehension.

Dyslexic people have often not developed such an approach but its application can make a significant difference to their performance.

Specific visual difficulties

Visual difficulties can cause additional problems with reading. They should be investigated by a vision specialist but can be compensated for and accommodated in a number of ways.

Compensations These can include:

- changing the colour of the paper or the computer display background
- using coloured overlays
- changing the font on the computer
- sub-vocalizing to provide auditory feedback
- using aids such as Text to Speech software.

Accommodations These can include:

- providing a reader
- ensuring that instructions are provided in pictorial or diagrammatic form
- ensuring lighting is very good.

Underlying performance at work are affective factors such as confidence and freedom from stress. These issues have been addressed in earlier chapters but they, as well as ways of dealing with them, are summarized in Table 9.2.

Written work in the office

The writing tasks in the office can range from notes and memos to recording telephone messages, taking minutes at meetings, letter writing and report writing. For many dyslexic people, it is the written aspect of their work that causes them the most humiliation. In all written work it is important to know who it is being written for and whether it will be proofread constructively. Some people have extremely helpful and supportive colleagues or line managers who will look over work and make constructive suggestions; others

Table 9.2 Performance issues

Stress

Skill development	Compensations	Accommodations
relaxation techniques identifying sources.	increased technological support.	take breaks extra time have job coach or mentor decrease work load extra supervision.

Problems with memory

Skill development	Compensations	Accommodations
learn memory strategies, e.g. mind-mapping, note-taking.	put on tape use Dictaphone.	instructions to be written down.

Confidence

Skill development	Compensations	Accommodations
set own goals review performance self talk.	list of positive statements on walls.	review with supervision mentor/coach.

have to cope with managers who are overly critical. The dyslexic person needs to recognize that this may be happening.

Knowing to whom the written work is going is important: if writing memos and emails to a colleague, then a casual and informal style is acceptable. The appropriate style needs to be chosen for the task. In general, most written tasks should be clear, structured and precise – often bullet points will suffice. All written work should be planned. This involves knowing the nature of the communication, its purpose, gathering the ideas and information, ordering and linking them and then writing the document. A simple 'who, what, when, where, why and how' approach can clarify the ideas. Using pro formas for memos and emails can help but they all require the date, name of writer and recipient, and the subject matter. Writing business letters requires even more careful planning and it is important to try and adopt the organizational format and language. Any letter to be sent out should of course be proofread, ideally by somebody else as this is good practice for everyone.

Record-keeping

Many jobs now require that records of all activities be kept, including phone calls made or visits carried out. Developing pro formas to provide a structure for the details is a solution and can speed up the process. The more the format is planned the easier it is for dyslexic people to manage the information, and they will be more efficient in producing a written report when this is required.

Report writing

Report writing is a skill that can be learned and developed. Reports can be lengthy and complex, so their production is daunting. It is essential, therefore, that they are made manageable by being broken into stages. Reports are structured and have a specific purpose so planning can be easier. They usually contain an introduction, main body, conclusion and/or recommendation, and appendices. They may have additional sections such as a background section, a financial section, or a research and results section. The precise format should be discussed with the line manager so that it is known exactly what is required of the report. Nearly all reports are drafted: the first draft can often be information gathering and an exploration of ideas, the end result being quite different. Often, several people will collaborate on a report: this can cause difficulties for dyslexic people as they sometimes perceive the revision of a draft as criticism when it might not be. The editing process can be improved by the use of a checklist which includes questions such as:

- Are the introduction and conclusion appropriate?
- Is each section clear in its aim and expression?
- Is the style correct and not repetitive?
- Is there enough material or evidence?
- Are the important sections and the argument easy to follow?

It is not unusual for dyslexic people to have planning strategies for dealing with written work. Graduates, for example, are used to writing essays. Nevertheless, when they move on to work, they do not always apply the skills they possess to new tasks. The former student whose work is shown in Chapter 5 was required to produce a proposal for a community arts project. It was suggested he use the visual techniques he had developed for essay writing. His first attempt is shown in Figure 9.1.

He was encouraged to make the plan more graphic and he eventually produced the drawing shown in Figure 9.2, which then enabled him to produce the report 'Ways forward' shown in Figure 9.3.

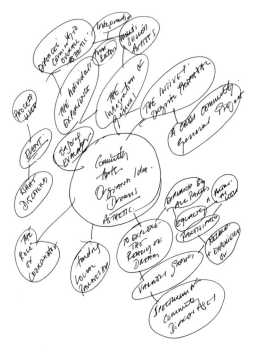

Figure 9.1 First mind map of Community Arts Project.

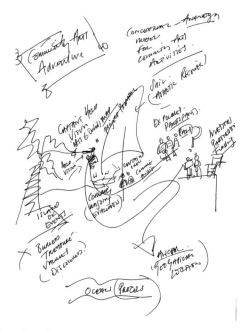

Figure 9.2 Visual plan of project concept.

Ways forward

It was felt by most groups that the project and the working process was very effective and productive for both the clients involved and also the employees. Both the concept and the employment of art forms within particular settings was experienced as beneficial, in that it allowed people to find value in their own artwork as well as working collaboratively in group work.

One of the main positive areas of growth was in the appreciation of participants who, for the first time for many, were engaged in activities which allowed them to experience themselves in a new way and also be perceived by others in a new light.

It is important here to realize the potential of the arts within any structure as another way of accessing people and open possibilities, awakening abilities that previously remained dormant. There were, however, some areas in which participants felt they could have progressed further and these should be taken into account in future projects. The primary one was time. Many felt there was insufficient time and this affected development. Another was the relationship between staff and artists, and communication of ideas and clear planning for the event. Many participants felt they would have benefited greatly if their employers were more included within the working process of the artists, and stated that in future projects training for the employees would be an essential part of the process.

It is recommended that the following areas be addressed for future projects:

Time: sufficient time is given to allow the on-going development of the project, taking into account the clients' needs.

Training: staff would benefit from workshops and training in the initial stages, in order to work alongside the artists and develop structures that can guarantee on-going projects if so desired.

Criteria: from the onset it is important that working expectations and concept ideas are clearly communicated to all involved in projects of this type. That all participants are allowed to voice their opinions and also are given an arena where their ideas are valued. Also, that the artists themselves are made aware of the needs of settings in which they may work.

Figure 9.3 Report.

Skill development Each occupation is likely to have a different format or procedure for report writing. General principles of writing in bullet points, keeping the sentences short and simple, and using summaries, will however always be applicable. Being able to extract the main idea and express it lucidly and cogently is a skill that also needs to be developed, as are the abilities to gather and sift information, identify specific issues, edit, and structure and plan. Dyslexic people should be encouraged to develop an awareness of their own style, the emphasis being on communication, and adapt it as necessary to the style required.

Compensations These involve the use of technology, including planning software, as well as having standard formats and pro formas.

Accommodations These involve providing the appropriate secretarial support and/or delegation of the task. Many dyslexic people are extremely good at coming up with ideas but are less good at recording them. One man, working for a media company, said that his department would always come to him for the ideas to go into a report but they sent him to somebody to dictate them to, since if they waited for him to write it down, he would miss every deadline.

Numeracy

Most occupations involve numeracy skills of some kind, even if this just relates to how much one earns and understanding a pay slip. The complexity of numeracy tasks will vary according to the demands of the job, for example:

> ... salespeople and cashiers need to know how to give correct change to buyers, total sales for the day and balance the cash drawer with receipts. A person who works for a delivery service must be very skilful at knowing addresses, managing time, and maintaining a log.
>
> (Patton et al. 1997: 179)

As indicated in Chapters 2 and 6, dyslexic people do not usually have conceptual problems with numeracy. Readers should refer to the section on improving quantitative literacy in Chapter 6 as the suggestions made there are relevant to the workplace, but some of these are reiterated here.

Skill development There are those who have very poor backgrounds in maths and will need to go over the basics but, essentially, helping a dyslexic person with maths problems should ensure that (a) they understand the language, and (b) they have strategies for dealing with:

- symbols
- sequences
- calculations.

Maintaining the place when dealing with series of numbers can often be a problem, and there is a need to use a guide, such as a ruler. The multisensory principle could be adopted and this includes subvocalization when dealing with symbols and numbers.

Compensations These can include very basic strategies, such as using fingers, but much will be resolved by the efficient use of an electronic calculator. When possible, a calculator that has a voice-chip in it, so that auditory feedback is provided, can be particularly useful.

Accommodations These can include delegation and reducing the demands in this regard, and relying on an accountant.

Proofreading and checking

It is often difficult for dyslexic people to check their own work. Proofreading one's own work is difficult because one anticipates what should be, rather than what actually is, written.

Skill development Structured approaches to proofreading can include COPS – checking Capitalization of letters, examining the Overall appearance, Punctuation, checking Spelling (Schumaker et al. 1981). Other skills can include keeping a list of errors one consistently makes, as well as reading from right to left when checking for spellings, to prevent anticipation. It can often be best to leave proofreading till well after the document has been prepared, certainly at a time when one is not tired.

Compensations Sometimes proofreading work can be more effective if the font on the computer is changed for the individual so that it looks like a new report. Equally, changing the colour on the background can make proofreading easier. Reading the letter or document into Speech to Text software so that proofreading can be undertaken by listening through Text to Speech software. Using grammar checks can also be helpful, but some knowledge of grammatical structure is required.

Accommodations The simplest accommodation is to have someone else proofread one's work.

Listening skills at work

Good listening skills are an essential part of success at work. Remembering instructions, coping with telephone calls, minutes of meetings and, indeed, meetings themselves require effective listening skills. Hearing what is being said, and remembering it at the same time, places demands on dyslexic people and often requires some note-taking. It is important for dyslexics to think about what they are about to listen to. If, for example, it is a list of instructions, then they perhaps need to use some concrete aid such as their fingers, noting how many things they have to remember; if it is a telephone call, then a notepad and pen will help; taking minutes in a meeting demands other strategies, as does listening to information given at meetings and presentations.

Listening and recording telephone messages can present dyslexic people with many difficulties as they often rely on visual clues to help them understand what is being said. Unfamiliar voices at the end of an anonymous telephone can create a panic situation for a dyslexic person. Not being able to hear or process the information clearly may be assumed by a dyslexic person to be his or her own fault rather than that of the person speaking. Dyslexics need to develop the confidence to ask people to slow down or repeat what has just been said. If necessary, they can blame the crackly telephone line or distractions in the office. If a major part of the job is concerned with telephone messages, pro formas can be developed to prompt the specific information that might arise during a phone call, e.g. name of caller, time of call, aim of call, points 1, 2, 3, 4 and so on, action to be taken, etc., and how urgent or important the message is.

Skill development Effective listening and remembering for dyslexics depends on how much they can control the flow of information. When taking instructions or telephone messages they need to develop the skill of being able to slow down the rate at which information is being given. If, for example, it is an address or telephone number then they need to be able to say, 'Could you repeat that, or start with the 0207 ...', which will automatically slow the speaker down. Instructions for work tasks can be repeated back. Learning to listen for signal words – the obvious ones being 'one', 'two' and 'three' – is also helpful. It is nearly always essential for the dyslexic person to make some form of note to help with the recall of the information that has just been given. A list of instructions demands chronological note-taking which can be in words or pictures.

Compensations The simplest compensation involves the use of a tape recorder or electronic memo device.

Accommodations These can include the provision of information visually, as well as written instructions.

Taking notes or minutes

Taking notes or minutes can be a particularly difficult skill for a dyslexic person as it places a heavy load on working memory.

Skill development In general, dyslexic people should adopt a minimalist approach to this activity, focusing on listening. Too many people take notes at the expense of 'noting'. Similar strategies can include the use of mind-maps, drawing pictures, noting key points and using abbreviations. It is first important to identify the purpose of taking notes, using the agenda to provide a structure.

Compensations These can include using a tape recorder as a back-up to minimalist strategy, as well as using a laptop computer in lecture/training sessions.

Accommodations These should include relying on other people's notes, being provided with a note-taker and ensuring that employees are given handouts.

Meetings

Meetings require one to listen to what is going on and to formulate ideas and arguments during the course of the meeting, and then to remember what has been said and what actions are to be taken: this can be a nightmare for some dyslexic people.

Skill development Coping with meetings, presentations and training courses can be made easier by using systematic approaches, including PQLR – tuning in, questioning, listening and reviewing. That is, the participant tries to identify the position the speaker will be taking and listens for evidence of this; generates questions about the topic at the end of the session or meeting; and mentally reviews the material to ensure that important points are remembered. Dyslexic people should seek clarification, use cross-questioning and seek an overview. It is important for them to be aware of how good they are at listening and how often they need to seek clarification. With different people they will need to seek different levels of clarification. They also need to have a list of phrases or ways of asking for clarification or repetition without causing irritation. Often it can be useful to take in projections or predictions of what the meeting might cover. Some people find it extremely useful to draw a map of where other individuals are sitting at the meeting, and have the information of the meeting on the place settings.

Compensations These can involve taking a tape recorder to the meeting, presentation or training session, to allow the person to listen to and control the information more readily.

Accommodations These can include providing overviews or diagrams, allowing recording, encouraging discussions and questions. It is important for the dyslexic person to know following a meeting what is remembered and where there are gaps, so that they can ask specific questions. They do need to be reassured that it is all right to acknowledge that there is a gap. No one takes in all the information in a meeting.

The way in which skill development, compensations and accommodations can be applied to a variety of work-related tasks is summarized in Table 9.3.

Working in a team

Working in a team can either cause a dyslexic person a great deal of difficulty or, conversely, can be a very positive experience. In a good team, a dyslexic person may be allowed to display strengths, including presentation and speaking skills, as well as creative and problem-solving abilities. Teamwork can be good for a dyslexic person as it can enable them to focus on their talents while other people deal with the areas that present them with difficulty. Working in a team can, however, involve having to display areas of weakness to colleagues who may be unaware of the difficulties with written language. If the dyslexic person is unable to give an explanation, any lack of performance may be misconstrued, which can undermine the performance of the team in general as well as the dyslexic individual's confidence. Some dyslexic people find working with other people extremely difficult because they like to have control over their own work routines. It is for this reason that self-employment is sometimes a good option for dyslexics, provided they create an infrastructure which helps them deal with tasks they find difficult.

Interviews

Although some dyslexic people are good at expressing themselves verbally, because of their information-processing difficulty interviews can be especially stressful. Their lack of confidence can undermine the way they present themselves and, at times, exacerbate their difficulties in areas such as

Table 9.3 Work skills

	Skill development	Compensations	Accommodations
Telephone work	listening skills note-taking using pro formas.	use Dictaphone, answerphone, voice mail.	ask someone else.
Filing	sequencing skills verbal reinforcement visual scanning.	colour-coding highlighters technology.	administrative support.
Organized desk	filing daily organization goal planning use of space.	in/out trays urgent or important trays laptop.	secretary or PA.
Following instructions	listening skills visualization skills notes.	on tape or diagram.	broken into small sections.
Taking minutes	listening skills memory strategies note-taking.	using pro formas Dictaphone.	someone else to do it.
Meetings	preview meetings prediction of outcome note-taking memory strategies/place.	Dictaphone.	collaborate with others.
Presentations	speaking skills memory aids/mind- mapping key notes.	role rehearsal video.	presentation software presentation training.
Report writing	purpose planning drafting editing.	software pro formas Dictaphone.	collaborate with others dictate to another.

word-finding and clarity of expression. It is important for a dyslexic person to be able to answer the following questions about the job they are being interviewed for:

- What is the job description?
- What are the task demands?
- What do I have to do?
- What skills do I have?
- What skills do I need to develop?
- Can I transfer any skills from my previous experiences, either at work or home?
- What are the potential difficulties?
- What type of supervision and support systems are there?

At the interview it is important to try and 'get a feel' for the job and address the question 'Is this job good enough for me?'.

The issues of disclosure must be considered and this is raised again in Chapter 10. Dyslexic people do need to consider how they might answer some of the following questions:

- What does dyslexia mean?
- How exactly does it affect you?
- What problems will it present you in this job?
- What would you need to help solve these problems?
- How do you work best?
- Will being dyslexic interfere with your output?
- If we need to train you, how do you learn best?
- Can you work well in a team?
- Can you be given a lead role in a team?
- Why should I employ you when I can hire another person who does not have any difficulties?
- What are you good at?

It can be helpful for dyslexic people to role-play an interview situation or to rehearse what they are going to say, and some people feel that visualization techniques can help them deal with a stressful situation. It can be useful, although somewhat painful, to have feedback on why the interview was not a success.

A note on the use of technology

There is no doubt that the use of technology has made an enormous difference to the lives of dyslexic people. It does, however, demand that people develop new skills, including typing, as well as the appropriate use of hardware and software. There has also been a reduction in the availability of secretarial support; those who have been able to rely on this are left vulnerable and exposed once they are responsible for all their own written work. Nevertheless, there is a wide range of technological aids available that many dyslexic people find useful including Speech to Text and Text to Speech software, and time management, planning and organization packages. Many employers are happy to provide technological aids as a way of making adjustments, allowing the dyslexic person to compensate. This can be supported by the Employment Service, an Assessment of Need being conducted to determine suitable provision. Perhaps the most important aspect, however, is ensuring that appropriate training in the use of technology is provided. An example of a workplace assessment report follows.

A sample workplace evaluation report

Introduction

G is an Executive Officer in the Civil Service and has an honours degree in Marketing. He was diagnosed as dyslexic during the first year of his university degree. He has been in his post in a government department for 18 months. He has found the job demanding and there are concerns about his performance at work. G and his line managers are aware that some of his difficulties are a result of being dyslexic.

Aims of the evaluation

- To assess what aspects of G's work are affected by his being dyslexic and what support he requires
- To assess the skills G needs to develop to work more effectively
- To suggest what compensations can be provided in the form of technological aids to help him
- To recommend what accommodations could be made.

Job description

G's job involves:

* the development and supply of a data base
* coordination and recruitment of companies
* management of a small team consisting of two administrative staff.

Work objectives

G's work objectives include:

* organizing the administrative staff files
* responding to general inquiries
* drafting correspondence
* inputting on the data base
* liaising with and briefing travel officers
* organizing training and development for his staff.

Areas of difficulty

Many aspects of the job make demands on G's literacy skills. Much of his work is research-based, involving finding out how things have been done in the past and what should be done now. G would find this work harder and take longer than others as reading is more difficult for him. In addition, he would research more widely than others, or more than might be necessary, as he needs to understand the 'whole picture' to be able to abstract the relevant information. G reported that he often asked other people for their views so that he could build up the picture more quickly.

G also has to write letters, memos, emails, draft reports, etc. and this is harder for him. He has had trouble meeting deadlines.

G is experiencing difficulty with inputting of data on the data base. He is not familiar with this yet and, at present, finds it somewhat overwhelming.

G is a person who likes a high level of organization and he has to work hard to achieve this. He is experiencing problems at present organizing his work, the work of his team, and all the new information that has to be processed when beginning a new job.

Like many dyslexic people, G has some trouble with verbal communication. He has been unable to communicate his needs effectively to his line managers, and communication with his team has been difficult.

G's difficulties at work have been exacerbated by the stress that has accumulated in response to the problems he has experienced.

Recommendations and skill development

- G needs to develop his understanding of his dyslexia and how it affects him at work. Transitions always place greater demands on dyslexic people than others. The change in environment, people, procedures and general understanding is sometimes overwhelming initially. For S the situation has been made more complicated by a lack of understanding of what the job really involves. He knows his skills lie in marketing but there are other aspects of his job that are hard for him.
- G needs to develop a better understanding of his abilities and skills so he can transfer them to his work. For example, he used mind-mapping techniques effectively at university and would find this a useful strategy when organizing information at work.
- G would benefit from developing his task analysis and organizational skills to help him balance the varying elements of his job.
- G would benefit from learning efficient reading strategies so that he can extract information from text more quickly. He also needs to learn planning strategies to help him draft written work more quickly.

Compensations

The compensations that will enable G to work more effectively include the use of technological aids. I have suggested the following:

- a desktop computer that has sufficient memory to run voice-activated software.
- a colour printer, as it will enable him to code and highlight key information.
- a scanner with OCR software that will allow G to input material into his computer directly and also enable him to read by listening.

Software

- voice recognition software that will enable a direct match between G's verbal skills and his written work
- a mobile microphone that will link directly to his computer so that he can record meetings. He then has an aide-mémoire and this will also enable him to take minutes more effectively
- 'textHELP! Read and Write' to help him check the spelling and grammar of his work
- 'Inspiration Idea Organizer' to help him plan and draft his work
- CD-ROM dictionary.

Other hardware

- Hand-held English Talking Dictionary/Thesaurus. This will help G with vocabulary and spellchecking.

There was some discussion as to whether G would benefit from a laptop computer. This would be an advantage, in that he would be able to choose to work at home if necessary. However, it does mean that he may then feel that he has to work at home, and this is not what his managers would wish as it may increase the pressure on him.

Training

- To enable G to make the best use of the technology, I recommend that he has three days' computer training at his office which will familiarize him with the speech to text software.
- G would also benefit from six sessions of computer training at the Centre to consolidate this and help him make the best use of the other software.

Accommodations

The accommodations that could be made to help G include:

- temporarily prioritizing his work and relieving him of some of the more difficult aspects. This would allow him to feel less pressurized and restore his confidence
- allowing him to work in a quiet environment, perhaps another office, when he has work that demands a lot of concentration
- providing him with a mentor with whom he can discuss any problems
- G learns best through experience – when asking him to do new work, providing him with an example to work from or a pro forma will help. He should then be able to adapt this to suit his way of working.

Conclusion

G does have many skills and he is determined and hard working. When he is confident, his people skills are good.

G has found the transition to his present job very hard and, at times, overwhelming. Nevertheless, with the appropriate training and technological support, as well as greater understanding all round, his performance should improve.

A dyslexic's perspective

Some of the best advice of course can come from dyslexic people themselves, especially those involved in management. One of our former clients is a Human Resources Manager and made the following suggestions:

- Extract information easily from any textbook, read intros and summaries/conclusions first, scan book looking at headings and major words, diagrams and pictures, do not necessarily read the whole book but dip in and out or read the best way for you.
- Overlearn words which are central to the subjects/profession in which you find yourself.
- Learn to have a core number of words that you use and are able to spell without spellchecker but also be prepared to slowly expand this vocabulary over time.
- Do not get embarrassed when others correct your pronunciation (I just say oh I'm not very good with foreign names and words).
- Plan all written work – beginning, middle and end and then the main headings in each of these sections.
- e-mail (I hate to write long ones – but had to work for a boss who only wanted e-mail) – write them as if you were talking to the person verbally and fairly informally but not too familiar.
- Learn the limitations of your memory – if someone gives you a tel number over the phone, when they get to the 2/3 digit – interrupt and stop them by repeating those digits and at the same time write them down. This can also be done for any name or difficult word.
- Learn where you make mistakes and be particularly careful in these areas – mine are transposing letters and numbers and the sound between 'm' and 'n'.
- During college and work I've used various technological aids:
  - computer – spellchecker, rewriting notes, e-mail and electronic presentations and diaries with reminders
  - Dictaphone for all lectures, if possible keep the main lectures until exams and replay them at revision – making it multisensory
  - voicemail – able to repeat messages
  - videos
  - walkie phone.
- Studying/working for short periods of time with a very short break, this facilitates retention of work hence multitasking type jobs are best as there are always different things to do for approximately 20 minutes each.
- Found someone during my first week at college who was prepared to let me photocopy their notes from the course once a week – be careful who you choose – this was great, as before I was always missing the lecture as I was trying to write notes which turned out to be very bad and I missed the main point of lecture. Give the person a present at the end for letting you have their notes.
- Redo your own notes from other persons and Dictaphone, at the same time write an index card for each lecture and fit main points on the index card – go

through these regularly and in particular very useful for revision.

- Never be afraid to ask questions - the others probably don't understand it either.
- Learn how to be prepared to try things for yourself and when to ask for help/advice.
- I prefer linear notes/brainstorming to mind-maps and I love flipcharts and marker pens.
- During my revision for my exams my flat was covered in flipchart paper with the main topics again, favourite places were in front of the toilet, kitchen walls, above the TV and across from the bed - it also helped to move them around every so often and use different colours and pictures.
- I've also found it good to analyse what I find useful and what is not working. An example of this was the use of an audiotypist. As I have very good verbal skills it was an obvious choice - but in a modern working environment and the fact that there are very few administrators and that everyone does their own e-mail and typing - this has not been possible and may never be in my working life.
- Putting a lot of effort into improving perceiving, understanding and remembering as well as an interest in how you and others around you operate.
- Use examples as much as possible and analogues.
- Any change involves - undoing change, make change, stabilize change.
- I'm a list person and could not live without my Filofax with diary, notes, to do list and addresses in it.
- Another invaluable aid is my Birthday calendar (available in Holland) or use a blank calendar which does not have days just has number of the month - it is much more visual than a Birthday book.
- I love bullet points and lists, especially in business writing.
- Always have a pen and paper by the phone.
- Post-Its, great invention.
- Large A3 blotter on my work desk which acts for all voicemail messages and a to do list and when you have filled page it can be put in the back and referred to at a later date if needed.
- Dish with all unpaid bills and things I want from post or to do - look through it once a week.
- Use other people at work (i.e. someone else takes the minutes - do not ever volunteer for this job or let anyone else volunteer you, when reading out list of names - get other person to do it).
- Be a pragmatist as the best way to remember is to do something - therefore try and learn by doing this.
- Any task, I find it easier to break it into bits and I always reward myself when I achieve a particularly difficult bit.
- I sometimes hear things wrong - so by summarizing back to the person what they have said it confirms the understanding - I tend to only do this when the information is very important.
- For my lecture notes or work files - I used dividers for each section and a list of contents at the beginning, which was updated each time a new section is added.
- I always put things in a file with the most recent at the back - so I always know how the files are ordered in date.

- I'm an evening person – so learn to do the easy tasks in the morning and the harder ones between 2pm – 5.30pm. When doing recruitment I never did an interview before 10am – it would not be fair on the candidate!!!
- Due to better experience I would not own up to being Dyslexic to anyone I did not know (including employer to be under Disability Act). This is due to the fact that during a two month assignment at which I owned up to being Dyslexic at the beginning I was discriminated against by an employer even though they were not practising HR best practice. It is better to prove you can do the job and then drop in conversation – after probationary period and when you are respected – that you have a problem with that as you are slightly dyslexic – make a joke of it and then they are not sure if you are being serious or not.

It has been great in the past four years to be aware and become more aware of my difficulties and make a conscious decision to create/develop strategies to overcome them and gain promotion within my profession.

Training course outline

Following the kind of evaluation described above a dyslexic person can embark on a course of training. The programme should be planned with the client, in discussion with their manager/supervisor, but should cover most of the following areas.

Initial consultation

This involves goal-setting. Long-term goals are discussed and short-term aims are planned. Particular problems are raised and possible ways of solving them are considered. How the experience and the skills the person has can be built upon, and the compensations and accommodations that are available, are also considered.

Personal development modules

Understanding dyslexia This module focuses on the nature of dyslexic people's difficulties: how they affect them now, how they have affected them in the past, and what solutions they have found to help them. Having some understanding and an explanation for their difficulties helps dyslexic people feel in control, and can give them confidence.

Self-advocacy Understanding their skills and abilities, their thinking skills, as well as their learning and working style, enables dyslexic people to utilize their strengths more effectively. It is important they know how to explain the nature of the difficulties they have, what problems they encounter, and the solutions that they can offer. It is also important that they know how to promote their abilities.

Skill development modules

Organizational skills These skills underpin success. Dyslexic people have to work hard at this as it is not automatic. This module includes:

- organization of time – developing the awareness of time, the effective use of time, prioritizing, goal-setting
- organization of work – setting up an appropriate filing system, and record-keeping
- personal organization – organization at home, coping with chores, and personal issues such as health, etc.

Task analysis and metacognitive skills Analysing a task so they recognize its components enables dyslexic people to match their skills to the task with the right strategy. It enables them to improve their performance by developing previewing, monitoring and reviewing skills. It helps to focus concentration.

Memory skills Understanding what memory is, how an individual remembers best, and developing visual and auditory memory skills, enables a person to feel more in control. A range of strategies such as visualization, mnemonics and memory systems are looked at. The three principles that aid memory – making things manageable, multisensory skills, and making use of memory aids, are discussed.

Specific work training skills This module looks at the job description, the task demands of the job, and developing specific skills, e.g. filing, recording information, coping with meetings, telephone skills, interview skills, presentation skills, working in a team, remembering instructions. It considers transferable skills.

Basic literacy skills This module works on developing basic literacy skills. It also focuses on the skills for daily living, e.g. form-filling, reading timetables.

Efficient reading strategies This module aims to develop the client's reading skills to enable him or her to extract information more quickly from text. Skimming, scanning and finding the main idea are covered. It can also cover critical and analytical reading. It is based on the four levels of reading – Functional, Vocational,Technical and Professional.

Writing skills This module includes understanding the nature of the task, writing with a purpose, looking at different styles of writing (descriptive, reports, memos, use of bullet points, presentations), planning and editing written work, and proofreading.

Spelling, punctuation and grammar This is based on a diagnostic assessment with the focus being largely on learning strategies for specific, personal or technical spellings required by the individual. Some spelling rule instruction will be included.

Social skills This module covers effective communication skills, including listening skills, developing concentration, awareness, non-verbal communication, appropriate responses, controlling anger and frustration, and working in a team.

Coping strategies The module explores a range of strategies which can be used to manage stress in the workplace. It includes identifying the source, relaxation techniques, dealing with motivation, coping with panic and with change.

Numeracy The first step is to establish whether the problem is conceptual or procedural, and the implications for training. Training focuses on specific areas, with practical applications of maths.

The programme should be formulated as a personal development plan and a suggested format is set out in Figure 9.4.

	Areas of potential difficulty for employment
Name	
Address	Training
Educational attainments	Attitudes to learning
History	Knowledge of abilities/skills/style

Employment details	Possible job options
	    Job title:
	    Job context:
	    Job description:

Present job	1. 2. 3.
Personal profile	Key skills required
Aptitudes	Skills to develop Compensations Accommodations
Interests	
Social skills	Training considerations
Personality characteristics	Training options
Transferable skills	Recommendations
Other factors (e.g. family considerations)	Objectives
Areas of strength	Action
Level of literacy	Outcome

Figure 9.4 Personal development plan: employment

Case study H

Reason for referral

H was an administrative assistant in the Civil Service. She was referred by her employer. There were queries about her performance and attitude. She was being threatened with dismissal. She had recently been assessed as dyslexic.

Education history

H's schooling had been interrupted. She had always experienced difficulty with reading and writing and had often been in trouble. She left school at 16 with no qualifications.

Employment history

H worked as a hairdresser for four years and then decided to get a job in the Civil Service because she wanted to get a mortgage. She had spent six months struggling to keep up with the demands of the job and had already been transferred from another department because of a 'personality' clash.

Assessment results

H's diagnostic assessment revealed that she was of at least average ability. Her reading skills were at the Vocational level. Her spelling was well below average; her handwriting was weak. Her computer skills were satisfactory.

Strengths

H had good spoken language skills and was very determined. She had good visual skills.

Areas of difficulty

H was very angry about being dyslexic. She often misunderstood instructions. Her social skills were good but she often misread situations. Her problems at work included time-keeping, work organization, sequencing, filing and writing memos.

Goals

To keep her job and be promoted. To develop her literacy skills and complete a Business Studies Course.

Programme

Twenty week course, one hour per week.

Personal development

- To understand dyslexia and how it affected her
- To increase her awareness of her skills in order to improve her self-confidence
- To improve her interpersonal skills.

Skill development

Spelling

Skill development Basic spelling course; strategies; mnemonics; visual imagery.
Compensations Handheld spellchecker.
Accommodations Proofreader.

Memory

Skill development Development of visual skills; linking; association semantics.
Compensations Lists; diary.
Accommodations Supervisor or colleague to check.

Organization of time

Skill development Estimation of timed exercises; planning a day.
Compensations Diary; clock on desk; whiteboard on office wall.
Accommodations Flexitime; prioritization of work.

Organization of work

Skill development Sequencing skills.
Compensations Colour-coding; filing system.

Writing

Skill development Memos; drafts; purpose/format; technology.
Compensations Spellchecker.

Accommodations Proofreader.

H completed the course and was finally promoted. Her skills improved significantly.

H was then sent by a new line manager to the Access to Work scheme. She was assessed again by a psychologist who indicated in his report to her employers that her literacy skills were weak and her intelligence very low. This report destroyed H; all her previous defensive/aggressive behaviour returned. After a period of difficult communication, she asked a dyslexia consultant to visit her office and explain the report to her employers. In fact H was able to explain the nature of her difficulties and her needs so effectively that her employers reinstated her.

H then had a further period of skill development training. Her reading skills improved to the Professional level and her writing skills to the Technical level.

Outcome

H completed a two year Business Studies course and now runs her own business very successfully.

Case study J

Reason for referral

J came to the Centre on her own initiative. She was experiencing significant difficulty in her job as an interior designer overseas. She had known throughout school that she had some type of problem but it had never been formally identified and she now wished to know what it was that was causing her problems at work. She was quite anxious at the beginning of her course and her self-esteem and self-confidence were extremely low. An assessment revealed that she was dyslexic.

Background information

J had not particularly enjoyed school. Her written language skills had always been weak and, despite working hard, she did not produce work she felt pleased with. Her handwriting was 'terrible'. However, she did enjoy art. She left school with GCSEs in Art and Design, and low passes in most of her other subjects. She did a foundation course at a College of Art where she could continue to develop her artistic talents.

Assessment

J's assessment revealed that she was of above average ability with a significant weakness in her working memory. Her Coding score was particularly low. She had strengths in both verbal and non-verbal areas. Her literacy skills were weak – her reading comprehension was low, her spelling was erratic and she produced written work slowly. She also reported having difficulty with handwriting, proofreading, organizing her work, and remembering things.

Goals

J's goal was to develop the specific skills she needed to enable her to do her job more effectively.

Programme plan

J followed a six session course over three weeks. The first part focused on developing her understanding of dyslexia and why she experienced these problems. It also explored the nature of her difficulties so she could avoid certain situations. This was particularly important as she was having difficulty with her manager. The second part of her course looked at the organization of her work, prioritization, time management, proofreading, and checking reference codes and numbers. J's skills lay in her ability to use pattern, shape, design and colour. It was these skills which were tapped in helping her with her work. For example, her organization became highly colour-coded, her time management, planning and prioritization skills were developed through the use of mind-mapping. Checking reference numbers and codes were also done through colour and looking at the pattern. Her problem with handwriting was addressed through practice and using a variety of pens.

Outcome

On finishing the course, J had a far greater understanding of how to explain her skills and avoid focusing on her weaknesses. She had experimented with various pens and found one which made a significant difference to her handwriting. She had also recognized the importance of improving her word-processing skills. She had designed and set up her own system of filing and was using colour-coding, indexes and wall lists. She also armed herself with a list of contingency phrases and plans to give herself time to explain herself or formulate her thoughts whilst presenting ideas.

In the long term, there had been a significant improvement in her relationship with her boss. J was working more efficiently and was applying for a more senior position.

Summary

- Dyslexic people can be successful in most, if not all occupations. This is, however, reliant on a combination of the support they receive at work as well as their own personal development.
- A whole-organization approach to supporting dyslexic people can be the most effective way of ensuring that they are able to capitalize on their talents.
- The problems they experience with literacy can continue to undermine the performance of dyslexics at work, but difficulties in organization, time management and coping with the work environment can also contribute to them performing less well then expected.
- There is a wide range of skills and compensations dyslexic people can develop which will enhance their performance.
- Relatively simple and cost-effective adjustments can be made for dyslexic people and these ensure that they are able to fulfil their potential.

Chapter 10
Advocacy

This chapter focuses on the empowerment of dyslexic people and the way in which this is fostered through the legislative framework, specifically the Disability Discrimination Act 1995. The role of advocacy and self-advocacy groups is also described.

Introduction

The preceding chapters have described the interventions which can enable dyslexic people to become successful. The underlying philosophy of this book is empowerment, which has been defined as a 'process of personal consciousness raising, resulting in an ability to solve one's own problems' (Cox 1991). In particular, the emphasis has been on self-empowerment, which is fostering the 'process of becoming increasingly more in control of oneself and one's life, and thus increasingly more independent' (Fenton and Hughes 1989). Correct interventions should facilitate this process. Empowerment is also fostered through advocacy, especially self-advocacy:

> Advocacy is the representation of the views, feelings and interests of one person or group of people by another individual or organisation. Self-advocacy is the action of a person on their own behalf without the intervention of another. The shift in focus from advocacy to self-advocacy is a natural extension of the process of empowerment.
>
> (Garner and Sandow 1995)

The past 20 years have seen an increased interest in advocacy and self-advocacy. To some extent this is a response to the policies of governments which have promoted individualism and an ethic which values things, including people, on the basis of how they are of benefit to others and/or how much they cost. The rights of the individual have been promoted at the expense of the community (Wolfensberger 1994).

Advocacy for dyslexic people in the UK has been best represented by the work of organizations such as the British Dyslexia Association. Self-advocacy is reflected in the work of adult support groups. The former have argued for help, support and equal opportunities. The latter have argued for rights and equity. Essential to the improvement of provision for dyslexic adults are the three 'U's. That is:

- Understanding – by parents and partners
- Understanding – by teachers/tutors and employers
- Understanding – dyslexic people's self-understanding.

Organizations advocating in the interests of dyslexic people have been quite effective in promoting the first two, but without allowing for self-advocacy, they can find that the very people they are trying to help become aggressive towards them. At the same time self-advocacy needs to be based in self-understanding and empathy – otherwise those seeking their rights and greater equity can alienate those who are trying to help them. It should be recognized that rather than there being 'experts in dyslexia', there is a variety of people who have an expertise. There are, for example, professionals who know how to diagnose, advise and train dyslexic people. Dyslexic individuals, however, do have their own views and an understanding based on their personal experience. The way forward is therefore to ensure that there is partnership between advocates, including professionals, and those engaging in self-advocacy.

Advocacy and self-advocacy are also fostered by legislation. The legislative framework can underpin rights, equity and equal opportunities. The policy and practices of government departments will foster appropriate help and support.

The legislative framework

In general terms the rights of dyslexic people are supported by the European Human Rights Act 1998. Article 14, 'Prohibition of discrimination', states:

> . . . the enjoyment of the rights and freedoms set forth in this convention shall be secured without discrimination on any grounds, such as sex, race, colour, language, religion or other opinion, national or social origin, association with a national minority, property, birth or other status.

More specific provision is made under the terms of the Disability Discrimination Act 1995. Section I of the Act defines 'disabled person' as a person with 'a physical or mental impairment which has a substantial and long-term adverse effect on his ability to carry out normal day-to-day activity'. Dyslexia is not listed as a disability but can be covered under the heading of 'memory or ability to concentrate, learn or understand'. There is, however, an illustrative example in the Code of Practice which refers to dyslexia as a specific case of a disability. The Act recommends that account should be taken of the person's ability to remember, organize his or her thoughts, plan a course of action and execute it or take in new knowledge. This includes considering whether the person learns to do things more slowly than is normal.

In some ways this is more satisfactory than the use of labels. However, concern has been expressed at the parameters recommended by the legislators. The examples given are that it would be reasonable to regard as a substantial effect:

* persistent inability to remember the names of familiar people such as family or friends
* inability to adapt to minor change in work routine.

It would not be reasonable to regard as a substantial effect:

* occasionally forgetting the name of a familiar person such as a work colleague
* inability to concentrate on a task requiring application over several hours
* inability to fill in a long, detailed technical document without assistance
* inability to read at speed under pressure.

The DDA and employment

Registration as disabled and the Quota Scheme established by the Disabled Person (Employment) Act 1944 have now been abolished. Under the new Act, employers with 15 or more employees, trade organizations such as unions, as well as professional organizations:

* may not discriminate against a disabled person in recruitment, promotion or dismissal
* must make reasonable adjustments to the job or the workplace to help a disabled person do a job.

If employees feel that they have been discriminated against illegally, they can take their employer to an Employment Tribunal.

Dyslexic people have successfully and unsuccessfully lodged complaints with Employment Tribunals. At a Tribunal three specific issues are considered. These are:

- whether dyslexia is a disability for the purposes of the Act
- whether the person's dyslexia affects their ability to carry out normal day-to-day activities
- whether an employer has made reasonable adjustments for the dyslexic person.

These issues are discussed below and illustrated by reference to a specific example (Case No. 3202838/98) of a matter taken to a Tribunal.

The case involves a young woman who accused her employers of unfair dismissal and discrimination. She had been working for the same organization for ten years, and had done sufficiently well to gain promotion, becoming an assistant manager. As well as demonstrating how the Act works, the case highlights issues referred to earlier. That is, promotion led to increased demands on paperwork and the applicant's problems with written work became more obvious. There was also a change in personnel, her line manager being replaced by someone who was less understanding and supportive. Rather than benefit from her employers acting on professional advice, the applicant faced more criticism, the threat of demotion and eventually what amounted to constructive dismissal.

Dyslexia as a disability

Establishing that dyslexia is a disability should not be difficult. Paragraph 4.12 of the Code of Practice expressly contemplates it as such in a given example. Further, although not specifically mentioned in the World Health Organization International Classification of Diseases or the Diagnostic and Statistical Manual (IV), the behavioural characteristics of dyslexia are listed under headings such as 'Specific Reading Disorder'.

With regard to the issue of dyslexia being a disability, the Tribunal hearing the case referred to above decreed that:

> Mental impairment covers a wide range of impairments relating to mental functioning including what are often known as learning difficulties. In our judgment, these words are apt to cover dyslexia. Indeed, paragraph 4.12 of the

Code of Practice expressly contemplates dyslexia as a disability in the example there given. It is not suggested by the Applicant that she has any mental illness and therefore the point taken by the Respondents that dyslexia is not included in the World Health Organization International Classification of Diseases does not go to the point. We find the Applicant has a mental impairment.

Day-to-day effects

Establishing that there are adverse effects on the ability to carry out normal day-to-day activities can be more difficult. Dyslexia is not well understood as an information-processing difficulty, and employers as well as lawyers are likely to focus on literacy skills alone. If someone does have very basic reading, writing and spelling skills this inevitably has an effect on day-to-day functioning. Literate dyslexics are, however, in a more difficult position:

> I find it really hard to express to people to what extent being dyslexic makes me the person I am, and how much it effects my confidence. The Majority of people may understand that it means I have poor reading and writing skills, but it has probably never occurred to them how much it effects my day to day living. The number of times reading and writing are involved in an average day. For example something as simple as the invention of the printed cheque has made shopping a lot easier, for I do not have to worry about spelling numbers incorrectly or feeling embarrassed if I have to ask for help. There are numerous times that I have got lost driving a car or gone the wrong direction on the tube.

Those supporting dyslexic people need to focus on the extent of the information-processing problem, particularly the impact on executive functioning. The Act does specifically refer to the person's ability to remember, organize his or her thoughts, plan a course of action and execute it, or take in new knowledge. Impaired executive functioning can have an impact in all these areas. Someone who has good academic qualifications and advanced literacy skills but who needs to get to work much earlier than everyone else and leave later, in order to complete all the tasks which would be required in a normal day, is being affected on a day-to-day basis. A company director who is also a mature student commented:

> My day to day experience as a dyslexic can be compared to a tangled ball of string. Some days I am able to unravel the ball of string. Those are the good days when I am able to find the correct words to articulate myself. On the other days the ball of string seems to stay tangled. On those days I am aware that I am not expressing myself as well. I also experience what I call 'one off' dyslexic encounters. The 'one off' experiences are usually mispronouncing a word or mixing up a group of words as I speak or stumbling over reading something out load. I become embarrassed and frustrated especially if what I have said or read out load creates laugher. I know people aren't really laughing at me because when I mix up words or mispronounce them they often do sound funny! I also find that on most days I need to read things several times in order to understand what I have read.

In considering whether the applicant's dyslexia had substantial and long-term adverse effect on her ability to carry out normal day-to-day activities, the Tribunal in Case No. 3202838/98 outlined the arguments of the two sides as being:

The respondents argued that the Applicant's ability to carry out normal day-to-day activities is not subject to a substantial adverse effect because:

- The Applicant has reasonably good GCSE qualifications in English, Maths and History, as well as in Cooking and Biology. They accepted that she took a year longer than others and had special remedial lessons.
- The Applicant listed reading as one of her interests.
- The Applicant had held a number of jobs since the age of 18 and she had never told an employer that she suffered from dyslexia prior to becoming employed. She gave evidence that she had no difficulty carrying out the jobs she had done. She had never asked any of her employers for reasonable adjustments and had never been disciplined for failure to carry out her duties adequately.
- The Applicant was proud of her work record and of the praise she has received in the past. This was not praise for her conduct and capability taking into account her disability, but praise for her performance from people who had no idea that, one day, she would be claiming to be disabled.
- The only period in her working life of over 18 years when she had claimed to have any sort of mental impairment affecting her ability to carry out her work, or indeed any other normal day-to-day activities was recent.
- On two separate occasions in answer to questions the Applicant said that she had no difficulty in carrying out day-to-day activities. She drives a car, manages a home and has a normal social life.

- The Applicant did not mention her dyslexia to her new prospective employer.
- The Applicant's demeanour and behaviour throughout the hearing indicated she had had no difficulty in remembering things in great detail and she spoke about them with great clarity. She had also written notes to assist her representative throughout the hearing.
- The Applicant had carried out training and had been proud of the fact that she had sorted out health and safety files successfully.

It was submitted as a matter of law that the term 'normal day-to-day activities' does not include work of a particular form because no particular form of work is normal for most people. Consequently, it was submitted that an Employment Tribunal must not judge whether or not a person has a disability by what she is able to do at work and the fact that an impairment disables a person from doing her job does not necessarily mean that she is disabled under the Disability Discrimination Act 1995.

To counter these arguments, Counsel for the applicant advanced that:

- 'Substantial' means more than minor or trivial, and
- Adverse effect is concerned with the ability to carry out activities. The fact that a person can carry out such activities does not mean that his ability to carry them out has not been impaired. It is not the doing of acts which is the focus of attention but rather the ability to do or not to do the acts.

Counsel submitted that the Applicant's ability to carry out normal day-to-day activities was affected because her dyslexia affected her memory or ability to concentrate, learn or understand. A psychologist's report stated that tests showed that in spelling the Applicant reached the level of a 9.8-year-old. In calculation skills she reached the level of a 10.6-year-old. Her spelling was weak, her reading was weak, she had a slow reading speed. She had a weak short-term memory especially auditory. She searched for words and lost track when speaking. She had poor sequencing skills, illustrated by the fact that she could not remember her own car registration number. In addition it pointed to the fact her school reports showed that she was in remedial class and needed extra time to take her examinations.

The Tribunal decided that the report provided the clearest evidence that her dyslexia affected her in her normal day-to-day activities. That evidence was supported by evidence that she had to get assistance from her father to write to her employers, and her partner confirmed he checks her letters and that when she is reading the Applicant has to interrupt his television-watching to ask him about words which she does not understand. There was also evidence that she was making errors in her job.

In considering the issue of 'day-to-day' effects, the Tribunal, citing an earlier case (*Goodwin* v. *The Patent Office*), took into account the warning that disabled persons are likely habitually to play down the effect that their disabilities have. They concluded that:

> In our judgment the applicant is a person who has a disability because she has a mental impairment which has a substantial and long-term adverse effect on her ability to carry out normal day-to-day activities. In our judgment the [psychologist's] report shows that there is a substantial long-term adverse effect of the dyslexia because it affects her memory or ability to concentrate, learn or understand. The effect is not limited to her work.
>
> The circumstances which gave rise to her resignation and therefore to her constructive dismissal all arose, in our judgment, from her dyslexia and the manner in which she was treated by the Respondents because of the results of her dyslexia. In our judgment she was dismissed because of her disability. This is nonetheless true because the dismissal was a constructive dismissal. By virtue of section 4(2)(d) of the Disability Discrimination Act, a dismissal is an act of discrimination under section 5(1) if the employer cannot show that the treatment in question (the dismissal) was justified.

Reasonable adjustments

The matter of 'reasonable adjustment' is also contentious. Under Section 5(2) of the Disability Discrimination Act 1995, if an employer fails to make reasonable adjustments under Section 6 of the Act, that failure in itself is an act of discrimination. There is a duty on employers not to discriminate against disabled people in recruitment, selection, promotion, retention and dismissal. As part of 'retention' employers are required to act on the recommendations made to support dyslexic people. This can include the provision of training, equipment and supervision.

In the case referred to here, the Tribunal also considered the issue of reasonable adjustments, finding as follows:

> The Applicant's professional advisors made a number of recommendations at modest costs which were not taken up. In our judgment the Respondents could have allocated to another person the duties with which the Applicant had difficulty because of her dyslexia. This might have been necessary for only a limited period while she attended a course of training. The Respondents' main objection to this would appear to be a financial one, namely that though the Respondent is a large organization, each site has a relatively small number of employees and must pay its own way. It might have been necessary for this particular site to make a little less profit for a while. It appears to be the intention of Parliament that the burden of making adjustments should fall on employers. If this results in a financial burden on employers, then that is part of the price of this legislation. In our judgment there was discrimination against the Applicant by the Respondents' failure to make reasonable adjustments.

The applicant was successful in this case, the unanimous decision of the Tribunal being that:

- she was unfairly dismissed by the Respondents and
- they discriminated against her for a reason which related to her disability. The Respondents were ordered to pay compensation.

The implications of this case for practitioners working with dyslexic people are that:

- They need to be very specific about the nature of dyslexia in its widest context if:
  (a) it is to be interpreted as a disability, and
  (b) day-to-day effects are to be established.
- They need to make very specific recommendations about appropriate skill development training, compensations and adjustments.
- It also demonstrates that dyslexic people must understand their needs if they are to advocate for themselves in employment settings.

The DDA and recruitment/selection

Another way in which employers are required to make adjustments is in the process of recruitment and selection. The Employers' Forum on Disability recommends flexibility, as often minor changes can make a significant difference, and a focus on 'what' is to be achieved in the job rather than 'how' it is to be achieved, allowing for a dyslexic person's different working style.

Usually the recruitment process begins with the completion of an application form. A simple format with a clear typeface, acceptance of emailed applications so that they can be typed and checked for spelling and perhaps the use of different coloured paper can all accommodate the needs of dyslexic people.

There have been particular concerns where psychometric tests measuring abilities and attainments are used. Dyslexia does affect performance in test situations, especially where there are time constraints, and dyslexic people might therefore be prevented from demonstrating their abilities. Someone could, for example, be very good at verbal reasoning but this might not be reflected in his or her performance on a 'pencil and paper' test. It is not unusual for dyslexics to gain lower scores on group administered tests of ability than those they achieve when tests are administered individually and verbally.

In making adjustments the key issue is to 'obtain an accurate assessment of those job-relevant abilities/aptitudes, while minimizing the influence of job-irrelevant factors' (Meehan et al. 1998:6). Adjustments for dyslexic people during the selection process could include the following:

- Applicants should be contacted to provide information about the assessment process and the different types of task involved. This would enable them to say if they are likely to have any difficulties and how these can be best overcome.
- Applicants should be encouraged to provide information about the ways in which they would normally deal with a 'pencil and paper' task.
- Test publishers should be contacted as they might have materials required in the format the candidate can use.
- Un-timed tests could be used or candidates could be given extra time. Changing time allowances can, however, create problems in interpretation, especially when speed is integral to the test. Determining how much extra time should be allowed is difficult. Too little might not lessen the disadvantage; too much might increase it, fatigue being a factor (Nester 1993).
- How the person would use the skill being measured on the job and whether the adapted version of the test measures the same ability is a key consideration.
- A qualitative view should be taken in making decisions, integrating all the information about the candidate, including test scores, exercise results and ratings. The skills the candidate may have gained from just managing his or her disability should not be underestimated.
- Employers who use methodology such as an interview could allow dyslexic people to refer to notes.

Dyslexia and negligence

Many dyslexic people justifiably feel aggrieved about the way they were treated during their school years. Some have successfully sued those responsible for their education, because of the failure to identify and/or provide for their dyslexia. The law concerning the issue of negligence, especially as it relates to the duty of care professionals, has been clarified by the House of Lords (Friel and Hay 1996) and the position of dyslexic people has been strengthened through case law.

Establishing negligence and securing compensation is, however, no easy matter. It has to be demonstrated that individuals, including teachers and psychologists, failed to exercise their professional duties in a manner which could be expected of them. To establish this detailed records are required and people rarely have these.

Further, the financial and personal costs involved in litigation are considerable. The former can be mitigated by seeking Legal Aid but the lengthy process involved is stressful, time-consuming and potentially destructive as, in defending themselves, those accused of negligence can become personal.

Dyslexic people do, therefore, need to think very carefully before they pursue negligence through the courts, as it can be counterproductive

Dyslexia and criminal law

A good deal of publicity has been given to the possibility of there being a disproportionate number of dyslexic people in the prison population. Studies in the UK and abroad have suggested that the incidence could be up to as much as 50 per cent. For a review of the literature, readers are referred to Reid and Kirk (2000). Suffice it to say here that the issue is controversial, systematic studies having been criticized on a number of counts.

Dyslexia does not cause criminal behaviour and is never an excuse for it. It does, however, make sense to assume that where secondary characteristics such as frustration have become marked dyslexic people could 'go off the rails', and that the effect of their dyslexia on their experience might be a mitigating factor.

It is important that individuals who are likely to encounter dyslexic people in the course of their work, including lawyers and police officers, are aware both of the nature of dyslexia and its impact on both verbal and written communication and also of the fact that difficulties in these areas can be exacerbated when someone is under stress. People with literacy difficulties will sign documents they have been unable to read and/or understand even when they have been read to them. The problems with verbal communication described earlier can affect the way someone performs in an interview.

Even if the incidence of dyslexic people amongst the prison population has been exaggerated by studies, one of the encouraging aspects is that such studies have led to the recommendation that awareness training be provided for lawyers, magistrates and probation officers.

Disclosing dyslexia

Dyslexia is a 'hidden disability' and this means that dyslexic people often have to advocate for themselves, their difficulties being less obvious and less well understood. Many struggle with the issue of 'disclosure' – that is, the question of whether they should tell an employer or a prospective employer that they are dyslexic. If they wish to access resources and be protected under the terms of the Disability Discrimination Act 1995, they must. It is interesting to note, however, that the members of the tribunal panel in the case cited earlier acknowledged that it is often difficult for people with disabilities to admit to the problems they experience.

To avoid discrimination, and to ensure that they are properly understood, dyslexic people need to be able to explain what dyslexia is, how it affects them, the way in which they work best, and what an employer can do to assist them. This applies during the process of selection and whilst in the job. Positive re-framing has been referred to in earlier chapters. Whilst it is never easy to know how much to say or when to say it, dyslexic people must:

Understand themselves:

- Know their strengths. We all have talents and abilities, and dyslexic people need to know what theirs are and feel positive about them.
- Know their weaknesses. We all have these and need to work around them. It is important to be realistic and know one's limitations.
- Know what adjustments enable them to do their best. Employers and colleagues can only know what to do if they are aware exactly what is being asked for.
- Know what situations to avoid. There are those which will present difficulties which cannot be overcome.

Be specific:

- Dyslexic people should only tell what is necessary to those who need to know. They should therefore be discreet and selective. There will be people who are not ready to hear what they have to say.
- They should talk about what they can do. If they have particular needs, they should tell people what they need rather than what their problem is.
- *Dyslexic people should try to give a complete picture*, and be able to describe the problem, the cause and the solution.

Provide information:

It can be helpful to others to provide information, both verbally and in written form. Authoritative handouts provided by appropriate organizations can add credibility. These can include articles and books or videos about dyslexia, and suitable adjustments.

Essentially, dyslexic people will get what they need by telling people what they need – not what their problem is.

Policy and practice in employment

Responsibility for supporting dyslexic people at work lies within the Employment Service of the Department of Work and Pensions. The Employment Service can offer a wide range of programmes and services designed to help people find and maintain employment, including:

* The Disability Services Team. These were formerly known as PACT (Placement Assessment Counselling Teams) which can provide specialist help and advice for disabled people and their employers. They offer a variety of services, including practical help directed towards enabling dyslexic people to find work for the first time or to return to work.
* Occupational Psychologists work within the Disability Services Division and they provide specialist assessment, counselling and training for people with disabilities, including dyslexics.
* Disability Employment Advisers. These are people based in Job Centres and are engaged to help and advise individuals who are encountering barriers to employment because of their disabilities. They work with the Occupational Psychologists.

The Employment Service conducts a number of programmes, the most recently developed being the New Deal, which was designed to help unemployed people generally but has specific provision for people with disabilities. The programme is delivered with the aid of Personal Advisers.

Access to Work is designed to provide help for people with disabilities securing and maintaining employment with practical support such as the provision of special aids and equipment and adaptations to premises, support workers and other assistants in meeting personal needs. For a comprehensive review of provision in employment readers are referred to Reid and Kirk (2001).

The DDA in education and training

The DDA did not originally outlaw discrimination on grounds of disability in education. However, as a result of the Act, further and higher education institutions did have to publish disability statements. Training providers were covered under services and therefore they were not able to discriminate against disabled people on their training schemes. The Special Educational Needs and Disability Bill has now strengthened the Act, placing anti-discrimination responsibilities on schools and colleges, as well as providers of further education.

Policy in higher education

Students in higher education can apply for funding from the Disabled Students Allowance which consists of three major supplementary allowances that can be claimed by a full-time or part-time student. These are:

- A special equipment allowance to cover the duration of the student's course. This will pay for technical support.
- A non-medical helper's allowance to enable the student to hire the services of someone to assist their academic work, for example a Learning Support tutor. They could also employ proofreaders, etc.
- There is also a General Disabled Students Allowance to cover items which are not covered by the other two allowances.

Disabled Students Allowances are available to any student who can prove that they have a disability. This may be temporary or lasting.

Self-help and self-help groups

Self-help is an attempt by people with a mutual problem to take control over the circumstances of their lives. It is founded on the principle that people who share a disability have something to offer each other that a professional cannot provide. Self-help can take many forms including formal self-help groups. They are based on the independent living paradigm. A self-help agency's role is to empower its clients through the following related activities at three levels of organization (Segal et al. 1993):

- Individuals are directly provided or helped to gain access to resources and skills necessary to reach desired goals, and alternative models are provided to counter stigma.
- Organizations are structured to give clients access to roles that permit them to take responsibility for and exercise discretion over policies that affect them, collectively within agencies.

- Changes are sought in the larger society that both better the condition of people with disabilities as a class and that empower them to participate in making decisions concerning policies that affect them.

Self-help groups can represent a demanding challenge even to professionals who wish to establish cooperation with them. The reality is that they exist and professionals need to accept the challenge of relating to and cooperating with them. Self-help groups may be distinguished from individual self-help in that they represent a mutual helping process, with members supporting and helping others whilst at the same time helping themselves. The benefits of such groups have been referred to in Chapter 4.

Self-help groups are not an alternative to professional services. They aim at and represent something quite different, namely the support which an equal relationship can give and the personal development which follows from the combination of giving and receiving support. Self-help groups show that resources for help may be found in people themselves, provided that a framework and professional support is available. Clarification of professional and voluntary approaches can be expressed thus:

Lay persons' use:

- feelings and experiences
- intuition and common sense
- here and now perspective
- identification

Professionals' use:

- knowledge and insight
- systematic assessment
- long-term perspective
- awareness

The three main factors which seem to hold professionals back from self-help groups are:

- They may not be aware that groups sometimes need professional support, because groups often do not know how to ask for help without risking being overwhelmed by too much professional benevolence.
- Professionals frequently feel annoyed and provoked by the different values of self-help groups and think that it may be irresponsible to send their clients to such groups.
- Another excuse for not getting involved with self-help groups is that they claim to want to be independent and often voice this by saying that they do not want professionals to help them. However, helping does not have to mean intervening, and many self-help groups do need support (Habermann 1990).

Summary

- The emphasis of any intervention designed to support dyslexic people should be on empowerment, specifically self-empowerment.
- The rights of dyslexic people can be promoted through the provision of the Disability Discrimination Act 1995.
- There needs to be an effective partnership between advocacy and self-advocacy groups, as they are working for a common goal.
- Whilst dyslexic people can be supported in many ways, ultimately they each have to advocate for themselves. Being able to do so requires that they understand how to ask for what they need.

Chapter 11
Epilogue

Authors such as West (1997) have suggested that the technological revolution is providing opportunities for those dyslexic people who have visual strengths to capitalize on their talents, and be more valued than ever before.

Whilst this might be true, that same revolution has brought about a great deal of rapid change. It has also created greater demands on literacy, the use of most technology requiring some reading and writing. At the same time as technology is providing solutions it is also creating new problems.

We hope that the way in which we have described dyslexia and the interventions which can support dyslexic people will facilitate the processes they need to go through to adapt to the changes and challenges they face. Many of the solutions might seem obvious but that should not be construed as a simplification of what many dyslexic people find complex.

We also hope that what we have written will contribute to all dyslexic people being valued 'for their difference', as well as the persistence, determination and resilience they demonstrate when faced with tasks most of us take for granted.

Appendix 1
Sample interview schedule

Name D.O.B.   Age

Address

Occupation

Source of referral

Reason for referral

Have you ever been formally assessed before?   Yes   No
Do you know the outcome?
Do you have a written report?   Yes   No

Medical history

Is your general health good?

Have you ever had any problems with the following?

- Vision
- Hearing

Family history of learning difficulties

Has anyone in *your family* had difficulty with any of the following?

			Comment
Reading	Yes	No	
Writing	Yes	No	
Spelling	Yes	No	
Maths	Yes	No	
Memory	Yes	No	
Organization	Yes	No	
Coordination	Yes	No	
Spoken language	Yes	No	

Educational history

At what age did you leave school?

What were your school years like for you?

Was your schooling disrupted in any way?

What were you good at, at school?

What did you enjoy at school?

What did you find difficult?

Did you need/have extra help at school?

Did you work hard at school?

Do you have any qualifications from school? What are they?

Have you tried to learn other languages? Did you find it difficult?

Characteristics of a learning difficulty

Have you ever had a problem with:

			Comment*
Remembering people's names	Yes	No	
Using a dictionary?	Yes	No	
Using a telephone directory?	Yes	No	
Following directions?	Yes	No	
Using a street map?	Yes	No	
Time keeping?	Yes	No	
Organizing yourself?	Yes	No	
Taking telephone messages?	Yes	No	

Writing letters or memos?	Yes	No
Concentration?	Yes	No
Dealing with money?	Yes	No
Remembering your tables?	Yes	No

* Have you any specific strategies for dealing with these tasks?

Communication and social skills

Comment

Do you ever mispronounce or use the wrong words?

Do you have trouble finding the right word?

Do you often lose track of what you want to say, or of what other people are saying?

What is your social life like?

Do you have any hobbies or interests?

Do you think you are a confident person?

In which situation are you most confident?

What situation do you avoid?

Do you think you know how you learn best?

Do you get on well with people?

Employment history and experience

Do you have any professional/vocational qualifications? If so, what?

What jobs have you held?

What difficulties did they present you with, if any?

What are your short-term employment goals?

What are your long-term employment goals?

Do you enjoy training courses?   Yes   No

At work have you had trouble with:

Remembering instructions/ new information?	Yes	No
Taking notes?	Yes	No
Organizing your work space?	Yes	No
Prioritizing your workload?	Yes	No
Understanding what you have read?	Yes	No
Remembering what you have read?	Yes	No
Writing?	Yes	No
Proofreading?	Yes	No
Spelling?	Yes	No
Transferring information from one source to another?	Yes	No
Presenting your ideas?	Yes	No
Concentration?	Yes	No
Interference with background noise?	Yes	No

** Do you use any specific strategies for dealing with these tasks?

What are your technological skills like?

Do you enjoy teamwork?	Yes	No
Can you supervise others?	Yes	No

Coping with pressure

Do you cope easily with:

Changing demands?	Yes	No
Meeting deadlines?	Yes	No
Alterations to routine?	Yes	No
Doing several things at once?	Yes	No

Appendix 2
Checklist for dyslexic adults

The checklist – interpretation of results

It is important to remember that this does not constitute an assessment of one's difficulties. It is just an indication of some of the areas in which you, or the person you are assessing, may have difficulties. It is important to stress that only through an extensive assessment carried out by those that have a real understanding of the potential difficulties can an understanding of the difficulties be fully understood. However, this questionnaire may provide a better awareness and understanding of the nature of the difficulties. If you use this questionnaire it should be for personal interest and should not as yet be used to decide whether to seek further support.

Whilst we do stress that this is not a diagnostic tool, we can state that our research suggests the following:

Score less than 35 - probably non-dyslexic

Research result: no individual who was diagnosed as dyslexic through a full assessment was found to have scored less than 30, and therefore it is unlikely that if you score under 30 you will be dyslexic.

Score 35-54 - showing signs consistent with mild dyslexia

Research result: most of those who were in this category showed signs of being at least moderately dyslexic. However, a number of persons not diagnosed as dyslexic (though they could just be undetected) also fell in this category.

Score greater than 54 - signs consistent with moderate or severe dyslexia

Research result: all those who recorded a score of more than 50 were diagnosed as moderately or severely dyslexic. Therefore we would suggest that a score greater than 50 suggests moderately or severely dyslexic. One person who considered themselves non-dyslexic and has not been independently assessed scored 55.

Checklist for dyslexic adults

For each question circle the box which is closest to your response from **Rarely** *to* **Most of the time**. *For example, if you frequently have trouble filling in forms, put a circle around 3 (the number in the 'Frequently' column), and write the number again under the 'Total' column.*	Rarely	Occasionally	Frequently	Most of the time	Total
Do you confuse visually similar words when reading (e.g. tan, ton)?	3	6	9	12	
Do you lose your place or miss out lines when reading?	2	4	6	8	
Do you confuse the names of objects (e.g. table for chair)?	1	2	3	4	
Do you have trouble telling left from right?	1	2	3	4	
Is map reading or finding your way to a strange place confusing?	1	2	3	4	
Do you re-read paragraphs to understand them?	1	2	3	4	
Do you get confused when given several instructions at once?	1	2	3	4	
Do you make mistakes when taking down telephone messages?	1	2	3	4	
Do you find it difficult to find the right word to say?	1	2	3	4	

For each question circle the box which is closest to your response from **Easy** *to* **Very difficult**. *For example, if you find sounding out words difficult, put a circle around 9 (the number in the 'Difficult' column), and write the number again under the 'Total' column.*	Easy	Challenging	Difficult	Very difficult	
How easy do you find it to sound out words? (e.g. el-e-phant)	3	6	9	12	
When writing, do you find it difficult to organize your thoughts on paper?	2	4	6	8	
Did you learn your multiplication tables easily?	2	4	6	8	
How easy is it for you to learn to write a foreign language?	1	2	3	4	
How easy do you find it to recite the alphabet?	1	2	3	4	
How easy is it to think of unusual (creative) solutions to problems?	1	2	3	4	
How hard do you find it to read aloud?	1	2	3	4	

Total Score

Appendix 3
Useful contact addresses

Advocacy

The Adult Dyslexia Organisation
336 Brixton Road
London SW9 7AA
tel: 020 7924 9559 Helpline
tel: 020 7737 7646 Admin.
fax: 020 7207 7796
email: dyslexia.hq@dial.pipex.com

The British Dyslexia Association
98 London Road
Reading
Berkshire RG1 5AU
tel: 0118 966 8271 Helpline
tel: 0118 966 2677 Admin.
fax: 0118 935 1927
email: info@dyslexiahelp-bda.demon.co.uk

Dyspraxia Foundation
8 West Alley
Hitchin
Herts. SG5 1EG
tel: 01462 454 986
fax: 01462 455 052
Adult Support Group tel: 020 7435 5443
email: p-colley@cableinet.co.uk

Disability Law Service
39–45 Cavell Street
London E1 2BP
tel: 020 7791 9800
e-mail: advice@dls.org.uk

Employers Forum on Disability
Nutmeg House
60 Gainsford Street
London SE1 2MY
tel: 020 7403 3020
e-mail: esd@employers-forum.co.uk

RADAR
12 City Forum
250 City Road
London ECV1 8AF
tel: 020 7250 3222
e-mail: radar@radar.org.uk

SKILL
National Bureau for Students with Disabilities
Chapter House
18–20 Crucifix Lane
London SE1 3JW
tel: 0800 328 5050 Information Service
email: info@skill.org.uk

Assessment and tuition

Adult Dyslexia and Skills Development Centre
5 Tavistock Place
London WC1H 9SN
tel: 020 7388 8744
email: dyslexia@adsdc.freeserve.co.uk

Dyslexia Assessment Service
22 Wray Crescent
London N4 3LP
tel: 020 7272 6429

Dyslexia Institute
133 Gresham Road
Staines TW18 2AJ
tel: 01784 46385
email: info@dyslexia-inst.org.uk

Dyslexia Teaching Centre
23 Kensington Square
London W8 5HN
tel: 020 7937 2408

Dyslexia Tuition for Adults
20A Pymmes Green Road
London N11 1BY
tel: 020 8368 3634

Helen Arkell Dyslexia Centre
Frensham
Farnham
Surrey GU10 3BW
tel: 01252 792400
email: general_enquiries@arkellcentre.org.uk

Hornsby International Dyslexia Centre
Wye Street
London SW11 2HB
tel: 0800 328 1357 Freephone
email: dyslexia@hornsby.co.uk

References

Aaron PG, Baker C (1991) Reading Disabilities in College and High School. Philadelphia, PA:York Press.

Adelman KA, Adelman HS (1987) Rodin, Patton, Edison, Wilson, Einstein: were they really learning disabled? Journal of Learning Disabilities 20(5): 270-79.

ALBSU (1995) Assessing Reading and Maths. London:The Adult Literacy and Basic Skills Unit.

Alster EH (1997) The effects of extended time on algebra test scores for college students with and without learning disabilities. Journal of Learning Disabilities 30(2): 222-27.

Armstrong M (1999) A Handbook of Human Resources Management Practice. London: Kogan Page.

Authier J (1977) The psychoeducation model: definition, contemporary roots and content. Canadian Counsellor 12: 15-22.

Backman L, Dixon RA (1992) Psychological compensation: a theoretical framework. Psychological Bulletin 112: 259-83.

Baddeley AD (1986) Working Memory. London: Oxford University Press.

Baddeley AD, Hitch GJ (1974) Working memory. In Bower G (ed.), Recent Advances in Learning and Motivation, Vol. VIII. New York: Academic Press. pp 47-90.

Baltes PB, Reese HW, Lipsett LP (1980) Life span developmental psychology. Annual Review of Psychology 31: 65-100.

Bannatyne A (1974) Diagnosis: a note on recategorization of the WISC scaled scores. Journal of Learning Disabilities 7: 272-74.

Barton RS, Fuhrmann BS (1994). Counselling and psychotherapy for adults with learning disabilities. In Gerber PJ, Reiff HB (eds), Learning Disabilities in Adulthood. Austin, TX: Pro-Ed. pp 82-92.

Battle J (1990) Self-Esteem: The New Revolution. Edmonton: James Battle and Assoc.

Battle J (1992) Culture-Free Self-Esteem Inventories (2nd edn). Austin, TX: Pro-Ed.

Beaton A, McDougall S, Singleton C (1997) Editorial: Humpty Dumpty grows up? – diagnosing dyslexia in adulthood. Journal of Reading Research 20(1): 1-12.

Beck AT (1990) Beck Anxiety Inventory. London: Psychological Corporation.

Beck AT, Rush AJ, Shaw BF, Emery G (1979) Cognitive Therapy of Depression. New York: Guildford.

Best M, Demb JB (1999) Normal planum temporale symmetry in dyslexics with magnocellular pathway deficit. NeuroReport 10: 607-12.

Bigler ED (1996) The neurobiology and neuropsychology of adult learning disorders. In

Patton JR, Polloway EA (eds), Learning Disabilities: The Challenges of Adulthood. Austin, TX: Pro-Ed.

Borkowski JG, Burke JE (1996) Theories, models and measurements of executive functioning. In Reid Lyon G, Krasnegor NA (eds), Attention, Memory and Executive Function. Baltimore, MD: Paul H Brookes. pp 235-61.

Borkowski JG, Muthukrishna N (1992) Moving metacognition into the classroom: 'working models' and effective strategy teaching. In Pressley M, Harris KR, Guthrie JT (eds), Promoting Academic Literacy: Cognitive Research and Instructional Innovation. Orlando, FL: Academic Press. pp 477-501.

Bowden SC, Fowler KS, Bell RC, Whelan G, Clifford CC, Ritter AJ, Long CL (1998) The reliability and internal validity of the Wisconsin Card Sorting Test. Neuropsychological Rehabilitation 8(3): 243-54.

Brown AL (1980) Metacognitive development and reading. In Spiro RJ, Bruce B, Brewer WF (eds), Theoretical Issues in Reading Comprehension. Hillsdale, NJ: Lawrence Erlbaum. pp 453-81.

Bryant BR, Patton JR, Dunn C (1991) Scholastic Abilities Test for Adults (SATA). Austin, TX: Pro-Ed.

Buchanan M, Wolf JS (1986) A comprehensive study of learning disabled adults. Journal of Learning Disabilities 19(1): 34-38.

Burns D (1980) Feeling Good: The New Mood Therapy. New York: New American Library.

Carey S, Low S, Hansboro J (1997) Adult Literacy in Britain. London: OCNS.

Carter R (1998) Mapping the Mind. London: Weidenfeld and Nicolson.

Cavalier AR, Ferretti RP, Okolo CM (1994) Technology and individual differences. Journal of Special Education Technology 12: 175-81.

Chimel N (1998) Jobs, Technology and People. London: Routledge.

Chinn SJ (2000) The Informal Assessment of Numeracy Skills. Mark, Somerset: Markco Publishing.

Chinn SJ, Ashcroft JR (1993) Mathematics for Dyslexics: A Teaching Handbook. London: Whurr.

Cohen G, Kiss G, Le Voi M (1993) Memory: Current Issues (2nd edn). Buckingham: Open University Press.

Cohn P (1998) Why does my stomach hurt? How individuals with learning disabilities can use cognitive strategies to reduce anxiety and stress at the college level. Journal of Learning Disabilities 31(3): 514-16.

Cooke A (2001) Critical response to dyslexia, literacy and psychological assessment. Dyslexia 7(1): 47-52.

Cordoni BK, O'Donnell JP (1981) Wechsler Adult Intelligence Score patterns for learning disabled young adults. Journal of Learning Disabilities 14(7): 404-7.

Cottrell S (1999) The Study Skills Handbook. London: Macmillan.

Cox EO (1991) Advocacy and empowerment. Social Action in Groupwork 14: 77-90.

Crawford JR (1998) Introduction to the assessment of attention and executive functioning. Neuropsychological Rehabilitation 8(3): 209-11.

Davis RD (1997) The Gift of Dyslexia (2nd edn). London: Souvenir Press.

DECP (1999) Dyslexia, Literacy and Psychological Assessment. Leicester: British Psychological Society.

de Fries JC (1991) Genetics and dyslexia: an overview. In Snowling M, Thomson M (eds), Dyslexia: Integrating Theory and Practice. London: Whurr.

de Fries JC, Alarcon M, Olson RK (1997) Genetic aetiologies of reading and spelling deficits: developmental differences. In Hulme C, Snowling M (eds), Dyslexia: Biology, Cognition and Intervention. London: Whurr. pp 20-37.

Dunn R, Dunn K, Price GE (1996) Learning Styles Inventory. Lawrence, KS: Price Systems.

Egan GE (1994) The Skilled Helper (5th edn). Monterey, CA: Brooks/Cole.

Ellis A (1962) Reason and Emotion in Psychotherapy. New York: Lyle Stuart.

Ellis ES (1993) Integrative strategy instruction: a potential model for teaching content area subjects to adolescents with learning disabilities. Journal of Learning Disabilities 26(6): 258-383.

Eslinger PJ (1996) Conceptualizing, describing and measuring components of executive function: a summary. In Reid Lyon G, Krasnegor NA (eds), Attention, Memory and Executive Function. Baltimore, MD: Paul H. Brookes.

Evans BJW (1998) Assessment of visual problems in reading. In Beech JR, Singleton E (eds), The Psychological Assessment of Reading. London: Routledge.

Everatt J, Smythe I (2001) Checklist for dyslexic adults. The Dyslexia Handbook. Reading, Berks: BDA. pp 73-78.

Everatt J, Steffert B, Smythe I (1999) An eye for the unusual: creative thinking in dyslexics. Dyslexia 5(1): 28-46.

Faas LA, D'Alonzo BJ (1990) WAIS-R scores as predictors of employment success and failure among adults with learning disabilities. Journal of Learning Disabilities 23(5): 311-16.

Fawcett AJ, Nicolson RI (1998) Dyslexia Adult Screening Test. London: The Psychological Corporation.

Fawcett AJ, Nicolson RI, Dean P (1999) Performance of dyslexic children on cerebellar and cognitive tests. Journal of Motor Behaviour 31: 68-78.

Fenton M, Hughes P (1989) Passivity to Empowerment. London: RADAR.

Fink RP (1998) Literacy development in successful men and women with dyslexia. Annals of Dyslexia 48: 311-43.

Fisher S, Marlower A, Lambe J, Maestrin E, Williams D, Ason A, Weeks D, Stein JF, Monaco A (1999) A quantitative trait locus on chromosome 6p influences different aspects of development dyslexia. American Journal of Human Genetics 64: 146-56.

Flowers DL (1993) Brain basis for dyslexia: a summary of work in progress. Journal of Learning Disabilities 26: 575-82.

Forness SR, Kavale KA (1991) Social skills deficits as primary learning disabilities: a note on problems with the ICLD diagnostic criteria. Learning Disabilities Research and Practice 6: 44-49.

Frederickson N (1999) The ACID test: or is it? Educational Psychology in Practice 15(1): 3-9.

Friel J, Hay D (1996) Special Educational Needs and the Law. London: Sweet and Maxwell.

Frith U (1995) Dyslexia: can we have a shared theoretical framework? Educational and Child Psychology 12(1): 6-17.

Frith U (1999) Paradoxes in the definition of dyslexia. Dyslexia 5(4): 192-214.

Galaburda AM (1999) Developmental dyslexia: a multilevel syndrome. Dyslexia 5(4): 183-91.

Galaburda AM, Sherman GF, Rosen GD, Aboitiz F, Geschwind N (1985) Developmental dyslexia: four consecutive cases with cortical anomalies. Annals of Neurology 18: 222-33.

Gardner H (1996) Extraordinary Minds. London: Weidenfield and Nicolson.

Gardner H (2000) 'Now that the battle's over . . .' Informal remarks by Howard Gardner on the occasion of his receipt of the Samuel T. Orton Award by the International Dyslexia Association. Annals of Dyslexia 50: ix–xvi.

Garner P, Sandow S (1995) Advocacy, Self-Advocacy and Special Needs. London: Fulton.

Garnett K (1985) Learning disabilities come of age: transitions in adulthood. Rehabilitation World (Spring): 32–33.

Gerber PJ (1994) Researching adults with learning disabilities from an adult development perspective. Journal of Learning Disabilities 27(1): 6–9.

Gerber PJ, Ginsberg R, Reiff HB (1992) Identifying alterable patterns in employment success for highly successful adults with learning disabilities. Journal of Learning Disabilities 25(8): 475–87.

Gerber PJ, Reiff HB, Ginsberg R (1996) Reframing the learning disabilities experience. Journal of Learning Disabilities 29(1): 98–101.

Gerber PJ, Schneiders CA, Paradise LV, Reiff HB, Ginsberg RJ, Popp PA (1990) Persisting problems of adults with learning disabilities: self-reported comparisons from their school-age and adult years. Journal of Learning Disabilities 23(9): 570–73.

Getzel EE, Gugerty JJ (1996) Applications to youth with learning disabilities. In Wehman P (ed.), Life Beyond the Classroom. Baltimore, MD: Brookes. pp 337–92 .

Goulandris NK, Snowling M (1991) Visual memory deficits: a plausible cause of developmental dyslexia? Evidence from a single case study. Cognitive Neuropsychology 8: 127–54.

Greenfield S (1997) The Human Brain. London: Phoenix.

Gregg N (1983) College learning disabled writers: error patterns and instructional alternatives. Journal of Learning Disabilities 16(6): 334–38.

Gregg N, Ferri B (1998) Hearing voices – witnessing pain: why does my stomach hurt? Journal of Learning Disabilities 31(3): 517–19.

Gunn L (2000) The Dyslexia Adult Screening Test (DAST): a review. Journal of the Application of Occupational Psychology to Employment and Disability 2(2): 37–44.

Habermann U (1990) Self help groups: a minefield for professionals. Groupwork 3(3): 221–35.

Hales G (1995) Stress factors in the work-place. In Miles TR, Varma V (eds), Dyslexia and Stress. London: Whurr.

Hearne JD, Poplin MS, Schoneman C, O'Shaughnessy E (1988) Computer aptitude: an investigation of differences among junior high students with learning disabilities and their non-disabled peers. Journal of Learning Disabilities 21(8): 489–92.

Heaton RK, Chelune GL, Talley JL, Kay GG, Curtis G (1993) Wisconsin Card Sorting Test Manual Revised and expanded Odessa, FL: Psychological Assessment Resources.

Hedderly R (1996) Assessing pupils with specific learning difficulties for examination special arrangements at GCSE, 'A' level and degree level. Educational Psychology in Practice 12(1): 36–44.

Hoffman FJ, Sheldon KL, Minskoff EH, Sautter SW, Steidle EF, Baker DP, Bailey MB, Echols LD (1987) Needs of learning disabled adults. Journal of Learning Disabilities 20(1): 43–52.

Holland JL (1973) Making Vocational Choices. Englewood Cliffs, NJ: Prentice-Hall.

Holland JL (1985) Making Vocational Choices: A Theory of Vocational Personality and Work Environments. Englewood Cliffs, NJ: Prentice-Hall.

Honey P, Mumford A (1986) The Manual of Learning Styles. Maidenhead: Honey.

Hopson B, Anderson J, Kibble D (1998) Learn to Learn. Leeds: Lifeskills Associates.

Hornby G (1990) A humanistic developmental model of counselling: a psychological approach. Counselling Psychology Quarterly 3(2): 191–203.

Howard J, Howard P (2000) Human resource optimisation: creating training and development that sticks. Selection Development Review 16(6): 8–13.

Hughes W, Dawson R (1995) Memories of school: adult dyslexics recall their school days. Support for Learning 10: 181–84.

Hulme C (1986) Memory development: interactions between theories in cognitive and developmental psychology. Bulletin of the British Psychological Society 39: 247–50.

Hynd GW, Hiemenz JR (1997) Dyslexia and gyral morphology variation. In Hulme C, Snowling M (eds), Dyslexia: Biology, Cognition and Intervention. London: Whurr. pp 38–58.

Jastak S, Wilkinson G (1993) Wide Range Achievement Test – Third Edition. Los Angeles: Western Psychological Services.

Jorm AF (1983) Specific reading retardation and working memory: a review. British Journal of Psychology 74: 311–42.

Kandola R, Fullerton J (1994) Managing the Mosaic: Diversity in Action. London: Institute of Personnel and Development.

Katz L, Goldstein G, Rudshin S, Bailey D (1993) A neuropsychological approach to the Bannatyne recategorization of the Wechsler Intelligence Scales in adults with learning disabilities. Journal of Learning Disabilities 26(1): 65–72.

Kaufman AS, Lichtenberger EO (1999) Essentials of WAIS-III Assessment. New York: Wiley.

Kay Runyon M (1991) The effect of extra time on reading comprehension scores for university students with and without learning disabilities. Journal of Learning Disabilities 2: 104–7.

Kephart NC (1968) Let's not misunderstand Dyslexia. The Instructor, Aug/Sept, 78: 62–63.

Kihl P, Gregerson K, Sterum N (2000) Hans Christian Andersen's spelling and syntax: allegations of specific dyslexia are unfounded. Journal of Learning Disabilities 33(6): 506–19.

Kitz WR, Nash RT (1992) Testing the effectiveness of the Project Success Programme for Adult Dyslexics. Annals of Dyslexia 42: 3–42.

Klein C (1991) Setting up a learning programme for adult dyslexics. In Snowling M, Thomson ME (eds), Dyslexia: Integrating Theory and Practice. London: Whurr. pp 293–301.

Klein C (1993) Diagnosing Dyslexia. London: Avanti.

Knowles M (1990) The Adult Learner: A Neglected Species (4th edn). Houston, TX: Gulf Publishing Co.

Kreiner DS, Gough B (1990) Two ideas about spelling: Rules and Word-Specific Memory. Journal of Memory and Language 29: 103–18.

Kronick D (1983) Social Development of Learning Disabled Persons. Toronto: Jossey-Bass.

Krumboltz JD (1976) A Social Learning Theory of Career Selection. The Counselling Psychologist 6 (1) 71–81.

Langdon DW, Warrington GK (1995) A verbal and spatial reasoning test (VESPAR). Hove: LEA.

Lashley C (1995) Improving Study Skills. London: Cassell.

Lefly DL, Pennington BF (1991) Spelling Errors and Reading Fluency in Compensated Adult Dyslexics. Annals of Dyslexia 41: 143–62.

Lenkowsky LK, Saposnek DT (1978) Family Consequences of Parental Dyslexia. Journal of Learning Disabilities 11, 1, 47–53.

Leonard FC (1991). Using Wechsler data to predict success for learning disabled. Learning Disabilities Research & Practice 6(1): 17–24.

Levine M (1990) Keeping A Head in School. Toronto: Educators Publishing Service.

Levinson DJ (1978) The Seasons of a Man's Life. New York: Ballantyne.

Lewis RB (1998) Assistive technology and learning disabilities: today's realities and tomorrow's promises. Journal of Learning Disabilities 31(1): 16–26.

Logie RH (1999) Working memory. The Psychologist 124: 174–78.

McCormick EJ, Ilgen D (1985) Industrial and Organisational Psychology (8th edn). London: Allen and Unwin.

McLoughlin D, Fitzgibbon G, Young V (1994) Adult Dyslexia: Assessment, Counselling and Training. London: Whurr.

McLoughlin D, Beard J (2000) Dyslexia support in a multilingual environment. In Peer L, Reid G (eds), Multilingualism, Literacy and Dyslexia. London: David Fulton Publishers.

Manzo AN, Manzo UC (1993) Literacy Disorders. Orlando, FL: Holt Rinehart and Winston.

Marsiske M, Lang FR, Baltes PB, Baltes MM (1995) Selective optimisation with compensation: life-span perspectives on successful human development. In Dixon RA, Backman L (eds), Compensating for Psychological Deficits and Declines. Mahwah, NJ: Lawrence Erlbaum Associates.

Mather N (1998) Relinquishing aptitude–achievement discrepancy: the doctrine of misplaced precision. Perspectives (Winter): 4–7.

Meehan M, Birkin R, Snodgrass R (1998) Employment assessment (EA): issues surrounding the use of psychological assessment material with disabled people. Selection Development Review 14(3): 3–9.

Miles TR (1993) Dyslexia: The Pattern of Difficulties. London: Whurr.

Miles TR (1996) Do dyslexic children have IQs? Dyslexia 2(3): 175–78.

Miles TR, Miles E (1990) Dyslexia: A Hundred Years on. Milton Keynes: Open University Press.

Miles TR, Miles E (1992) Dyslexia and Mathematics. London: Routledge.

Miles TR, Varma V (1995) Dyslexia and Stress. London: Whurr.

Miles TR, Haslum MN, Wheeler TJ (1998) Gender ratio in dyslexia. Annals of Dyslexia 48: 27–57.

Miner JB (1992) Industrial and Organisational Psychology. Singapore: McGraw-Hill.

Morgan E, Klein C (2000) The Dyslexic Adult in a Non-dyslexic World. London: Whurr.

Morris RG, Craik FM, Gick ML (1990) Age differences in working memory tasks: the role of secondary memory and the central executive system. Quarterly Journal of Experimental Psychology 42A: 67–86.

Mosberg L, Johns D (1994) Reading and listening comprehension in college students with developmental dyslexia. Learning Disabilities, Research and Practice 9(3): 130–35.

Myers IB, McCauley MH (1985) Myers-Briggs Type Indicators. Palo Alto, CA: Consulting Psychology Press.

Nathan R, Hill L (1992) Career Counselling. London: Sage.

Nelson H, Willison J (1991) National Adult Reading Test (NART). Windsor: NFER-Nelson.

Nelson-Jones R (1995) The Theory and Practice of Counselling. London: Cassell.

Nester MA (1993) Psychometric testing and reasonable accommodations for persons with disabilities. Rehabilitation Psychology 38(2): 75–85.

Nicolson RI, Fawcett AJ (1995) Dyslexia is more than a phonological disability. Dyslexia 1: 19–37.

Nicolson RI, Fawcett AJ (1999) Developmental dyslexia: the role of the cerebellum. Dyslexia 5(3): 155–77.

Nicolson RI, Fawcett AJ (2001) Dyslexia as a learning disability. In Fawcett AJ (ed.), Dyslexia:Theory and Good Practice. London:Whurr.

Patton JR, Polloway EA (1992) Learning disabilities: the challenges of adulthood.Journal of Learning Disabilities 25(7): 410–15.

Patton JR, Polloway EA (1996) Learning disabilities: the challenges of adulthood.Austin, Texas: Pro Ed.

Patton JR, Cronin ME, Bassett DS, Koppel AE (1997) A life skill approach to mathematics instruction: preparing students with learning disabilities for the real-life math demands of adulthood.Journal of Learning Disabilities 30(2): 178–87.

Peel M (1992) Career Development and Planning. Maidenhead: McGraw-Hill.

Pennington BF (1990)The genetics of dyslexia.Journal of Child Psychology and Psychiatry 31: 193–201.

Pennington BF, Bennetto L, McAleer O, Roberts RJ (1996) Executive functions and working memory. In Reid Lyon G, Krasnegor NA (eds), Attention, Memory and Executive Function. Baltimore, MD: Brookes. pp 327–48.

Plata M, Bone J (1989) Perceived importance of occupations by adolescents with and without learning disabilities.Journal of Learning Disabilities 22(1): 64–71.

Pressley M (1991) Can learning disabled children become good information processors? How can we find out? In Feagans L, Short E, Meltzer Y (eds), Subtypes of Learning Disabilities. Hillsdale, NJ: Erlbaum. pp 137–62.

Quandt IJ (1977)Teaching Reading:A Human Process. Chicago: Rand McNally.

Rack J (1997) Issues in the assessment of developmental dyslexia in adults: theoretical and applied perspectives.Journal of Research in Reading 20(1): 66–76.

Reid G, Kirk J (2000) Dyslexia in Adults: Education and Employment. Chichester:Wiley.

Reid M (1999) Career Assessment: Choosing the Right Tools. Dyslexia Handbook. Reading: British Dyslexia Association.

Reiff HB, Gerber PJ, Ginsberg R (1993) Definitions of learning disabilities from adults with learning disabilities: the insiders' perspectives. Learning Disability Quarterly 16: 114–25.

Riddick B (1996) Living with Dyslexia. London: RKP.

Riddick B, Sterling C, Farmer M, Morgan S (1999) Self-esteem and anxiety in the educational histories of adult dyslexic students. Dyslexia 5(4): 227–48.

Roberts R, Mather N (1997) Orthographic dyslexia: the neglected subtype. Learning Disabilities Research and Practice 12: 236–50.

Rogan LL, Hartman LD (1990) Adult outcomes of learning disabled students ten years after initial follow-up. Learning Disabilities Focus 5: 91–102.

Rogers C (1951) Client-centered Therapy. Boston, MA: Houghton Mifflin.

Rosenblum L (1987) An experiment in group therapy with learning disabled adults. In Johnson D, Blalock J (eds),Adults with Learning Disabilities: Clinical Studies. Orlando, FL: Grune and Stratton. pp 233–37.

Roth AD, Fonagy P (1996) What Works for Whom? A Critical Review of Psychotherapy Research. New York: Guildford Press.

Salvia J, Gajar A (1988) A comparison of WAIS-R profiles of non-disabled college freshmen and college students with learning disabilities.Journal of Learning Disabilities 21(10): 632–35.

Sanders P (1994) First Steps in Counselling. Manchester: PCCS Books.

Schumaker JB, Deshler DD, Nolan S, Clark FL, Alley GR, Warner MM (1981) Error Monitoring:A Learning Strategy for Improving Academic Performance of Learning Disabled Adolescents. Lawrence, KS: University of Kansas.

Scott MJ, Dryden W (1996) The cognitive behavioural paradigm. In Wolfe R, Dryden W (eds), Handbook of Counselling Psychology. London: Sage. pp 156-79.

Scott SS, Gregg N (2000) Meeting the evolving needs of faculty in providing access for college students with LD. Journal of Learning Disabilities 33(2): 158-67.

Shaywitz SE (1996) Dyslexia. Scientific American (Nov): 98-104.

Segal SP, Silverman C, Tembin T (1993) Empowerment and self-help agency practice for people with mental difficulties. Social Work 38(6): 705-12.

Siegel LS (1992) An evaluation of the discrepancy definition of dyslexia. Journal of Learning Disabilities 25(10): 618-29.

Singleton CH (1991) Computer applications in the diagnosis and assessment of cognitive deficits in dyslexia. In Singleton CH (ed.), Computers and Literacy Skills. British Dyslexia Association.

Singleton CH (1996) Dyslexia in higher education: issues for policy and practice. Paper presented at Dyslexic Students in Higher Education Conference, Huddersfield, January.

Skottun BC, Parke LA (1999) The possible relationship between visual deficits and dyslexia: examination of a critical assumption. Journal of Learning Difficulties 32(1): 2-5.

Smith JD (1996) Adult development theories: an overview and reflection of their relevance for learning disabilities. In Patton JR, Polloway EA (eds), Learning Disabilities. Austin, TX: Pro-Ed.

Smith P, Whetton C (2000) Skillscape. Windsor: NFER-Nelson.

Snowling MJ (2001) From language to reading and dyslexia. Dyslexia 7(1): 37-46.

Spadafore GJ (1983) Spadafore Diagnostic Reading Test. Novato, CA: Academic Therapy Publications.

Spekman NJ, Goldberg RJ, Herman KL (1992) Learning disabled children grow up: a search for factors related to success in the young adult years. Learning Disabilities Research and Practice 7: 161-70.

Spreen O, Strauss E (1991) A Compendium of Neuropsychological Tests. New York: Oxford University Press.

Stanovich KE (1991) Discrepancy definitions of reading disability: has intelligence led us astray? Reading Research Quarterly 26: 1-29.

Stanovich KE (1996) Towards a more inclusive definition of dyslexia. Dyslexia 2: 154-66.

Stein J (2001) The magnocellular theory of developmental dyslexia. Dyslexia 7(1): 12-36.

Stein J, Talcott J (1999) Impaired neuronal timing in developmental dyslexia - the magnocellular hypothesis. Dyslexia 5: 59-77.

Sterling C, Farmer F, Riddick B, Morgan S, Matthews C (1997) Adult dyslexic writing. Dyslexia 4: 1-15.

Super, D. E. (1969) Vocational Development Theory: Persons, Positions and Processes. Counselling Psychologist 1: 2-9.

Swanson HL (1994) The role of working memory and dynamic assessment in the classification of children with learning disabilities. Learning Disabilities Research and Practice 9(4): 190-202.

Swanson HL, Cooney JB, O'Shaughnessy TE (1998) Learning disabilities and memory. In Wong BYL (ed.), Learning about Learning Disabilities (2nd edn). San Diego, CA: Academic Press. pp 107-62.

Taymans JM (1991) The use of the self-directed search and the self-directed search form E with people with learning disabilities. Learning Disabilities Research and Practice 6: 5-58.

Thomas M (2000) Albert Einstein and LD: an evaluation of the evidence. Journal of Learning Disabilities 33(2): 149-157.

Thomson ME (1990) Developmental Dyslexia. London:Whurr.

Tonnessen FE (1997) How can we best define 'dyslexia'? Dyslexia 3: 78-92.

Vanderiendonke A, Franssen V (2000) Cognitive deficits affecting time perception. Paper presented at The British Psychological Society London Conference, December.

Venneri A (2000) Cognitive deficits affecting time perception. Paper presented to The British Psychological Society London Conference, December.

Vogel SA, Forness S (1992) Social functioning in adults with learning disabilities. School Psychology Review 21(3): 374-85.

Walker BA (1994) Valuing differences: the concept and a model. In Mabey C, Iles P (eds), Managing Learning. London: Routledge. pp 211-23.

Webster RE (1997) Learning Efficiency Test II - Revised. Novato, CA: Academic Therapy.

Wechsler D (1944) The Measurement of Adult Intelligence (3rd edn). Baltimore:Williams and Wilkins.

Wechsler D (1976) The Wechsler Intelligence Scale for Children. Windsor: NFER.

Wechsler D (1981) The Wechsler Adult Intelligence Scale (Revised). New York: Psychological Corporation.

Wechsler D (1999a) The Wechsler Adult Intelligence Scale (3rd edn). New York: Psychological Corporation.

Wechsler D (1999b) Wechsler Memory Scales (3rd edn). New York: Psychological Corporation.

Wehman P (1996) Life Beyond the Classroom. Baltimore, MD: Brookes.

West TG (1997) In the Mind's Eye (2nd edn). Buffalo, NY: Prometheus Books.

White WJ (1992) The postschool adjustment of persons with learning disabilities: current status and future projections. Journal of Learning Disabilities 25(7): 448-56.

Wilkins A (1995) Visual Stress. Oxford: Oxford University Press.

Wilson AM, Lesaux NK (2001) Persistence of phonological processing deficits in college students with dyslexia who have age-appropriate reading skills. Journal of Learning Disabilities 34(5): 394-400.

Wilson BA, Alderman N, Burgess P, Emslie H, Evans J (1996) Behavioural Assessment of the Dysexecutive Syndrome. Bury St Edmunds, Suffolk:Thames Valley Test Company.

Winner E, von Karolyi C, Malinski D (2000) Dyslexia and visual-spatial talents: no clear link. Perspectives 26(2): 26-29.

Wolfensberger W (1994) The growing threat to the lives of handicapped people in the context of modernistic values. Disability and Society 9(3): 395-413.

Wong BYL (1986) Metacognition and special education: a review of a view. Journal of Special Education 20: 19-29.

Wray D (1994) Comprehension monitoring, metacognition and other mysterious processes. Support for Learning 9: 107-13.

Yost EB, Corbishley MA (1987) Career Counselling. London: Jossey-Bass.

Zdzienski D (1997) StudyScan. London: PICO Educational Systems Ltd.

Zeffiro TJ, Eden G (2000) The neural basis of developmental dyslexia. Annals of Dyslexia 50: 1-30.

Index